EMERGENCES: WOMEN'S STRUGGLES FOR LIVELIHOOD IN LATIN AMERICA

UCLA LATIN AMERICAN STUDIES
VOLUME 82

Emergences

WOMEN'S STRUGGLES FOR LIVELIHOOD IN LATIN AMERICA

Edited by
John Friedmann
Rebecca Abers
Lilian Autler

UCLA Latin American Center Publications
University of California, Los Angeles

UCLA Latin American Center Publications
Box 951447
University of California
Los Angeles, CA 90095-1447

Copyright © 1996 by The Regents of the University of California
All rights reserved
Printed in the United States of America

All translations from the Spanish, except chapter 5, by Lilian Autler

Cover design by Linda M. Robertson

Cover photograph by Allison Lange
Courtesy of the Inter-American Foundation

Library of Congress Cataloging-in-Publication Data

Emergences: women's struggles for livelihood in Latin America /
   edited by John Friedmann, Rebecca Abers, Lilian Autler.
      p.   cm. — (UCLA Latin American studies; v. 82)
   Includes bibliographical references and index.
   ISBN 0-87903-083-6
   1. Women—Latin America—Social conditions.   I. Friedmann,
John.   II. Abers, Rebecca.   III. Autler, Lilian.   IV. Series.
HQ1460.5.E47   1996
305.42'098—dc20   96-12920
                                                              CIP

To the memory of
Elisabeth Souza-Loba,
Brazilian feminist scholar and activist

Contents

Acknowledgments ix
The Contributors xi
Editors' Introduction 1

I. Context

1 The Foreign Debt Crisis and the Social Costs of Adjustment in Latin America
LOURDES BENERÍA / 11

II. Collective Social Action and Labor Markets

2 Women Confronting the Crisis: Two Case Studies from Greater Buenos Aires
MARÍA DEL CARMEN FEIJOÓ / 31

3 Industrialization and Changing Gender Roles in Rural Michoacán, Mexico
GAIL MUMMERT / 47

III. Political Practice

4 Women, Collective Kitchens, and the Crisis of the State in Peru
MARUJA BARRIG / 59

5 In No-Man's Land: Poor Women's Organizations and Political Violence in Lima's Neighborhoods
CECILIA BLONDET / 79

6 Power and Patriarchy: The Long Struggle to Forge a Coordinated Women's Movement in Nicaragua
MALENA DE MONTÍS / 91

7 The Difficult Path toward Organizing Household
   Workers: A Dialogue
                ELSA M. CHANEY AND AÍDA MORENO VALENZUELA / 107
8 Concluding Reflections: "Redrawing" the Parameters
   of Gender Struggle
                                       SONIA E. ALVAREZ / 137

IV. Bibliography

Women's Struggles for Livelihood: An Annotated
Bibliography, 1980–1992
                                        REBECCA ABERS / 155

Index   / 193

Acknowledgments

This volume of essays is the outgrowth of an international conference, "Learning from Latin America: Women's Struggles for Livelihood," held at the University of California, Los Angeles, February 27–29, 1992. The conference was cosponsored by UCLA's Center for the Study of Women, Latin American Center, Chicano Studies Research Center, and Graduate School of Architecture and Urban Planning. Its purpose was to bring together women scholars from two continents engaged in research on poor women's struggles for livelihood. At the same time, we wanted to begin building bridges with the Latina communities of Los Angeles, in the hope that an exchange of information among North American, South American, and Angelina women activists might be useful to all concerned.

Conference participants included twelve Latin American women scholars and activists and ten North American counterparts. In addition, we invited nine Latina community leaders from Los Angeles, including street vendors, domestic workers, housewives, and union organizers. During the two days of academic meetings they participated as discussants and were the focus of a workshop held at Dolores Mission in East Los Angeles. Altogether, in this major North-South encounter of women scholars on the question of women's organizations and livelihood struggles, a total of four countries from South America (Brazil, Argentina, Chile, Peru), two countries from Mesoamerica (Nicaragua, Mexico), and the United States were represented by one or more participants. Explicitly interdisciplinary, the conference involved economists, sociologists, anthropologists, psychologists, political scientists, as well as multifaceted urbanists, along with activists and community leaders.

We would like to thank the several institutions that made our meeting financially possible: The John D. and Catherine T. MacArthur Foundation, the Inter-American Foundation, The Ford Foundation, and the National Science Foundation. Research support was also made available through the UCLA Latin American Center, the Academic Senate of the Los Angeles Division of the University of California, and the Graduate School of Architecture and Urban Planning at UCLA. Furthermore, our warmest thanks are extended to Helen Astin, Acting Director of the Center for the Study of Women, for her unstinting support of this endeavor, and the present and past members of her staff, including Millie Loeb, Lynn Naliboff, Evelyn Barnes, and Van Do-Nguyen. We would like to recognize Marsha Brown for the splendid conference poster she designed as well as for preparing the final manuscript of this volume, and Teri Bond Michael for her fine publicity work. Dolores Mission in East Los Angeles hosted the Saturday workshop which brought together scholars and community activists. We are especially grateful to Eduardo Vilches and Maria Teixeira for making this encounter possible. Finally, we would like to acknowledge a group of graduate students in Urban Planning whose assistance throughout the conference and workshop was a vital contribution to its success: Jacqueline Chase, Tess Colby, Ana Goicolea, Ivelisse Gorbea-Class, Dan Klooster, Kori Kanayama, Alberto Lourenço Pereira, and Billi Romain.

This collection of essays is dedicated to the memory of Elisabeth Souza-Lobo, a Brazilian feminist scholar and activist who died on March 15, 1991, in an automobile accident while in the Northeast of Brazil conducting research. Along with her died a local feminist and rural union activist, Marília da Penha Nacimento Silva, who had received death threats.

Throughout her life, Souza-Lobo combined academic research with activism. Her research on women industrial workers and their union activities filled an important gap in feminist studies in Brazil and Latin America. She also published a biography of Emma Goldman and wrote extensively on sociological methodology and gender theory and on work, identity, and language. At the same time, she was a militant activist in Brazil's Partido dos Trabalhadores (Workers' Party) and conducted numerous courses and seminars for union, church, and political organizations. She was a professor of sociology at the Universidade de São Paulo from 1982 until her death, and began teaching in the graduate program of the social history of labor at the Universidade de Campinas in 1989. Shortly after her death, a group of Souza-Lobo's academic and activist colleagues published in her memory a volume of her essays, *A classe operária tem dois sexos: trabalho, dominação e resistencia* (São Paulo: Secretaria Municipal de Cultura, Prefeitura do Municipio de São Paulo, 1991).

The Contributors

REBECCA ABERS is a doctoral student in the Urban Planning Program at the University of California, Los Angeles. She has written on development and migration in the Amazon, and is currently conducting research on local government and democratization in Brazil.

SONIA ALVAREZ is a professor of Politics at the University of California, Santa Cruz, and has written extensively on women and the democratization process in Brazil. Major recent publications include *Engendering Democracy in Brazil: Women's Movements in Transition Politics* (1990). Currently, she is associated with the Ford Foundation in Brazil.

LILIAN AUTLER graduated from the Urban Planning and Latin American Studies programs at the University of California, Los Angeles, and is currently the director for economic development of El Rescate, a Los Angeles-based non-governmental organization. She has studied social movements and women's organizations in Mexico and Nicaragua, and has written about street vendors and the informal economy in Los Angeles.

MARUJA BARRIG is a journalist, activist, and researcher in the areas of women's work and political participation in Peru. She received a degree in Literature and Journalism from the Universidad Católica del Perú, and is currently the coordinator of the Working Group on Urban Services and Low Income Women (SUMBI) in Lima.

LOURDES BENERÍA is a professor in the Department of City and Regional Planning at Cornell University. She has written extensively about household economics and women's work in Latin America. She co-edited the volume titled *Unequal Burden: Economic Crisis, Persistent Poverty and Women's Work* (1992), and was co-author of *The Crossroads of Class and Gender: Industrial Homework, Subcontracting and Household Dynamics in Mexico City* (1987).

CECILIA BLONDET is director of the Instituto de Estudios Peruanos in Lima, Peru. Her major research interests include the limits and possibilities of urban women's organizations in Peru.

ELSA CHANEY is a professor of Anthropology and chair of the Women in International Development program at the Center for International and Comparable Studies, University of Iowa in Iowa City. She has done research on working women in many parts of Latin America, and has collaborated with and written about household workers and their organizations. She co-edited one of the major volumes on this topic, *Muchachas No More: Household Workers in Latin America and the Caribbean* (1989), and is co-author of *Sellers and Servants: Working Women in Lima, Peru* (1985).

MARÍA DEL CARMEN FEIJOÓ is a sociologist and researcher in CEDES in Buenos Aires, Argentina. Her research interests have included the history of women's movements in Argentina, and household and community responses to prolonged economic crisis in Buenos Aires.

JOHN FRIEDMANN is professor emeritus and former head of the Urban Planning Program at the University of California, Los Angeles. He has written extensively on regional planning, alternative development, household economics and urban social movements, with special reference to Latin America. His major publications in these areas include *Empowerment: The Politics of an Alternative Development* (1992) and *Life Space and Economic Space: Essays in Third World Planning* (1988).

MALENA DE MONTÍS is founder of the research institute CENZONTLE in Managua, Nicaragua. In 1992–93 she was a resident scholar at the Radcliffe's Bunting Institute at Harvard University. Her major interests are popular education and women's political mobilization in Nicaragua.

AÍDA MORENO VALENZUELA has been a domestic worker and activist in Chile for many years. She is Secretary General of the Confederation of Latin American and Caribbean Household Workers (CONLACTRAHO) and runs a cooperative cleaning service, employing 40 ex-household workers.

GAIL MUMMERT is a researcher at the Centro de Estudios Antropológicos of the Colegio de Michoacán, Mexico.

Editors' Introduction

This collection of essays is about Latin American women of working class and peasant backgrounds. In different ways, it reflects a growing awareness during the 1980s of women's emergence from the cocoon of domesticity—their traditional lot in life—into an enlarged public sphere. In local communities, women have struggled for the self-provisioning of livelihood; as breadwinners, they are gaining access to both formal and informal markets; and as citizens, they are defending their right to livelihood and social justice in the political arena.

The stories that follow tell of neither victory nor defeat but of women's continuing and tenacious efforts, grounded in relations of kinship and community, to wrest a living for themselves and their families from a hostile environment. The battle is being waged simultaneously on a number of fronts: against patriarchy at home; against the state; and even against movements that wrap themselves in the mantle of social revolution. Of the thousands of stories that might have been told, we have included here only a small, essentially random sample. Nevertheless, we believe that our case studies open a few windows onto the broad transformative changes being worked on the lives of poor and still largely disempowered women in Latin American societies.

Two terms are central to these accounts: livelihood and citizen rights. Livelihood struggles take place over the means of subsistence; they are struggles for the reproduction of life itself and have traditionally been centered in the household, that is, in what was and still is predominantly women's space. As employed here, the concept of livelihood is broad and inclusive, embracing both production and consumption. It is a culturally mediated, multidimensional concept that covers a great deal more than the customary measure of household income. A decent or adequate livelihood, by community standards, endeavors to balance a variety of claims, some originating from outside the household itself (conformity with social norms), some from within. Where this "moral economy" of social relations predominates,[1] livelihood means having access to a safe and secure territorial base; getting enough food and drink on the table; having some money as well as unencumbered time for investment in housing, durable household goods, and the education of the young; caring for and nurturing infants, children, the sick, and the elderly; maintaining close relations with kin and neighbors; and, in the most general sense, having time for the celebration of life. In a household perspective, then, the problem of producing a livelihood is much more complex than simply securing a steady flow of income. In market economics money is a necessary element for the good life, but it is far from enough.[2]

In the classical scenario of the capitalist economy which conceives of economic relations exclusively in contractual terms articulated through the universal medium of exchange, men would work for wages outside the domestic sphere, while women, cloistered in their homes, would manage, without compensation, the consumption side of the equation. This scenario, of course, assumes the ability of male workers to earn a family wage sufficient for the social reproduction of both their own labor and the unpaid labor of their households. But what if this condition should not be fulfilled? The assumption of a "family wage" has always been counter-factual. But in Latin America during the 1980s, it was becoming clear that livelihoods could no longer be sustained without disrupting the gender division of labor implied by the classical scenario. As economic circumstances, especially for the laboring classes, progressively worsened, the spatial separation between production in the public sphere and consumption in the private sphere was beginning to break down as the standard model of the capitalist order. As women sought to meet their daily needs through collective actions in concert with other women, livelihood struggles spilled over into neighborhoods. Some organized collective kitchens, production cooperatives, child care services, and community gardens in what María del Carmen Feijoó calls an "economy of solidarity." Others went to work, finding low-wage employment in factories and middle-class households, or venturing into small, informal businesses on the street.

With this intensification of the livelihood struggle, the traditional separation of the money economy (markets) from the moral economy (households) has begun to blur. With their respective codes of behavior, markets and households are intersecting and merging, giving rise to the new social reality of a community-based economy and, contained within it, of a household economy no longer defined by passive consumption but by the production of livelihood and life itself (Friedmann and Salguero 1988). Women are playing the dominant role in this reconfigured space of production and, in doing so, are beginning to challenge the gendered division of labor which, as a principle, still underlies the classical conception of capitalist relations.

Alongside livelihood, citizen rights constitute the second main object of women's struggles. The term came increasingly into use during the 1980s as a number of authors began to reconsider the set of rights and obligations that should define membership in a political community (Dietz 1985; Mouffe 1992). Political rights were the most important of these and led to demands by organized sectors of "civil society" for active participation in decision making and for holding politicians to reasonable standards of honesty and accountability. But claims were beginning to be staked out for economic and social rights as well, such as the right to work, to housing, and to the equal treatment of women before the law. This politics of claiming involved all sectors of society but, as several of the essays in this volume show, specifically women of the "popular sectors."[3] This new insistence on universal rights, rather than special favors, challenged the traditional order of clientelistic relations that continues to be deeply ingrained in Latin America's political ethos (Durham 1984).

The 1980s were a preeminently conflictive decade in Latin America, particularly for women. It is true, of course, that historical changes cannot be arrayed into neat decadal clusters. There is nevertheless good reason to look at the 1980s as the decade of women's "emergences." What happened on the larger historical canvas helps to explain why it is specifically this and no earlier decade that marked a turning point in the history of Latin American women. Three points stand out in particular. First, the mass impoverishment of working-class, popular sector, and peasant households: as Lourdes Benería shows in her lead essay, most of them had significantly less real income at the end of the decade than at its start. Second, the "retreat of the state" from its social obligations, in part, a result of the structural adjustment policies championed by the World Bank and of the worldwide revival of neoliberal ideology. Third, a weakening of central state powers as a result not only of a loss of traditional functions but also of high-level corruption (intensified by the upsurge of the international drug trade), prolonged civil conflict and, toward the end of the decade, the withdrawal of military regimes in a number of leading countries and a return to formal democratic rule. It was this specific combination of circumstances that, we believe, gave rise to the intensified struggles for livelihood and citizen rights mentioned above, and to the part played in them by women.

A contextualizing force in women's social and political mobilization during the decade was the continuing incorporation of the population into urban life. In the major countries of the region, the glacial shift from rural to urban finally culminated in a substantial majority of urban population and, in some cases, even in absolute rural declines. For a variety of reasons, identified below, urbanization tends to raise the probability of social and political mobilization:[4]

- the segregation of the poor in very large peripheral settlements typically deprived of even the most basic services;

- the consequent high accessibility of the urban poor to politicians on the Left, to students, and to radical priests whose encouragement, mediations, and support in mobilization episodes are usually required;

- the social learning that urban settings promote: the impact of the media, the visibility of the rich, the contrast between political rhetoric and actual performance, the experience of successful mobilizations, etc.;

- the higher average levels of social development that prevail in cities, especially literacy and education, by contrast with rural areas, making deprivation and disempowerment more onerous to bear (see UNDP 1993);

- the greater political visibility of the poor when they take to the streets and the role of the media in reporting on these events: poverty in cities is more difficult to hide than that in rural areas.

Women are part of the general mobilization of the poor. Except in rare cases, such as the Madres de la Plaza de Mayo in Buenos Aires, women do not mobilize by themselves; they join in the general mobilization of poor communities.

The essays collected here are about both livelihood and citizen rights. Livelihood underlies all of them as the central concern of impoverished households, but the emphasis in four of the essays is on women's increasing role in the politics of livelihood. In this politics, women now play an increasingly visible role. As might be expected, their new role has grown out of the nurturing part of mother and housewife to which capitalism and older traditions have consigned them. The difference is that, in their old roles, women were publicly invisible and silent. In many Latin American cities that is no longer the case. Women have emerged, are still emerging, into the public sphere challenging the prevailing patriarchy. As a result, they have gained in stature on both lines of struggle: as visible providers, their contributions to household maintenance can no longer remain unacknowledged; as political actors, they are acquiring new capacities for collective leadership and action.

In a context-setting essay, Lourdes Benería, an economist, recounts the social impact of neoliberal structural adjustment policies. She shows how these policies, imposed by Latin American governments under pressure from international agencies, have disproportionately affected women. Austerity packages designed to ensure international debt repayments have produced a dramatic deterioration in living conditions throughout the region. Social services which, one would have supposed, had become all the more necessary under conditions of prolonged economic crisis have been sharply rolled back and in some cases, even eliminated. As caretakers of social reproduction and the domestic economy, women have been the most harshly affected by these policies. They have been forced into labor markets to supplement the declining value (if not disappearance) of men's wages, and have assumed increasing domestic responsibilities as well. As economic resources have declined, the domestic sphere has had to reorganize its efforts to ensure the survival of the immediate family. And with dwindling state support, it has again been women, organizing at neighborhood levels, who have provided the needed social services of food distribution, health care, and infant and child care. Whether or not alternative policy options were open at the time, and whether they would have had substantially different outcomes, remains a puzzling question. But structural adjustment continues to rework economy, society, and state in Latin America and constitutes the objective context for the stories that follow.

The two chapters of Part II explore women's emergence in community-based economic organizations (Feijoó) and industrial labor markets (Mummert). María del Carmen Feijoó's contribution discusses two community development projects in Greater Buenos Aires that attempted to respond to the "social emergency" by placing the responsibility for providing needed social services on the communities themselves. She suggests that such self-help approaches which organize women around caretaker roles reinforce traditional gender roles that subordinate them to men. Nevertheless, it is precisely in this extension of household responsibilities into the collective sphere that women learn to work together and to develop leadership capacities for which, in earlier times, there were no outlets.

For her part, Gail Mummert shows how global restructuring processes, such as those described by Benería, have affected the lives of inhabitants in a small rural community in Michoacán, Mexico. Covering three decades of its history, Mummert describes how the social fabric of the community has been transformed with the establishment of a U.S.-financed strawberry packing plant nearby. In this case, traditional gender relations were disrupted by the participation of young women in the agroindustrial work force. For these women, earning a wage outside the home opened new horizons and profoundly affected their self-image. Earning wages, even the low wages of strawberry packers, gave them a new understanding of themselves as producers and contributors to their households' livelihood, as the community passed from provincial obscurity into the mainstream of economic life.

Part III examines women's political practices. Maruja Barrig and Cecilia Blondet write from within the severe crisis of the Peruvian state. Barrig argues that as debt crisis and structural adjustment crippled the state's fiscal capacity, women's community-based organizations became a primary source of social services, especially in the provision of that most basic need, food. So-called popular kitchens are at the heart of her story. The food was donated by the official U.S. foreign assistance agency and distributed in Lima by CARITAS, a non-profit agency of the Catholic Church. In time, the Peruvian state tried to capture the increasingly autonomous community-based organizations by inserting itself as an intermediate agent in the process of food distribution. Barrig connects her story to the question of citizenship, but her conclusion is a pessimistic one. "The precarious notion of political citizenship," she writes, "is only a flimsy platform used as a starting point from which to appeal to the strengthening of group identities, making it difficult to construct an inclusive democratic order." In Peru, at least, the corporativist tradition is alive and well.

Cecilia Blondet's chapter is a straightforward account of the attempt by Sendero Luminoso, the terrorist, revolutionary movement of the Shining Path, to seize control of Lima's working class barrios. After first neglecting women's organizations as irrelevant for their purposes, the Shining Path movement began targeting them along with other organizations active in the barrios and *pueblos jóvenes* of Lima's periphery. Their primitive philosophy of "whoever is not for us is against us" allowed for no equivocation, and community leadership had either to be co-opted, cowed, or physically eradicated. Blondet shows how difficult women's livelihood struggles became when they were suddenly caught in the cross fire between a repressive and financially bankrupt regime and a terrorizing, largely male-dominated movement aiming to destroy anyone who stood in the way of their own march to hegemonic power. Although these conflicts have somewhat abated since the essay was written, women's lot has hardly been eased.

Malena de Montís gives us a detailed account of the official women's movement under the Sandinista regime and what happened to it once the traditional ruling class returned to power in Nicaragua. Her focus is women's political organizations and their struggle for autonomy from the state. Noting that the identities and personal relations among women are themselves the products of patriarchy, she shows how organized women were forced to address these deeply embedded aspects of gender in order to build a cohesive movement. Failing to be a true expression of grassroots sentiments, the movement was unable to challenge a state-imposed conception of women's emancipation. In postrevolutionary Nicaragua, these conflicts between an ideologized "revolutionary" women's movement and a grassroots-based democratic movement came into the open, characterizing the present phase of the struggle.

The dialogue between Elsa Chaney and Aída Moreno takes us out of these localized perspectives by discussing the efforts of domestic workers to organize on a Latin American scale. Chaney, a university-based researcher, and Moreno, a domestic worker, activist, and union leader, talk about the rise of the domestic workers' movement in the region and about the ways scholars have supported these efforts with their studies.

In her concluding essay, Sonia Alvarez explores various feminist strategies for "integrating women's rights into male-dominant political arenas." She challenges us to look "beyond and beneath" the nation state to forge a constructive collaboration between feminists and poor women's struggles over livelihood, and to move toward a transformative conception of citizenship. Hers is an explicitly activist perspective. She writes passionately about a subject that she knows intimately from firsthand experience on the battle lines of feminist struggle.

The narratives that follow don't fall neatly into a three-act structure, with a beginning, middle, and end. They are open-ended stories whose ultimate outcome and meaning cannot be foreseen. The writers are scholar-activists who cannot remove themselves to look "objectively" at the events they recount, but who report from close to the scene of the action itself; none are disinterested observers.

With the exception of the Chaney-Moreno dialogue, the stories reveal their authors' rage and sense of desperation. For Feijoó, community participation reinforces women's subordination to men. For Mummert, women's gains from industrial employment in rural Michoacán come at the expense of traditional cultural forms and security networks. For Barrig, women's self-help organizing is inherently linked to a retreating state, worse social conditions, and a fragile sense of citizenship; for Blondet, the story is even more straightforwardly tragic. And for de Montís, the women's movement in Nicaragua has splintered into multiple factions, few of which enjoy grassroots support.

In the end, the stories in this volume convey an ambiguous message. Although Latin American women from the so-called popular sectors are beginning to emerge into the public sphere, their struggles for livelihood, citizen rights, and social justice are far from being won. In some cases, the condition of women is worse today than it was ten or even twenty years ago. It is not surprising therefore that in her closing essay, Sonia Alvarez addresses issues of strategy rather than theory. Before the text can be interpreted, it must first be written.

ENDNOTES

1. The concept of moral economy refers to social relations that are mediated through a process of general reciprocity (see Scott 1976; Ekeh 1974).

2. For a historical and critical overview of the household economy in relation to markets, see Booth (1993).

3. In Spanish Latin America, the preferred descriptive term for the masses of poor families and households is the vague but widely understood term of *clases populares*.

4. Clearly, mobilization of the poor occurs also in rural areas as well as in the more rural countries of the continent. What we emphasize here is the greater probability of poor people's movements under conditions of rising levels of urbanization.

BIBLIOGRAPHY

Booth, William James (1993). *Households: On the Moral Architecture of the Economy*. Ithaca: Cornell University Press.

Dietz, Mary G. (1985). "Citizenship with a Feminist Face: The Problem with Maternal Thinking." *Political Theory* 133:1 (February), 19–37.

Durham, Eunice (1984). "Movimentos sociais: Construção da cidadanía." *Novos Estudos CEBRAB* 10 (October).

Ekeh, Peter (1974). *Social Exchange Theory: Two Traditions*. Cambridge, MA: Harvard University Press, 1974.

Friedmann, John, and Mauricio Salguero (1988). "The Barrio Economy and Collective Self-Empowerment in Latin America." In John Friedmann, *Life Space and Economic Space: Essays in Third World Planning*. Brunswick and Oxford: Transaction Books.

Mouffe, Chantal (1992). "Feminism, Citizenship and Radical Democratic Politics." In Judith Butler and Joan Scott, eds., *Feminists Theorize the Political*. New York: Routledge.

Scott, James (1976). *The Moral Economy of the Peasant: Rebellion and Subsistence in Southeast Asia*. New Haven: Yale University Press.

UNDP (United Nations Development Program) (1993). *Human Development Report 1993*. New York: Oxford University Press.

Part I. Context

1

The Foreign Debt Crisis and the Social Costs of Adjustment in Latin America

LOURDES BENERÍA

The Debt Crisis and Structural Adjustment

The debt crisis surfaced in August 1982 when Mexico made public that it could no longer meet its debt payments. At that time, Mexico was "rescued" with a financial package which included loans from the International Monetary Fund (IMF) and the U.S. government; in turn, the Mexican government adopted the first set of the IMF-inspired structural adjustment policies (SAPs) associated with the crisis. Such a package of policies would become the model followed by other countries, particularly in Latin America and Africa during the 1980s and, more recently, in Eastern Europe. Essentially, these policies have been high-powered austerity programs aimed at mobilizing the whole economy in order to generate resources that would help repay the debt. Some of the details may have varied from country to country, but the basic characteristics have been quite similar and can be grouped in four main policy areas.

First, a common starting point has been the adjustments in the area of foreign exchange, beginning with some degree of currency devaluation in order to deal with normally overvalued currencies. A devaluation automatically makes imports more expensive and exports cheaper and the result is felt immediately in price increases. This implies an automatic decrease in the purchasing power of fixed incomes; even for people with non-fixed incomes, purchasing power is likely to decrease unless their income rises faster than the inflation rate. Wage increases have lagged hopelessly behind the extremely high inflation rates that have prevailed in many countries, generating huge declines in the standard of living for the majority of the population and the impoverishment of many.

Second, drastic cuts in government spending have been used not only to reduce deficits in the public sector but also to restructure the economy, shifting resources and economic activity from the public to the private sector. These cuts have reduced or eliminated government services and subsidies—such as in education, health, and other sectors that tend to benefit particularly the lower income groups and increase their social wage—and they have been implemented at a rapid pace in most countries. For example, per capita public expenditures on education in Mexico declined by 66 percent between 1982 and 1984 while the corresponding figures for health and social security fell by 70 and 75 percent respectively (Benería 1992). A different aspect of policies geared to reduce the role of the government in the economy has been the process of privatization of public firms. Although it may have served the important function of eliminating inefficient and even corrupt operations in the public sector, privatization has also played the ideological role of responding to the dictates of the decade's neoliberal model and to the imposition of market over welfare and other criteria in the functioning of the economy.

Third, as part of the new emphasis on the market, structural adjustment policies have been used to open up the economy to foreign competition. There are two major parts to this process, namely, the reliance on trade liberalization to foster competition and the easing of rules regulating foreign investment in both the financial and the productive sectors. One result of these processes has been an increase in the internationalization of domestic economies, representing a dramatic shift from domestically oriented economies to an increase in their openness to foreign competition and global capital.

Fourth, the other side of the same coin is that structural adjustment policies have also been used as part of the shift from the import substitution models of the past to export promotion development strategies. The new emphasis is on the production of tradeables rather than non-tradeables. Hence the need for "modernization" or the drive toward more efficient and lower-cost production so as to be able to compete in international markets. Thus, the competitive pressures result from both the imports that compete with domestic production and from the need for exports to be competitive at the global level. This creates the need for restructuring production which includes the introduction of new technologies and the pressures to lower labor costs.

The lowering of labor costs is but one aspect of what some authors have referred to as "the crushing of labor" which results from a variety of factors. On the one hand, high levels of inflation have deteriorated living standards while the relative share of gross national product (GNP) going to wages has decreased drastically. In Mexico, for example, this share fell from 40 percent in 1976 to 32 percent in 1982 and continued to decline during the 1980s (Edel and Edel 1990). On the other hand, the rise in unemployment generated by the cuts in the public sector and the low or negative levels of investment that prevailed in many countries have increased the vulnerability of labor, reduced its bargaining power, and contributed to the informalization of the labor market. The informal sector therefore has played an increasing role in generating household income, while the sector itself has been transformed in the process (Roberts 1991).

To sum up, SAPs represent a series of measures that amount to: *(a)* getting the population to work hard and more productively, even though at lower real wages, so as to generate funds to repay the debt; *(b)* eliminating waste and inefficiency while "rationalizing" the economy according to the signals dictated by the market; *(c)* achieving a higher level of openness to foreign competition as well as a higher degree of integration with the global economy; and *(d)* returning to "normalcy" and growth through the invisible hand of the market.

Have these goals been achieved after more than a decade of SAPs? Since the early 1990s, the international development community has often expressed a great deal of optimism with regard to the Latin American debt crisis, frequently declaring that it is over. Much has been said about the emerging boom in financial markets, the return of capital previously sent abroad, and the positive rates of growth in several countries. As the weekly *The Economist* put it in 1992, "the re-emerging markets in Latin America have become hot business" while at the same time "nowhere are the celebrations of life after debt bigger than on Wall Street."[1] The article points out that inflows of new capital jumped from around $8 billion a year in the late 1980s to about $40 billion in 1992. Similarly, other reports on economic and social conditions in the region emphasized the beginning (in 1991) of the "long-awaited recovery . . . as favorable expectations generated by the reform process stimulated private investment, encouraged a boom in the equity markets, and attracted substantial financial flows from abroad" (Inter-American Development Bank 1992). These optimistic reports have emphasized the "spectacular" growth achieved by Argentina, Chile, Venezuela, and even Peru in recent years—to the extent of talking about the "found decade" and counterposing it to the "lost decade" of the 1980s—and have suggested that the sacrifices of the 1980s have begun to pay off.[2]

How should one interpret these optimistic reports? I want to argue three points: *(a)* the debt crisis is over for the banks but not for most countries; *(b)* although a turning point in these economic indicators has indeed been observed in several countries, an emphasis on social rather than economic indicators would hardly lead to such optimism; and *(c)* to the extent that progress has been achieved in some cases, it is still precarious and many countries continue to face a "crisis of development."

In order to elaborate the first point, we need to recall the seriousness of the foreign debt crisis in the early 1980s, a period when the fear of a collapse in the international financial system was intense among the high international financial circles. This was very explicitly noted by William Rhodes, vice chairman of Citibank, when he described this situation as it was viewed during the annual IMF/World Bank meeting in Toronto in September 1982: "The standing joke [at the time] was that the efforts to contain the crisis amounted to no more than rearranging the deck chairs on the Titanic" (Rhodes 1992). The fear was that a major bank would collapse, which would set off a chain reaction that would severely shock the international financial system.

These fears, Rhodes argued, did not materialize for a variety of reasons. First, SAPs started to be implemented and new loans to the countries that adopted these policy packages avoided default. Second, the key actors in the international financial community—commercial banks, government agencies, and international financial organizations—worked together as a common front to deal with the crisis. Third, the emphasis placed by the international community on a "one-by-one negotiation" contrasted with the "global solution" that would have led to a common front on the part of the debtor countries. This process gave strength to the international actors and weakened individual debtor countries with regard to the terms of debt negotiations.

As a result of this process, by the time the Baker Plan was announced in October 1985, the worst crisis had been avoided. New loans were granted in exchange for an intensification of structural reforms, as in the case of Chile, Mexico, and Brazil, which permitted the continuation of the process of debt repayment. And debt repayments continued to shift huge amounts of financial resources from the debtor countries to banks of high income countries, acting as a regressive international tax.

To illustrate, between 1979 and 1989 Brazil paid about $113 billion in interest only, and for Latin America as a whole estimates of debt repayments have ranged between $30 and $40 billion (Dussel-Peters 1993;

Nogueira 1994). The notion of "recolonization" seems quite appropriate to describe this drain of resources from the poorer to the richer countries. Thus, by the time the Brady Plan was announced in March 1989, the potential "for a serious international banking crisis" (Sachs 1989) had disappeared as debt repayment proceeded. The position of the lending commercial banks had improved considerably—to the extent that the Brady Plan, for the first time since the crisis emerged, called for voluntary debt reduction and debt forgiveness by commercial banks. Although faulty and short of mechanisms for implementation, the plan reflected the fact that international banks were by then "safe" and could afford some degree of forgiveness. Thus a long and complex process of debt renegotiations, debt swaps, and debt forgiveness began; the banks had been saved, and they could now afford some leniency even though the relative amount of debt that was reduced was not very significant (see below).

A similar story, though with different details, can be told about countries in Africa and other regions that have been subject to SAPs. In this sense, SAPs can be viewed as an unprecedented international effort to save the commercial banks that lent heavily and at a rate "difficult to justify" during the 1970s (Sachs 1989) by mobilizing entire countries and a large proportion of their population to avert a financial crisis of world proportions.

Yet, despite these efforts, heavy debts continue to burden most countries. According to World Bank figures, between 1982 and 1992 the total external debt outstanding increased in all Latin American countries. As Table 1 indicates, even Mexico, a country which successfully negotiated debt forgiveness through the Brady Plan mechanisms and which has managed to attract capital again since 1990, still carried a debt burden of over $113 billion in 1992. Although Mexico has been presented as a success story and a model for other countries to follow, it is difficult to draw this conclusion from these figures.

Table 1 also includes the proportion of debt to GNP, a way of expressing the debt burden in relative terms. Here the figures depict a mixed picture, indicating that some of the major debtor countries show an improvement (Argentina) or no change (Brazil). Other countries, however, like Mexico, Colombia, Venezuela, and some of the smaller countries, registered a clear decline in their relative position. In the case of Ecuador, Honduras, Jamaica, Nicaragua, Panama, and Peru this deterioration is dramatic—to the extent that the proportion of total debt to GNP is close to or more than 100 percent. For these countries, the question of designing

TABLE 1. CHANGES IN EXTERNAL DEBT OUTSTANDING, 1982–1992

Country	Total Debt Outstanding[a] (Millions of Dollars)		Total Debt to GNP (%)	
	1982	1992	1980	1992
Argentina	43,634	67,569	48.4	30.3
Bahamas	228	392[d]	15.2[b]	13.3[c]
Barbados	236	535[d]	23.8[b]	31.7[c]
Bolivia	3,329	4,243	93.3	61.2
Brazil	92,903	121,110	31.2	31.2
Chile	17,315	19,360	45.2	48.9
Colombia	10,306	17,204	20.9	36.9
Costa Rica	3,641	3,963	59.5	58.7
Dominican Republic	2,519	4,649	31.5	57.0
Ecuador	7,705	12,280	53.8	99.9
El Salvador	1,443	2,131	25.9	25.5
Guatemala	1,537	2,749	14.9	24.2
Guyana	956	1,924[d]	206.5[b]	313.6[c]
Haiti	536	906[d]	20.9	36.1[c]
Honduras	1,842	3,573	61.5	92.2
Jamaica	2,846	4,303	78.3	131.7
Mexico	86,019	113,378	30.5	34.1
Nicaragua	2,913	11,126	121.5[b]	750.3
Panama	3,923	6,505	92.3	107.2
Paraguay	1,296	1,747	20.7	24.6
Peru	12,305	20,293	51.0	92.7
Suriname	25	123[c]	2.4[b]	7.2[b]
Trinidad and Tobago	1,203	2,262	14.0	50.8[c]
Uruguay	2,647	5,253	17.0	46.7
Venezuela	32,153	37,193	42.1	61.1

a. Sum of long-term and short-term debt and use of IMF credit.
b. Debt/GNP data refer to 1982 and 1991.
c. 1990 figures.
d. 1991 figures.

Source: Inter-American Development Bank 1992, table E1; World Bank 1992, table 24; and World Bank 1994, tables 21 and 22.

alternative policies for the immediate future is urgent, since they will face prolonged hardships as orthodox SAPs continue to be implemented. Again, it is difficult to be optimistic about the debt crisis when looking at these data. For Latin America, the most we can say is that the crisis is over for the banks but not for most of the debtor countries.

The Social Costs of Adjustment

What began as a banking crisis, however, created other types of crises. The accumulated social costs generated by SAPs have been enormous and devastating for a large proportion of the population affected and particularly for the poor (Cornia et al. 1987; Commonwealth Secretariat 1990; Benería and Feldman 1992). Accompanied by the economic "shocks" caused both by the halt in investment and by the decrease in export prices, unemployment, and deteriorating economic conditions, the 1980s in Latin America reversed several decades of considerable, even if uneven, economic progress. During this "lost decade" most Latin American countries suffered a stagnant or negative growth rate. According to the Economic Commission for Latin America (CEPAL, Comisión Económica para América Latina), by 1989 the average per capita GNP for the region as a whole was 8 percent less than in 1980—equivalent, in real terms, to the 1977 level (CEPAL 1990).

Aggregate and average figures, however, are misleading. The devastating effects of the debt and subsequent social adjustment policies need to be disaggregated since the distribution of the burden of adjustment, as numerous studies have shown (including the essays in this volume), has been uneven. As pointed out above, government cuts, particularly in education, health, housing, and other social services, have affected the poor disproportionately, given poor people's greater reliance on such services and their inability to afford the substitutes provided by the private sector. In addition, the SAPs listed above, coupled with the greater reliance on the market, have intensified the traditional inequality in the distribution of resources in Latin America. For example, while in 1980, 32 percent of the population in the region lived below the poverty line, by 1985 the proportion had increased to 39 percent and continued to increase throughout the decade (CEPAL 1990). In Venezuela, the proportion of households in moderate poverty increased from 22.3 percent in 1982 to 32.6 percent in 1987, while the proportion living in extreme poverty increased from 10.3 percent in 1982 to 21.5 percent in 1987 (Cartaya and Delía 1991).

Similar figures can be quoted for other countries; the process has been accompanied with an increased polarization of income and social inequalities (Cortés and Rubalcava 1993).

The general deterioration of living standards for all but a small proportion of the population has generated social tensions at many levels of society, which are symbolized by the increase in crime and violence among the young, particularly in urban centers, and it has led to food riots and political tensions. Similarly, this deterioration has been at the root of the strong migratory pressures from Latin America and the Caribbean to North America during the 1980s (CEPAL 1990). Many studies and documentaries have given detailed accounts of the hardships generated by the social costs of adjustment.[3] Yet, not enough thought has been given to the search for and experimentation with policy alternatives. One cannot help but ponder the fact that bankers and officials making policy from government offices and international organizations are not, after all, among those suffering the hardships of adjustment.

It is also well known that the distribution of the burden of adjustment has been unequal within households. A variety of studies show that, for the people affected, daily survival has been organized at the micro level of the household. In Latin America, a "major gathering of forces" at the family level and a "privatization of the struggle for survival" have occurred.[4] Although important collective strategies have emerged, such as soup kitchens in Peru (*comedor popular*) and Bolivia (*olla comun*), it is at the household level that survival strategies have been centered. Therefore, a close look at the micro level of the household is useful in understanding the significance of the costs of adjustment in people's daily lives. I have argued elsewhere that these survival strategies have developed around three main areas: *(a)* labor market adjustments; *(b)* budget adjustments; and *(c)* the restructuring of daily life (Benería 1992). In addition, a great deal of organizing has taken place around household issues which can be viewed as part of these strategies. Each of them affects women in a special way.

A common response to the crisis has been the increase in the number of household members participating in the *labor market* in order to contribute to family income. The need to increase the pool of labor force participants has affected mostly women and young people. Married women, who generally had a particularly low participation rate, have joined the paid labor force in unprecedented numbers. In many cases, this has meant joining the informal economy, especially given the difficulties in finding work under less precarious conditions. A case study carried out in Mexico City in the summer of 1988 illustrates this point. Sixty-six percent of the mothers with a male partner earned some income, two-thirds of them from informal work (Benería 1992). This high degree of involvement in some form of paid activity has been documented by other studies as well (see CEPAL 1990; Safa and Antrobus 1992; Pérez-Alemán 1992). Given women's primary dedication to domestic work and the basically unchanging division of labor in the household, their participation in the labor force has represented an important increase in their work load, often the source of stress and physical exhaustion and part of the more intangible social costs of adjustment (González de la Rocha 1991).

Children and teenagers have been the second group most affected by labor force strategies. For them, participation in the labor market has often implied the interruption or termination of schooling, a loss that is likely to be permanent. While the discontinuation of schooling at the end of secondary education seems to have affected both young men and women, school interruption at younger ages has been found to be most common among girls who are often asked to stay at home to help with domestic work when the mother has a paid job or is involved in some other activity (Moser 1989). The cumulative effects of such interruptions are difficult to estimate but in the long run are likely to be substantial, since they have an impact on the educational level of those affected.

As a result of the crisis, heavy *budget adjustments* have affected not only the poorest sectors of the population but also a large proportion of the middle class as well (Benería 1992). As practically every Latin American person knows and many studies have amply documented, the crisis has required very drastic reductions in expenditures on food, clothing, shoes, transportation, drinks, and snacks, and so on (Safa and Antrobus 1992; Pérez-Alemán 1992). What exactly has been cut from the household budget varies according to income level, class background, and other factors. For the lower income groups, budget adjustments have led to deeper levels of poverty and hardship. In different degrees, hardships and anxieties resulting from budget adjustments have also been felt by stable working-class families that have seen many products excluded from their shopping lists and even by middle-class households that have had to reduce expenses previously taken for granted, such as imported goods and domestic help. In all these cases, women have carried very directly the burden of adjustment since they are primarily responsible for the household budget.

Budget adjustments have also led to the *restructuring of daily life*, that is, to changes in the way households organize themselves to carry out their daily activities and social life. This restructuring has taken different forms across Latin American countries. To illustrate with the case of Mexico, the adjustment of the 1980s generated at least three basic responses: *(a)* changes in purchasing habits; *(b)* intensification of domestic work; and *(c)* changes in social life.

Households have been forced to change their buying habits because of the increased need to look for the lowest prices, often in more distant markets or because of other factors. The crisis has also resulted in an increase in the number of, and often the length of time to complete, household chores; and it has contributed to the intensification of domestic work, such as the need to perform two or more tasks at the same time (Floro 1992), or, for the middle-class housewife, less domestic help. When budgets are tighter, homemade goods and services replace those purchased in the market, and more cooking, sewing, mending, and fixing needs to be done at home. When space is reduced, the need for cleaning and tidying increases.

Although all family members may participate in these tasks, a substantial proportion of the responsibility falls upon women. For women heading households, particularly those with small children, the burden often seems unbearable. For working daughters, the pressure to participate in the double load represented by domestic and market work intensifies the existing asymmetries with working sons, who are not asked to participate equally in domestic work, and generates gender-related tensions within the household (Moser 1989; Benería 1992; Safa and Antrobus 1992).

Finally, changes in social life can take different forms—from reducing the number of visits to relatives in order to save on transportation, to staying at home or in the neighborhood on Sundays instead of going to the movies, to eliminating parties and family celebrations. Although, taken individually, these changes may seem trivial, their cumulative impact has had an enormous effect on people's daily lives (González de la Rocha 1991). To the extent that women's lives are more centered around the household than men's, these changes have also affected them in a disproportionate way.

Women have also taken part in a different type of survival strategy by participating in grassroots organizations that deal with issues related to daily needs, such as social services and infrastructure (food, health care delivery, housing, transportation, water, electricity, etc.). Poor women have been in the forefront of many of these organizations, representing a collective effort of unprecedented proportions. The emergence of popular women's organizations was an important part of the new social movements in Latin America during the 1980s, an effort resulting from both the severity of the economic crisis and the new consciousness of women regarding their political role and place in society. A variety of studies have documented this effort and analyzed "the politicization of daily life" as well as the significance of these struggles for an understanding of gender politics and the new positioning of women in the political life of Latin American countries (Barrig 1992; Wappenstein 1992).

The cumulative effects of more than a decade of deteriorating living conditions are not easy to estimate, particularly in the long run. Standards of nutrition and health have declined in many countries and many trends of previous decades have been reversed; the reappearance of disease epidemics, such as cholera, has been an indication of this retrogression. To be sure, some studies are not conclusive regarding the impact of SAPs on health in Latin America (Langer et al. 1991), but the long-term effects in this area are very difficult to evaluate and need to be added to the list of the often intangible but nonetheless real impacts of structural adjustment policies. For millions of people, the increase in violence in the streets as well as in the home, mental and physical stress, anxiety around daily safety and survival, infrastructure and environmental degradation, and a general deterioration in the quality of life may bring long-lasting consequences, and not only for the poorest groups.

All of it, including the longer than initially expected period of adjustment which for most countries has not yet ended, seems a high price to pay for rescuing the banks which followed an irresponsible lending policy during the 1970s (Sachs 1989). The resulting increase in poverty in the countries that have adopted SAPs has led to growing criticisms of the IMF/World Bank model of adjustment even by establishment sources. The weekly *The Economist*, for example, accused the World Bank of "complacency" on the issue of poverty in Africa, claiming that it "has lost any claim to intellectual and political credibility" (March 5, 1994). Likewise, the current "Fifty Years Is Enough" campaign against the IMF and the Bank, organized around their fiftieth anniversary, indicates the extent to which SAPs are perceived as a source of hardship instead of a solution to debtor countries' problems.

This is especially so if we consider that even the countries that seem to have reached a turning point do not show clear signs of a healthy recovery, with the possible exception of Chile. Mexico's performance, for example, has been uneven, and the 1994 uprising in Chiapas, together with the assassination of the governing party's presidential candidate, show the precariousness and high degree of vulnerability of its recovery. In the same way, recent elections in Costa Rica, Colombia, the Dominican Republic, and Venezuela show that the majority of the population have voted for candidates critical of the orthodox adjustment packages.

Other Biases of Structural Adjustment Policies

I have argued that the unequal distribution of the burden of adjustment has resulted in class and gender biases. A third bias—related to race and ethnicity—is also apparent. Although they have not been analyzed in the studies of the costs of adjustment, the events in Chiapas have provided some evidence for it. To the extent that the indigenous populations and people of color are disproportionately represented among the poor, it is to be expected that there is a race and ethnicity bias as well.

In addition, there are at least two other types of biases in these processes. One has to do with the general imposition of market-related efficiency criteria to the virtual exclusion of other criteria in policy making. Thus, the objectives of adjustment are measured exclusively in terms of cost/benefit analysis, efficiency and productivity standards, competitiveness in domestic and international markets, economic growth, and the like. While these are important criteria in a world of scarcity and are valid for dealing with many of the problems of the Latin American economies, the failure to take into consideration human costs and effects on human (as opposed to economic) development has been disturbing, a fact emphasized by UNICEF in 1987 (Cornia et al. 1987). The fact is that SAPs have been imposed without correlative social policies to counteract the negative consequences derived from the functioning of the market.

Thus, in the same way that the industrial revolution and the growth of nineteenth-century capitalism generalized the imposition of market criteria in many areas, the internationalization of domestic economies during the late twentieth century has facilitated and intensified a similar process at the global level. As some authors have argued in favor of SPAs, the commonly assumed conflict between efficiency and equity has been dealt with by opting for efficiency, as reflected through the market mechanism (Cartaya and Delía 1991). This choice implies that, for the time being at least, income distribution and social polarization have not become a matter of political concern. To be sure, adjustment policies have been accompanied by some programs dealing with the poorest of the poor—such as the "emergency social funds" being implemented in several countries or Mexico's Programa Nacional de Solidaridad or PRONASOL (Solidarity Program). However, their objectives amount to avoiding conditions of extreme poverty and preventing social unrest that would jeopardize the implementation of the overall policies. The absence of social policies dealing with the social cost of adjustment (UNICEF's "adjustment with a human face") has been the norm rather than the exception—at a time when the voices calling for evaluating the development process with criteria that reflect human as well as economic indicators are growing louder.[5]

A different problem along these lines has to do with how efficiency is measured. The use of market criteria implies that efficiency is measured in terms of market prices/costs. Thus, as argued above, producing at the lowest possible prices for the international market has resulted in a "downward adjustment," resulting in lower wages, repressive trade union policies, intensification of household work, and other forms of cost reduction. In the same way, government budget cuts and privatization can be viewed as part of this downward adjustment to the extent that they generate, for example, new health problems and lower educational standards. These human costs are not taken into consideration despite the fact that many of them could be assessed in dollars and cents.

It can be argued, therefore, that greater efficiency and lower costs represent a transfer of costs from the market to the household. Market prices underestimate the true costs of adjustment. In theory, a social cost/benefit analysis should include all costs, including non-market costs, in order to arrive at a more comprehensive and human evaluation of the adjustment process. As Elson (1991) has eloquently argued, macroeconomic policies are not neutral, as policy makers commonly assume; their focus is not on people but on macroeconomic variables and on impersonal concepts such as productivity and efficiency. These apparently neutral concepts, Elson argues, assume that human resources are free and "costlessly transferable between different activities" and that "households and people will not fall apart under the stress of the decisions that adjustment requires" (p. 168). Thus, there is a bias not only against specific groups of people—mostly a class bias—but also "a deeper gender bias" owing to sexual divisions of labor and the special location of women in market production and in the household, as I argue here.

A second bias in SAPs is that they have responded to the needs and agendas of powerful international capital interests—represented by the large commercial banks, financial organizations, transnational capital, and institutions such as the IMF and the World Bank. Thus, at a time when the "new democracies" have been advertised widely in Latin America and elsewhere, packages affecting millions of people have been adopted practically overnight without "democratic" discussion. This is an example of what Europeans have called a "democratic deficit," referring to the undermining of democratic control as local decisions are shifted from the domestic sphere to the level of the European Union.

Was/Is There an Alternative?

One of the common responses from government and international development circles to criticisms of SAPs is that there was no alternative to the austerity programs of IMF-inspired adjustment packages implemented not only in Latin America but in Africa and other Third World countries that were carrying substantial foreign debt. To be sure, the 1980s witnessed an incredible homogenization of national policies dealing with foreign debt despite the very different conditions prevailing in the domestic economies that adopted them. The more recent implementation of similar packages in Eastern Europe is but the latest manifestation of such a trend; here, too, the social costs of adjustment have begun to emerge—raising once more the question of whether less painful alternatives could have been attempted.

It is not easy to speculate about what would have been the outcome if different policy packages and institutional settings had been tried as alternatives to SAPs. In Mexico, for example, the IMF-inspired package adopted in 1982 prevailed over the more progressive "managed adjustment" policies proposed by a team of Cambridge economists, which included a series of measures and controls aimed at dealing with the crisis without creating the painful shocks that followed. The proposed alternative policies ranged from exchange rate and trade controls to bank nationalization and direct negotiations with commercial banks. The alternative strategy also included the formation of a common front between Mexico and other Latin American countries to negotiate the debt from a "global position" of greater strength by acting together. The orthodox model has consistently emphasized the importance of a one-by-one negotiation that would prevent a common front.[6] But the historical opportunity to take this route was lost when the Mexican government agreed to the IMF-inspired package; the orthodox model prevailed and became the standard package for other countries.

Part of an alternative strategy, even at this late date, would imply the adoption of policies to induce growth and efficiency while distributing the burden of debt repayment more equitably. This would involve the implementation of a set of social policies along with fiscal reforms and redistributive measures. Taking into account the unequal burden falling upon women, alternative policies would need to incorporate gender as an integral part of the macroeconomic models used. This would mean paying attention to the prevailing division of labor in order to predict the differential gender impacts of adjustment and to prevent or compensate for any negative consequences on women. These objectives have not been taken seriously in the prevailing neoliberal model, which assumes that redistribution will have a trickle-down effect throughout the economic system, a phenomenon for which there is little evidence. This is why, even within the World Bank and other international organizations, the voices calling for such alternative policies have been growing louder (Blackden and Morris-Hughes 1993).

To be sure, some thinking has been done along these lines (Cornia et al. 1987; CEPAL 1990). Some analysts have called for alternative policies that would enhance education, skills, and productivity and which would redistribute resources and debt burden in a more egalitarian manner. One of the challenges of the 1990s is likely to come from the need to incorporate more democratic formulas into the process of policy making. If the democratic process is to be taken seriously, those who bear the consequences of decisions should be allowed to participate in making them. This means that the women who have struggled and actively searched for solutions since the onset of the debt crisis and the men who share their objectives need to make their voices heard at even higher levels of decision making.

ENDNOTES

1. "Falling in Love Again," *The Economist*, August 22, 1992, p. 63.
2. Inter-American Development Bank, Newsletter, March 1994.
3. See, for example, the collection of articles in Canak (1989), González de la Rocha and Escobar (1991), and Benería and Feldman (1992).
4. For more on these points, see Moser (1989), Benería (1992), Safa and Antrobus (1992), among others.
5. See, for example, *The Caracas Report on Alternative Development Indicators* (1990); UNDP (1990); and Escobar (1995).
6. For a banker's view of the process of debt negotiation, debt repayment, and SAPs, see Rhodes (1992).

BIBLIOGRAPHY

Barrig, Maruja (1992). "Nos habíamos amado tanto: Crisis del estado y organización femenina." Paper presented at the conference "Learning from Latin America: Women's Struggles for Livelihood," University of California, Los Angeles, February 27–29.

Benería, Lourdes (1992). "The Mexican Debt Crisis: Restructuring the Economy and the Household." In Lourdes Benería and Shelly Feldman, eds., *Unequal Burden: Economic Crises, Persistent Poverty, and Women's Work*. Boulder, CO: Westview Press. Pp. 83–104.

Benería, Lourdes, and Shelly Feldman, eds. (1992). *Unequal Burden: Economic Crises, Persistent Poverty, and Women's Work*. Boulder, CO: Westview Press.

Blackden, C. Mark, and Elizabeth Morris-Hughes (1993). *Paradigm Postponed: Gender and Economic Adjustment in Sub-Saharan Africa*. Technical Department, Africa Region, World Bank.

Canak, William, ed. (1989). *Lost Promises: Debt, Austerity and Development in Latin America*. Boulder, CO: Westview Press.

The Caracas Report on Alternative Development Indicators: Redefining Wealth and Progress (1990). Indianapolis: Knowledge Systems.

Cartaya, Vanesa, and Yolanda Delía (1991). *Pobreza en Venezuela: Realidad y política*. Caracas: Centro de Investigaciones en Ciencias Sociales.

CEPAL (Comisión Económica para América Latina) (1990). *Transformación productiva con equidad*. Santiago de Chile: United Nations.

Commonwealth Secretariat (1990). *Engendering Development for the 1990s*. London: Commonwealth Secretariat.

Cornia, Giovanni A., Richard Jolly, and Frances Stewart, eds. (1987). *Adjustment with a Human Face*. Oxford: Clarendon Press.

Cortés, Fernando, and Rosa María Rubalcava (1993). "Cambio estructural y concentración: Un análisis de la distribución del ingreso familiar en México, 1984–1989." Manuscript. Mexico City: El Colegio de México.

Dussel-Peters, Enrique (1993). "Quo Vadis, Señor Brady? The Brady Initiative: A Way Out of the Global Debt Crisis?" *The Review of Radical Political Economics* (March), 87–107.

Edel, Matthew, and Kim Edel (1990). "Un análisis de la crisis de acumulación mexicana." In Servio Aguayo Quesada and Bruce Michaels Bagley, eds., *En busca de la seguridad perdida: Aproximaciones a la seguridad nacional mexicana*. Mexico City: Siglo XXI Editores. Pp. 175–206.

Elson, Diane (1991). "Male Bias in Macroeconomics: The Case of Structural Adjustment." In D. Elson, ed., *Male Bias in the Development Process*. Manchester: Manchester University Press. Pp. 164–190.

Escobar, Arturo (1995). *Encountering Development: The Making and Unmaking of the Third World*. Princeton: Princeton University Press.

Floro, Maria Sagrario (1992). "Work Intensity and Women's Time: A Conceptual Framework." Manuscript.

González de la Rocha, Mercedes (1991). "Family Well-Being, Food Consumption, and Survival Strategies During Mexico's Economic Crisis." In Mercedes González de la Rocha and Augustín Escobar Lapatí, eds., *Social Responses to Mexico's Economic Crisis of the 1980s*. San Diego: Center for U.S.-Mexican Studies, University of California, San Diego. Pp. 115–128.

Inter-American Development Bank (1992). *Economic and Social Progress in Latin America: 1992 Report*. Baltimore: The Johns Hopkins University Press.

Langer, Ana, Rafael Lozano, and José Luis Bobadilla (1991). "Effects of Mexico's Economic Crisis on the Health of Women and Children." In Mercedes González de la Rocha and Augustín Escobar Lapatí, eds., *Social Responses to Mexico's Economic Crisis of the 1980s*. San Diego: Center for U.S.-Mexican Studies, University of California, San Diego. Pp. 195–220.

Moser, Caroline (1989). "The Impact of Recession and Adjustment at the Micro-Level: Low Income Women and Their Households in Guayaquil, Ecuador." In *The Invisible Adjustment: Poor Women and the Economic Crisis*. New York: UNICEF.

Nogueira, Jorge (1994). *Notes on the Debt Crisis: Brazil and the Dominican Republic*. Ithaca, NY: Cornell University.

Pérez-Alemán, Paola (1992). "Economic Crisis and Women in Nicaragua." In Lourdes Benería and Shelly Feldman, eds., *Unequal Burden: Economic Crises, Persistent Poverty, and Women's Work*. Boulder, CO: Westview Press. Pp. 239–258.

Rhodes, William (1992). "The Disaster That Didn't Happen." *The Economist*, September 12.

Roberts, Bryan (1991). "The Changing Nature of Informal Employment: The Case of Mexico." In Guy Standing and Victor Tokman, eds., *Towards Social Adjustment: Labor Market Issues in Structural Adjustment*. Geneva: International Labor Office. Pp. 115–140.

Sachs, Jeffrey (1989). "Introduction." In J. Sachs, ed., *Developing Country Debt and the World Economy*. Chicago: University of Chicago Press. Pp. 1–36.

Safa, Helen, and Peggy Antrobus (1992). "Women and the Economic Crisis in the Caribbean." In Lourdes Benería and Shelly Feldman, eds., *Unequal Burden: Economic Crises, Persistent Poverty, and Women's Work*. Boulder, CO: Westview Press. Pp. 49–82.

Standing, Guy, and Victor Tokman, eds. (1991). *Towards Social Adjustment Labor Market Issues in Structural Adjustment*. Geneva: International Labor Office.

UNDP (United Nations Development Program) (1990). *Human Development Report*. New York: Oxford University Press.

Wappenstein, Susana (1992). "Women, Violence and the Politics of Daily Survival: The Formation of a Gender-Based Culture of Resistance in Lima, Peru." Master's thesis, Cornell University.

World Bank (1992, 1993 and 1994). *World Development Report*. Oxford: Oxford University Press.

Part II. Collective Social Action and Labor Markets

2

Women Confronting the Crisis: Two Case Studies from Greater Buenos Aires

MARÍA DEL CARMEN FEIJOÓ

This essay discusses the alternative solutions in which women have participated or which they themselves have developed in response to Argentina's economic and social crisis. I refer specifically to collective solutions that, for the purposes here, do not include the survival strategies of individual households and families. The principal question is whether women's day-to-day activities, carried out against the backdrop of the economic crisis, correspond to the descriptions found in analyses of similar experiences in other countries. Are they productive projects or are they part of the family's reproductive activities? Can they be seen as a range of choices? Are they a basis for a collective empowerment of women? How are they articulated with local society and the state? Do they represent solidarity and resourcefulness inspired by structural adjustment policies? Or do they constitute an alternative social policy generated and managed by the groups most affected by structural adjustment and the economic crisis?

Given that such experiences are relatively new in Argentina compared with other Latin American countries, analyzing these processes is a first step toward the recognition of a phenomenon that deserves closer study, in terms of both its magnitude and its qualitative aspects. I refer to an economic sector—an "economy of solidarity"—which is emerging as a result of the diffusion of collective experiences, and about which we still know very little.

Editors' Note: Translated by Lilian Autler.
Author's Note: The author gratefully acknowledges the collaboration of Eleonor Faur in the research for and preparation of this report.

The Lost Decade: From Economic Crisis to "Social Emergency"

The "lost decade"—as the Economic Commission for Latin America (CEPAL, Comisión Económica para América Latina) has designated the 1980s—was a period of marked downturn for Latin America as a whole, for individual countries within the region, and for various sectors of the population, among them primarily, though not exclusively, the poor. In the context of a general drop in economic performance, the social costs of structural adjustment—related to the increase in foreign debt—fell especially hard on workers and on the middle classes (CEPAL 1990). The medium- and long-term impacts on these parts of the population must be evaluated. Women and children, who were affected in specific ways by the crisis, suffered its consequences more intensely. In the end, children are hurt most by the cuts in social spending which to a greater or lesser degree have been made by all the countries of the region. Women, in turn, have borne the costs of the "invisible adjustment," as they have been forced to increase their workload within and outside the family in order to take on many of the functions previously performed by the state.

Some figures help to give a sense of the magnitude of the problem. Between 1981 and 1989, per capita gross national product (GNP) fell 8.3 percent in Latin America (CEPAL 1990). In Argentina, a significant decrease in wage workers' share of GNP revealed a sharply regressive income distribution: in 1974, wages represented almost 45 percent of GNP; 13 years later the share was down to 30 percent. In addition, average income dropped by 40 percent between 1974 and 1987 (Minujin 1990).

The steady deterioration of the standard of living of the so-called popular sectors which marked the "lost decade" has affected countries differently. In some, the structural crisis has led to "social emergencies" in which impoverishment has intensified to the point where the historical reproductive mechanisms of the low-income population are endangered. These mechanisms have consisted of monetary income from employment, domestic production for household consumption, and state transfers in the form of social services. The crisis has seriously upset this triad and jeopardized the most basic consumption process of daily reproduction. The components most affected by the crisis were state transfer programs and household incomes, which fell drastically. Consequently, the survival of the poorest citizens came increasingly to depend on the resourcefulness of households themselves.

This has been the case in Argentina, where the skyrocketing hyperinflation which erupted in 1989 generated unprecedented social upheavals. The unrest culminated in looting which left about twenty people dead, most of them women and children. At the same time, we saw a flourishing of defensive actions aimed at softening the impact of the social emergency and developing the capacity of those hardest hit to respond individually or collectively to the situation.

One type of response has been known to social scientists since the 1970s as "survival strategies." These can take the form of changes in individual or family/household behavior, collective action, or both. Among the former are entry into the labor market of household members who previously devoted themselves exclusively to domestic work (such as women, children, and adolescents); changes in the structure of income and expenditures; migration; and changes in the composition of the domestic unit— that is, the incorporation or expulsion of household members as a function of economic imperatives, personal and family expectations, their ability to adapt to the crisis, and other conditions.

Survival strategies of a more collective nature, by comparison, imply the articulation of the family/household unit with a wide range of external actors, from state social programs and their agents to the world of diverse voluntary organizations which have proliferated in Latin America as a result of the crisis. For the purposes of this study, then, I define collective survival strategies as those responses to the crisis that involve some type of organizational entity which brings together several people or groups around activities with a neighborhood focus.

Women in the Context of the Crisis

By making it necessary for women to engage in both productive and reproductive activities, the crisis has pushed them into the social arena with greater intensity than would have resulted from the pace of growth during the 1970s. It has prompted women's incorporation into two particular realms of social activity: the labor market and neighborhood-based survival activities. In this process, some of the activities which had historically been carried out in the relatively private context of the family and the household were displaced into the public realm. Even while some groups of women have been stepping into this redefined public space, however, others have maintained traditional defensive strategies within the private sphere of the household.

Women's participation in the labor force grew significantly throughout Latin America during the 1980s, especially among married and middle-aged women (Arriagada 1990). In Argentina, the increasing number of women—particularly married women—holding paid employment can be understood as an active response to the crisis. Concomitantly, there has been a sharp drop in income among men and an increase in male unemployment (Minujin 1990).

Women of all groups have entered the labor force in great numbers. In non-poor households, women increased their participation by 33 percent between 1974 and 1987, while those in poor households did so by 11 percent during the same period. If these figures are analyzed in terms of the woman's position in the family, married women's labor force participation increased 53 percent among the non-poor and 33 percent among the poor (Minujin 1990).

The difference in the percentages of poor and non-poor women entering the labor force can be attributed to the fact that women from poor households face greater restrictions on their ability to work outside the home, such as the lack of satisfactory child care options as well as lower levels of education and training. Thus while levels of labor market participation are lower for all married women with children under six years of age, the difference is particularly notable among poor women. The combined conditions of poverty and gender limit their range of employment alternatives to low-paying occupations which are generally part-time and within the informal sector (Cortés 1990). The increase in the number of women employed in domestic service is a clear indication of this phenomenon. Nevertheless, their earnings are vital to the household, especially considering the rising unemployment and falling incomes among the male labor force.

Those women who do not meet their subsistence needs by entering the labor market might, in theory, be more inclined to participate in collective survival strategies. Obviously, willingness to join in such activities depends on more than just having free time available. It also has to do with personal attitudes such as an inclination toward group activities, a belief in the value of solidarity, perhaps some previous experience of belonging to and participating in organized groups, and a disposition for sociable interaction with one's neighbors. Given these conditions, whether one participates in collective strategies also depends on the existence of the kinds of opportunities and activities that comprise the "economy of solidarity."

The emergence of this economy is closely linked with the development and consolidation of non-governmental organizations (NGOs). In the case of Argentina, various levels of the state have played a historically significant role in stabilizing the standard of living of the popular sectors. Thus when discussing the factors behind the "economy of solidarity" it is important to take into account—in addition to the action of the NGOs—government welfare programs that rely for their implementation upon the organization of the beneficiaries.

Throughout Latin America, women play a central role in these experiences. To parody Bryan Roberts, we could say that the region's modern metropolises today are ringed by "cities of women" who lead their daily lives under conditions that are a far cry from those enjoyed by the more privileged sectors in the urban centers. Beyond this directly observable evidence, however, little is known about these forms of participation, with the exception of what has been learned in certain countries such as Peru and Chile from studies of grass roots economic self-help organizations and women's roles within them. In Argentina, perhaps because the "social emergency" is still a relatively novel phenomenon, little research has been carried out regarding either the functioning of the "economy of solidarity" generally or women's participation in it specifically.

The Actors, the Setting, and the Rules of the Game

If this characterization of women's actions in response to the economic crisis and the "social emergency" is correct, then a whole new set of issues arises regarding the role women play in developing these strategies, the impact which this role has on them, and the practical consequences of their participation.

The first set of questions is: Who are these women in terms of their socio-demographic profile and their place in the society and the community? Going on, we can inquire, on a case by case basis, about the kinds of activities they undertake: Do they barely cover the family's subsistence, or do they produce a significant monetary income? Are they part of a neighborhood- or community-wide experience which serves to strengthen and broaden social bonds and networks of solidarity? Or, on the contrary, do they involve the establishment of microenterprises which, though small, are guided by business motives and oriented toward the market? Which of these objectives is foremost in the minds of the actors? And what practical consequences does this mode of participation have on women's daily lives, identity, and self-esteem? Even more important, what parameters do we use to evaluate the consequences of women's participation in these types of projects? Is it sufficient that, after long hours of unpaid work, women feel more self-confident? Are there no other paths for achieving these ends that involve less sacrifice and are not so clearly determined by need? Beyond generalizations, which in many cases are no more than expressions of the ideology of the observers, the search for adequate responses to these questions can only emerge from a careful analysis of a whole family of related experiences.

The second set of questions refers to an analysis of women's activities in response to the crisis and reintroduces theoretical questions that concern the logic of articulation between productive and reproductive processes, and the boundaries of the public and private spheres of human life and of the state and civil society as settings in which women's activities are played out.

Two Case Studies

These two sets of questions—about the women themselves and about the social relations in which their actions are embedded—can be posed of each of the experiences to be discussed. Case studies are an especially suitable methodology for answering these questions.

The following discussion is based on the analysis of two projects in the province of Buenos Aires which emerged in response to problems related to reproduction, in its broad sense. Several means were used to gather information in each case: unstructured interviews with the actors involved in the projects and with key informants; participant and non-participant observation of activities related to the projects; and review of secondary information, including documents and reports, regarding the projects. In both cases, an attempt was made to contrast the actor's point of view with that of the observer in the analysis of the projects' impact on women's situations.

Itatí is a municipality of 17,000 inhabitants located on the southern edge of Greater Buenos Aires. From the highway, one can see an enormous stretch of precariously constructed homes with low roofs of sheet metal interspersed with vacant land and garbage heaps up to six kilometers long. Itatí's thirty-six blocks are set on uneven terrain which includes a low, sunken area, though most of the homes are on the higher plateau. In the mornings, the low zone is covered by a thick fog. Along either side of the road, one can see the carts of those who have turned to garbage-picking as a response to the crisis. The cars and trucks which speed by on the highway look upon the settlement with contempt and, in recent times, with increasing fear.

Itatí began to form thirty years ago in the same manner as other popular neighborhoods (*villas*) on the outskirts of Greater Buenos Aires. It started off as an empty lot with a few rickety houses. Little by little, collective efforts made it possible to install running water and an unstable drainage system, construct roadways, and develop the social conditions which have enabled the residents to coexist for so many years. Now there is even a popular communications network for disseminating the neighborhood news.

The project for training mothers as teachers' assistants (*madres educadoras*) emerged as part of a social development program initiated in 1985 as a joint effort of the local government and UNICEF: the Programa de Desarrollo Integral de Buenos Aires (Integral Development Program of Buenos Aires) (PRODIBA). Its aim was to provide basic services as medium-range solutions to some of the problems faced by neighborhoods in the greater metropolitan area, and in the process to provide women the opportunity to develop new skills. In Itatí, the project included the construction of three preschool centers which offered day care and primary health and nutritional services to children between two and five years old. The women involved in the project are trained to co-manage the centers, provide child care, offer basic workshops to parents regarding early childhood development, and act as health promoters.

The second project, Amasando la Esperanza (Kneading Hope), developed in the several neighborhoods which compose the municipality of Moreno. Many new settlements have sprung up in Moreno over the past five years because of the continued deterioration of workers' living standards and the availability of land in the area. Families that were expelled from other neighborhoods or that migrated from the country's interior arrived and at first constructed their houses haphazardly, according to personal preference, without any sort of land use plan for laying out blocks and streets. Later, neighborhood commissions were formed both to manage the inexhaustible demand for land and to design aspects of the villas.

In these newer settlements, most houses are either prefabricated or self-constructed. There is no running water (only communal faucets on the outskirts of the neighborhood), and electricity is obtained by tapping the power lines. Once the residents reach the paved roads, the local transportation system brings them to Moreno, where the municipality's administrative and commercial center is located.

In May of 1989, this area was at the center of the looting that took place in the outskirts of Greater Buenos Aires as a consequence of the hyperinflation which pushed monthly inflation rates to an unprecedented 196 percent. The memory of this experience, in which many people died, still frightens the residents. The desperation of the looting made clear the need to seek ways of confronting the crisis of reproduction which was affecting the poorest of the poor. The first spontaneous popular responses in Moreno were aimed at both taking greater advantage of existing food-oriented social policies as well as at organizing the community. It was Madre Tierra (Mother Earth), a local NGO linked to the Episcopal Church and funded by UNICEF, that introduced the project Amasando la Esperanza in response to the social emergency and the need for alternative sources of food in Moreno. The project initially involved thirty groups of ten families who operated "mini-factories" for the production of fresh pasta for the participants' consumption and later for income generation. In contrast to the first project, this one operates directly out of the homes of the women who participate.

Women play active, protagonistic roles in both projects. The latter involves exclusively women, and the former, while aimed at the community as a whole, has in practice come to be largely dominated by women.

Without elaborating on these experiences in detail, I will attempt to convey a general sense of the dynamics and daily functioning of the projects, especially with respect to the following points: (1) the profile of the protagonists, (2) what motivated them to participate, (3) the impacts of these experiences, and (4) the conditions which would allow women to improve their performance.

The Profile of the Protagonists

Both case studies refer to participants who are characterized by their historical and current condition of structural poverty. The family groups appear to have no memory of better times in terms of either formal sector employment, periods of accumulation of household stocks, or major intergenerational projects or enterprises. They may at times have had an easier existence with more money coming in and, consequently, more latitude in decisions regarding immediate necessities of everyday life such as clothing or food. But this relatively "better" situation did not allow them to resolve basic problems of housing or permanent employment. Even within this long-term perspective, however, the "social emergency" has meant a qualitative difference in their lives. This is true not so much because it provoked a drop in their already low consumption levels, but because the emergency introduced additional causes of uncertainty and fear in the form of lootings and greater labor market instability.

The women studied had given up their informal occupations because of the drop in earnings, or had lost their jobs. Their employment status is not surprising given their experiences, where having the available "free time" is a necessary condition for participation in collective projects. In this sense, the women's decision to get involved in the projects does not truly constitute a choice between alternative options, but rather the only available option.

One of the first meaningful questions that occurs to the observer is how these women were recruited, for although the willingness to participate may exist, it can only be translated into practice through a series of mediations in which external agents play a fundamental role. This role is conditioned by the nature of the program, the institution upon which it depends, the size of the budget, and the personal characteristics of those involved. The projects examined in these case studies were responding to two different challenges: in Itatí, PRODIBA seeks to implement solutions which transcend the immediate circumstances and promote an improved neighborhood life and the empowerment of women, among other goals. The project in Moreno, in contrast, directly inspired by the social emergency, attempts to respond to that immediate situation with food-related programs, although it too is concerned with developing organizational capabilities among the families involved.

Although all of the women come from a background of historical deprivation, we can distinguish between the purposes which participation in the projects serves for women of different age groups. In the case of Itatí, both "older" mothers and young women without children are involved. While participation constitutes a survival strategy for all of the women, for the younger women it also represents a vocational opportunity which can be followed up with specific training in order to facilitate their incorporation into the labor force. For both groups of women, the communal activity serves to institutionalize and legitimize their individual efforts to improve the living conditions of the neighborhood, such as providing child care in their own homes. In the other project, Amasando la Esperanza, younger women are involved as well, but women's status as mothers is more important than age in explaining their participation.

The Motivations of the Participants

To impute women's participation in the projects to a sole motivation would be to risk reductionism. Given the socioeconomic characteristics of the neighborhoods and groups involved, economic motivations are undoubtedly important; this does not mean, however, that women's interest in the projects ends there or can be reduced to a matter of economic benefit.

In both projects, the salaries women receive are low: in the child care centers of Itatí women are paid only about 20 dollars over a period of approximately two months; in the "pasta factories" of Moreno they earn 80 cents for three hours of work daily. Additional benefits include, in the first case, being able to feed their children and younger siblings in the day care centers, and in the second case, the leftover pasta at the end of each day.

It is puzzling that the women should be satisfied with this meager income. Their satisfaction can only be understood in terms of an extra-economic rationality which takes into account the advantages of not having to leave the house and of being able to use the time spent there lucratively. The near indigence in which the women live also helps to explain their relative satisfaction with the income they receive, no matter how small.

While the incomes in the two cases are comparable, the labor relations behind them are quite different. In Moreno, the women themselves expressed the initial desire to form enterprises and receive wages for their work, whereas in Itatí the idea that the mothers should be paid was proposed by the teachers and not by the madres educadoras.

As far as social and personal dimensions are concerned, PRODIBA in Itatí exposes the women to a whole new world because of the large number and variety of actors involved (including technicians and advisors from state agencies, UNICEF, and community organizations) and the scale of the project in terms of design and investment. The goal of having the women themselves co-manage the day care centers—which has yet to be fully realized—necessarily pushes them to learn and grow. In Moreno, by contrast, the principal goal is still to facilitate families' subsistence. Any progress in women's personal development can be attributed to the basic organizational skills required and promoted in the course of the project, and in some cases to the opportunity to practice skills acquired through other similar experiences.

The Impacts of the Projects

In what ways do the two projects empower women in the context of societal strategies to combat poverty? We can analyze the transformations produced on three different levels: the immediate results of the project, to which I have referred above; the project's impact on the women's identity as social subjects; and finally, the strategies used to consolidate this process of empowerment—strategies such as training and leadership development among women.

One of the more controversial points has to do with the women's ability to differentiate between their interests as women and those of the family as a collective organized around reproductive tasks. Beyond their explicit objectives, the projects—especially in the case of PRODIBA—engage women in their capacity as organizers of consumption. In this sense, the women play "vicarious" roles which imply *representing* the interests of their families. Mothers especially are defined by this role as defenders of the interests of the family group. As a survival strategy this makes perfect sense; as a means of empowering women, however, it demands further consideration. While in the case of Moreno, working with families was an integral part of the design and ideology of the project, in Itatí the initial goal of involving the entire population came in practice to mean working with family groups as well.

The advantages and disadvantages of working with families must be carefully analyzed. It is likely, however, that by operating within the framework of an institution such as the family, which is marked by gender-based and generational hierarchies, the projects themselves evolve in a way that is resistant to the goal of differentiating and elevating the interests of women. In fact, in Moreno, the woman who supervises the project behaves like a mother, caring for and organizing the activities of the less experienced participants in an almost domestic way. In the case of Itatí, women's maternal responsibility is expressed in the notion that their project is "for the good of the neighborhood." Despite the different initiatives and actors involved, both projects face the challenge of reaching out to more women in the neighborhoods in order to include a broader segment of the population and expand the scope of the project.

Improving Women's Performance

In the contexts described, the objective probability of promoting women's strategic gender interests is low. We can conclude that the way in which each project approaches the question of women's social development—whether explicitly as in Itatí, or without even posing it as in Moreno—has a strong impact on the way in which this process occurs, especially in terms of its collateral results. In both cases, however, participation in the projects seems to positively affect women's self-esteem because of the social value assigned to the activities they are engaged in. While these results are meaningful at a subjective level and valuable in and of themselves, they are only partial achievements in light of the complex and ongoing nature of the enterprises, and cannot define the social or collective significance of the projects.

Training is another important element in guaranteeing that the projects succeed in advancing women's interests. Otherwise, the sexual division of labor whereby the men in the community take responsibility for all public relations while the women devote themselves exclusively to the inner workings of the projects remains firmly entrenched.

Returning to Some of the Original Questions

Returning to the questions posed above about the nature of these activities, are the Buenos Aires projects productive or reproductive? To answer this question we must determine how the women themselves view their experience in the context of the economic crisis. Certain indications suggest a recognition of the productive aspect of their work—such as their demand for stable terms of employment, salaries, and training—while others, in contrast, reaffirm its reproductive nature, such as the fact that many of the activities closely resemble women's domestic tasks. How do the women see themselves? As workers? Or as complementing their family's subsistence with small contributions stemming from their household labor? How would they define themselves to a census taker? In the case of Moreno, it is the changes in scale and working relations that affirm the activity's potentiality as productive labor directed toward the market. In the case of Itatí, the potentiality lies in the formalization of the activity of child care.

To what extent are these projects "public" and to what extent are they "private"? Rigid schematic notions of what constitutes the public and private spheres do not accurately reflect the social relations produced in the communal context of poor neighborhoods. The relative importance of these arenas in the course of the projects' development depends in part on the ideology of the NGO involved, and in part on the participants' ability to transcend such divisions. If the project becomes defined as a private, women's activity, it will have great difficulty broadening its scope or becoming institutionalized, and is likely to be relegated to an informal circuit.

The redefinition of state-civil society relations in the context of the crisis can also be examined in light of these experiences. In Moreno, the project is purely societal, and links with the state have apparently not been contemplated. As an "alternative" project in the traditional sense of the term, it has great possibilities for expansion, although the question remains as to whether it is capable of making qualitative leaps. To be sure, this capacity is also determined by the level of development of popular organizations in the neighborhood and the surrounding area which, if advanced, could catalyze a drive toward more complex levels of organization. Until now, however, the project's impact has been felt mainly within the private realm of the family in the framework of a strategy for strengthening civil society.

In contrast, the case of Itatí is an important step in the search for alternative models of social policy that articulate the state with civil society. In this undertaking, each party exercises its comparative advantages: in the case of the state, its capacity for mobilizing material and human resources and planning activities; in the case of civil society, its enormous labor power which can be channeled into initiatives to improve the quality of life. Thus new forms of cooperation can be explored in which the state does not perceive of popular organizations as a threat, and where civil society can undertake the democratic exercise of positioning itself as an interlocutor with the state. Of course, new arrangements imply potential risks: the state could require the community's labor power and only admit their participation on a symbolic level; or the community could view with hostility the way in which the state selects human resources, gives orders, or designates funds. It is not an easy path but, as the crisis worsens, it appears to be the only possible means of satisfying the basic needs of large segments of the population.

Looking toward the Future

Although we are dealing with activities of different scales, objectives, and settings, we can draw a lesson from the case studies presented here: it is possible to devise alternative strategies for reducing the costs of the structural adjustment policies being implemented in the region. Moreover, these types of alternative responses are probably the only ones that allow the populations hardest hit by the crisis to not only improve their material standard of living, but also to preserve their self-esteem, identity, and history through activities that yield more than just monetary benefits.

It has often been mentioned that among these groups, it is women and children who end up paying the invisible cost of adjustment policies. Because they are in the shadow of society—relegated more to the private than the public sphere, associated more with reproduction than with productive activities, the labor market, or formal politics—poor women are less capable than other social actors of defending their own interests and those of their families. These two projects, in which women play a leading role, demonstrate that responses to adjustment policies can be found that do not imply passivity or resignation, and that simultaneously create a difficult but promising venue for addressing the specific problematic of women as social subjects beyond their conventional representation as guarantors of their families' welfare.

BIBLIOGRAPHY

Arriagada, Irma (1990). "La participación desigual de la mujer en el mundo del trabajo." *Revista de la CEPAL*, no. 40 (April).
Backhaus, Annette (1988). *La dimensión de género en los proyectos de promoción a la mujer: Necesidad y reto.* Enfoques Peruanos, Temas Latinoamericanos, 11. Lima: Fundación Friedrich Naumann.
Barrig, Maruja, and Amelia Fort (1987). "La ciudad de las mujeres: Pobladoras y servicios. El caso de Agustino." Documentos de Trabajo SUMBI. Lima.
Blondet, Cecilia (1989). "Las organizaciones femeninas y la política en época de crisis." Paper presented at the Seminario Mujer y Hábitat, Buenos Aires, CLACSO.
Briones, Guillermo (1985). *Evaluación de programas sociales: Teoría y metodología de la investigación. Evaluativa.* Santiago: Programa Interdisciplinario de Investigaciones en Educación (PIIE).
Buvinic, Mayra (1984). "Projects for Women in the Third World: Explaining Their Misbehavior." Washington, DC: International Center of Research on Women.
Caldeira, Teresa (1987). "Mujeres, cotidianeidad y política." En E. Jelin, ed., *Ciudadanía e identidad: Las mujeres en los movimientos sociales en América Latina.* Geneva: United Nations Research Institute for Social Development (UNRISD).
Calderón, Fernando, and Mario dos Santos (1990). "Hacia un nuevo orden estatal en América Latina: Veinte tesis socio-políticas y un corolario de cierre." Conclusion of the Regional Project, PNUD/UNESCO/CLACSO, RLA 86/001. Buenos Aires.
Campero, Guillermo (1987). *Entre la sobrevivencia y la acción política: Las organizaciones de pobladores de Santiago.* Santiago: Estudios Ilet.
CEPAL (1989). "La crisis del desarrollo social: Retos y posibilidades." In Bernardo Kliksberg, ed., *Cómo enfrentar la pobreza? Estrategias y experiencias organizacionales innovadoras.* Buenos Aires: CLAD/PNUD/Grupo Editor Latinoamericano.
———. (1990). *Transformación productiva con equidad: La tarea prioritaria del desarrollo de América Latina y el Caribe en los años noventa.* Santiago: Comisión Económica para América Latina.
Cornia, G.A., R. Jolly, and F. Stewart, eds. (1987). *Ajuste con rostro humano: Protección de los grupos vulnerables y promoción del crecimiento.* Vol. 1. Mexico City: Siglo XXI/UNICEF.
Cortés, Rosalia (1990). "Women's Work in Argentina in the Eighties: New Forms of Unprotected Work?" Buenos Aires. Mimeographed.

Egaña, Rodrigo (1985). "Aspectos económicos en proyectos de desarrollo de organizaciones económicas populares." Santiago: UNICEF.
Feijoó, María del Carmen (1988). "Y ahora qué? La crisis como ruptura de la lógica cotidiana de los sectores populares." Documento de Trabajo No. 4, Investigación Sobre Pobreza en la Argentina. Buenos Aires: IPA/INDEC.
———. (1990). "La pobreza latinoamericana en perspectiva." Documento CEDES/40. Buenos Aires: CEDES.
———. (1990). "Pobres y desorientados." *Diario Clarín* (Buenos Aires), January 12.
———. (1990). "Diciembre dolió en el corazón." *Diario Clarín* (Buenos Aires), January 17.
Feijoó, María del Carmen, and Elizabeth Jelin (1987). "Women from Low Income Sectors: Economic Recession and Democratization of Politics in Argentina." En UNICEF.
Forni, Floreal (1988). *Formulación y evaluación de proyectos de acción social*. Buenos Aires: Humanitas.
Gutman, Pablo (1987). "Pobreza urbana: Explorado algunas micro-soluciones para macroproblemas." *Desarrollo Económico* (Buenos Aires), no. 106, vol. 27. (July/September).
Guzman, Virginia (1990). "Proyectos productivos, empleo y cooperación." In P. Portocarrero, ed., *Mujer en el desarrollo: Balance y propuestas*. Lima: Innovación y Redes para el Desarrollo (IRED)/Flora Tristán.
Hardy, Clarisa (1985). "Estrategias organizadas de subsistencia: Los sectores populares frente a sus necesidades." PET, Documento de Trabajo, No. 41. Santiago.
Hartfield, Ann (1982). "In Support of Women: Ten Years of Funding by the Inter-American Foundation." Mimeographed.
Hintze, Susana (1989). *Estrategias alimentarias de sobrevivencia: Un estudio de caso en el Gran Buenos Aires*. 2 vols. Biblioteca Política Argentina, 270/271. Buenos Aires: Centro Editor de América Latina (CEAL).
Hirschman, Albert O. (1984). *Getting Ahead Collectively: Grassroots Experiences in Latin America*. New York: Pergamon Press.
IIED (1990). *Environment and Urbanization: Community Based Organizations. How They Develop, What They Seek and What They Achieve*. Vol. 2, No. 1 (April).
INDEC (1989). *La pobreza en el conurbano bonaerense*. Estudios INDEC, No. 13. Buenos Aires: INDEC.
Jelin, E., ed. (1987). *Ciudadanía e identidad: Las mujeres en los movimientos sociales en América Latina*. Geneva: United Nations Research Institute for Social Development (UNRISD).
Klenner, Arno, and Luiz Zúñiga (1984). "Generación de ingresos y vinculación a los mercados en la economía de la pobreza." Santiago: UNICEF. Mimeographed.
Kliksberg, Bernardo, ed. (1989). *¿Cómo enfrentar la pobreza? Estrategias y experiencias organizacionales innovadoras*. Buenos Aires: CLAD/PNUD/Grupo Editor Latinoamericano.
Minujin, Alberto (1990). "From Secondary Workers to Breadwinners: Poor and Non-Poor Women Facing the Crisis." Buenos Aires. Mimeographed.
Moser, Caroline (1989). "The Impact of Recession and Adjustment Policies at the Micro Level: Low Income Women and Their Households in Guayaquil, Ecuador." In *The Invisible Adjustment: Poor Women and the Economic Crisis*. Santiago: UNICEF.
Portocarrero, Patricia, ed. (1990). *Mujer en el desarrollo: Balance y propuestas*. Lima: Innovación y Redes para el Desarrollo (IRED)/Flora Tristán.
Quijano, Aníbal (1988). "Otra noción de lo privado, otra noción de lo público." *Revista de la CEPAL* (Santiago), no. 35.

Raczynski, Dagmar, and Claudia Serrano (1985). *Vivir la pobreza: Testimonios de mujeres*. Santiago: CIEPLAN-PISPAL.

Riofrio, Gustavo (1986). "La mujer y las políticas municipales de servicios." Documentos de Trabajo SUMBI. Lima.

Serrano, Claudia, and Dagmar Raczynski (1988). "Crisis y recuperación: Realidad cotidiana de algunos hogares pobres." *Apuntes CIEPLAN* (Santiago), no. 71.

SUMBI (1986). "Servicios para las mujeres: Programas y políticas." Serie Debates, Informativo No. 1. Lima: SUMBI.

SUMBI (1987). "Acciones municipales en torno a los servicios y las poblaciones de bajos ingresos: Necesidades de las mujeres." Serie Debates, Informativo No. 2. Lima: SUMBI.

Touraine, Alain (1987). *Actores sociales y sistemas políticos en América Latina*. Santiago: PREALC/OIT.

UNICEF (1986). *Del macetero al potrero (O de lo micro a lo macro): El aporte de la sociedad civil a las políticas sociales*. Santiago: UNICEF, Centro de Políticas Sociales y Planificación en Países en Desarrollo; Columbia University.

―――. (1989). *The Invisible Adjustment: Poor Women and the Economic Crisis*. Santiago: UNICEF.

Vergara, Pilar (1990). *Políticas hacia la extrema pobreza en Chile, 1973–1988*. Santiago: Facultad Latinoamericana de Ciencias Sociales (FLACSO).

Yudelman, Sally W. (1988). *Una apertura a la esperanza: Estudio de cinco organizaciones femeninas de desarrollo de América Latina y el Caribe*. Rosslyn, VA: Inter-American Foundation.

3

Industrialization and Changing Gender Roles in Rural Michoacán, Mexico

GAIL MUMMERT

Although rural Mexican women have long played a central role in assuring their families' livelihood, it is only relatively recently that they have done so through working in the wage economy on a substantial scale. Wage work has challenged traditional gender roles and has been linked to changing family structure and organization. In this case study of a U.S-bound migrant village in western Mexico,[1] I examine the impact of women's labor force participation on the standard of living of peasant families. Furthermore, I focus upon the ways in which women's wage labor—in conjunction with other trends—has led to incipient sociocultural change affecting nuptiality, fertility, postmarital residential arrangements, gender roles, intergenerational relationships, and domestic power.

The study community is particularly suited for such an analysis of profound sociocultural change. Here, as in some other parts of rural western Mexico, women have been engaged in salaried work for over a quarter of a century. The historical depth of two (and, in some families, three) generations of salaried workers allows us to perceive certain long-term effects perhaps not yet visible in other contexts. Thus, some useful lessons can be drawn from this case for future research on the overall societal impact of female salaried work.

This study analyzes young women wage earners in a rural village from a life course perspective that privileges "transitions in individual lives and the decisions associated with them" (Alter 1988:10). It is therefore essential to distinguish between different categories of women engaged in income-generating activities by marital status. Jobs and workplaces are culturally defined as appropriate to a particular marital status. In this case, young unmarried women are permitted to engage in nondomestic salaried work. Spinsters, widows, and the abandoned (all viewed as exceptional instances of women without men) may also do this type of work, but the place of married women is considered to be in the home. These distinctions by marital status will throw into greater relief the renegotiation processes that occur within the web of obligations that family members hold toward one another in peasant households.

The Study Setting: Male Migration, Female Salaried Work, and the Commercialization of Agriculture

A variety of forces has shaped the struggles for livelihood of peasant families in Quiringuicharo, an agriculturally based migrant community of some 3,000 persons located between two regional agroindustrial centers in the state of Michoacán in western Mexico. Over the past few decades, the villagers have witnessed and participated in the confluence of three major processes that have changed not only their forms of livelihood but also the very fabric of social interaction.

The first of these processes is male wage-labor migration to the United States. In the heart of the principal migrant-sending region of Mexico, Quiringuicharo has seen the departure of its able-bodied men (which began after 1941 with the bracero program) reach the proportions of a veritable exodus in the last three decades. Discouraged by the vagaries of rain-fed agriculture and encouraged by the prospect of building a nest egg of dollar earnings, the initial migrants were adult men who left families behind to take seasonal agricultural jobs in California. Especially since the 1980s, however, migration flows have been fueled by a growing number of younger, single males who prefer service jobs in Chicago's periphery. The typical migratory pattern is to shuttle back and forth over the course of several years, sending back remittances to support the family and often to finance house construction or improvement.

Second, in the mid-1960s, a demand arose for cheap, female labor at the new American-owned strawberry packing plants in the nearby urban center.[2] Rural women were recruited for this seasonal work which involved de-stemming and selecting strawberries for freezing and export to the United States. Despite strong male opposition, the unmarried women of Quiringuicharo welcomed the opportunity to enter the regional labor force and to contribute significantly to family income, until then based primarily on subsistence farming. This female labor force participation continues to an even greater extent today, though it is largely restricted to the period before marriage (roughly age 15–20); widows, spinsters, or mothers of extremely poor families are exceptions to the rule.

Third, with the drilling of wells for irrigation during the 1980s, local agriculture became more mechanized and commercially oriented. Cash crops such as tomatoes, wheat, and sorghum now link farmers to regional markets although in a disadvantageous position vis-à-vis large-scale merchants. Mostly in the hands of older, former migrants, the agricultural sector—now capable of producing two cash crops per year—nevertheless remains a risky business and not all are willing or able to invest in it.

Working Daughters: The First *Freseras*

In the mid-1960s, some 120 women from Quiringuicharo—motivated by economic necessity—flocked to the first packing plants. Overwhelmingly young and single, they generally came from large, landless families whose day laborer fathers struggled to support them. Most had little or no schooling, but the jobs required little more than manual dexterity. They worked despite the opposition of family and others whose concern over the moral consequences of factory work for women led to severe criticism of their behavior.[3]

Clearly, such entry of women into salaried work outside the village transcended traditional feminine boundaries, challenging existing gendered spatial divisions. Women—mainly those of courting age—moved outside of the house and into unknown environments beyond the vigilant eyes of their parents. The breakdown of traditional spatial barriers is aptly summed up by an old-timer who complains, "It used to be that pigs roamed the streets while women stayed at home. Nowadays women roam the streets while pigs are penned up at home."

The crux of male opposition to women working in the packing plants was that it called into question their manliness on two accounts: first, in their ability to support the family, and second, in their ability to control women's movements.[4] Common reactions of husbands and fathers were "Why do you want to work? What needs of yours do I not fulfill?" Innuendo suggested that outside of the watchful eye of the male guardians of their honor, the women would turn to illicit liaisons with unknown men. Therefore, the process of acceptance of the plant workers as respectable persons who contributed to their family's well-being through their earnings had to be based upon the dissipation of such fears and the gradual molding of new gender roles.

On the whole, the women workers (known as *freseras*) quickly demonstrated that they were capable of upholding family honor while channeling much-needed cash into otherwise ailing family coffers. Until this opportunity of female salaried work emerged, parents held greater expectations regarding possible financial aid from their sons than from their daughters. But, in this context, having a number of daughters earning salaries (even in this notoriously low-paying sector) was a valuable asset to a peasant family with ten or twelve mouths to feed. As domestic duties eased with the introduction of electricity and running water in many homes and of a well for drinking water by 1970, mothers could more readily forego some of their daughters' assistance during the six-month strawberry season.

Although women generated monetary income (supplementing goods and/or income produced by the male head of household) and enjoyed increased spatial mobility, their power to make decisions regarding the expenditure of the money they earned remained limited. Most of the first freseras dutifully turned over their entire earnings to their parents.[5] Typically, these earnings were used to cover daily living expenses or to buy furniture. In families with other sources of income (e.g., migrant remittances), the fact that daughters financed everyday needs set the stage for a more rapid building of family patrimony in terms of land, agricultural machinery, livestock, and the like. In a few cases, daughters' savings contributed directly to the buying of land or house improvements.

Working Daughters Today

Today, having lost much of their perceived danger as unfamiliar territory, the packing plants are considered workplaces suitable for young women. The number of workers from Quiringuicharo now surpasses two hundred and they come from all social sectors. In fact, this work has become a rite of passage, much as going North has for young males. For young women, the job represents an escape from the drudgery of household chores and the monotony of village life, a chance to meet new people and expand horizons and, above all, an opportunity to earn and spend money.

Over the course of one generation, the perception—both on the part of the worker and her parents—of the young woman's obligation to render earnings to her family has changed dramatically. While some do contribute as much as one-half of their salary directly to their household, others spend it entirely at their own discretion—usually on clothing and makeup.[6] In a very real sense, young women see this type of expenditure as an investment in their futures by allowing them to enter more effectively an increasingly competitive marriage market. Mothers (many of them former workers themselves) tend to support such use of income, favoring their daughters' immediate enjoyment of the fruits of their labor, in sharp contrast to their own experience of contributing to the family patrimony in which they— as members who married out—shared little.

Furthermore, local and regional opportunities for salaried work for women have been expanding. Partly because of the village's shortage of males, since the 1980s female agricultural day laborers are being hired for tomato picking in Quiringuicharo. Some freseras combine field work (physically more demanding, but paying more for fewer hours work) with factory work. Such role overlap—women doing work traditionally considered to be "men's work"—is on the increase throughout western Mexico (Arias and Mummert 1987).

Working Women without Men: Spinsters, Widows, and the Abandoned

The case of women without male partners is of particular interest to the extent that, as an in-between status, it necessitates a certain degree of bending the norms with respect to gender roles. Moreover, in this setting of massive male emigration and local violence (at least throughout the 1950s), the proportion of permanent spinsters is striking and widowhood was not an uncommon (nor necessarily a transient) experience for women.

Before 1965, women without men had few alternatives for supporting themselves and their family. Widows or those abandoned by migrant husbands generally eked out a living by resorting to extensions of the domestic role—washing and ironing clothes or grinding corn and making tortillas for better-off villagers. A few were seamstresses or worked in petty commerce of home production (e.g., eggs), groceries, or prepared food. Spinsters generally lived with aging parents and theoretically received support from married brothers. A spinster daughter would normally receive some type of inheritance (e.g., house, livestock, land) in gratitude for the succor she afforded her parents in their old age.

The opening of the packing plants marked a new role for these unmarried or no longer married women. Women who, out of personal preference or parental opposition, did not marry could legitimately engage in salaried work. While the pay was low and seasonal, it channeled much needed cash to their households and even allowed some to start small business ventures in the village (e.g., livestock raising, a grocery store, the sale of clothing).

Working Wives

Although a minority, some wives and mothers also joined the ranks of the first freseras. Invariably, their husbands were agricultural day laborers and initially opposed the idea. But the women argued that, the head's salary being insufficient to support the family, they would be helping the children eat and dress better. One mother accompanied her eldest daughter to the factory, leaving remaining daughters in charge of the younger siblings. Another wife eventually got a job for her husband in the plant. Some mothers worked until the eldest daughter reached the age of 13 or so and was able to replace her as a wage earner.

With the increasingly common phenomenon of the emigration of married males beginning in the 1960s, wives were called to assume new roles as de facto household heads during their husbands' absence.[7] As the recipients of migrant remittances, they developed new skills such as money management (involving banking in nearby cities), buying materials for house construction, and supervising land cultivation. With their husbands away for the majority of the year and sometimes even more extended periods, women "lived as widows," often carrying single-handedly the burden of raising children, attending to family holdings (land, animals, etc.), and making ends meet when remittances were not forthcoming. One way of making ends meet was precisely working as a fresera, sometimes without the husband's permission or knowledge. While the proportion of married freseras today is somewhat higher than in the early years, they are still a minority.

Although most married migrants prefer to leave their families behind (both to maximize earning power and to shield them from what they consider the corrupting effects of U.S. society), a growing number of wives have joined their husbands in Chicago or California. The number of single women from the village going North is also on the rise. Most women migrants seek employment in the United States, either in industry or services, in order to contribute to family income.

Long-Term Implications of Female Wage Labor for Household Structure and Organization

Family Formation: Courtship, Marriage, and Childbearing

Largely as a result of male exposure to U.S. culture and freseras' increased contact with non-villagers, courting patterns in Quiringuicharo have become more open: couples now meet in the plaza and may talk to each other at the gate to the girl's home. Dances and parties are daily occurrences at year's end when the majority of migrants return and matches are made and cemented in marriage. Although fathers seem to have a difficult time accepting the new mores,[8] mothers tend to agree that such openness is preferable to the surreptitious meetings of their own courting days, and the frequent elopements that resulted in order to circumvent parental disapproval.

The age at first marriage is on the rise. Whereas former generations of women were wedded as early as 14 or 15, today's brides are more likely to be 19 or 20. Apparently, youthful goals as well as parental and church pressure not to marry so young are responsible for this trend. With increased opportunities to meet potential partners from other places, exogamy is also spreading, although most continue to prefer a spouse from the village.

Family size is also declining. Despite continued opposition of the Catholic Church to contraceptive use, many women agree on the need to limit family size to three or four children, given Mexico's deteriorating economic situation. Contraceptives and family planning counseling are available at local health clinics and are presently used by over half of married women of child-bearing age, especially young mothers.[9]

Residential Patterns

Two forces have been contributing to a trend toward neo-locality among newly married couples. First, many single male migrants wish to have a home before marriage: they send remittances to their parents and instruct them to build a house for them. (No female contributions toward the future home are imaginable. Furnishings purchased by a single fresera will remain in her parents' house.) Second, the successive subdivision of family compounds to accommodate married sons has reached its limit. For the young wife, this means that the period during which she traditionally lived with and "served" her parents-in-law has been either drastically shortened or eliminated.[10] Neo-locality seems to be facilitating the redefinition of intergenerational relationships, particularly in terms of conformance to traditional patterns of conjugal decision making. Yet, ironically, if the husband migrates, the new bride may live with her parents-in-law or return to her own parents' household in order to avoid being in a situation of danger and to avoid being the subject of gossip.

Redefinition of Gender Roles and Domestic Power

In Quiringuicharo, traditional gender roles were called into question both by the opening of female salaried work and large-scale male emigration. Men struggled to retain their image as sole providers for the family, largely via emigration and remittances in dollars. Yet, they soon realized the contribution that women's work in the packing plants made to improving the family's lot. The resulting redefinition of long-standing gender roles and spatial schemes was surprisingly swift for a peasant society.[11] By limiting such employment in most cases to the years before marriage, the peasant society attempted to retain the basic gendered division of public and private spaces within married life.

As for the power relationship underlying gender roles, there are indications of an increased participation of wives and daughters in family decision making. Many villagers interpret this as a sign of the loss of respect of children for their parents and of wives for their husbands. Clearly, most of today's young wives are not willing to adopt a submissive role when faced with physical abuse or adultery on the part of their husbands.

Increased control over monetary resources by young persons of both sexes has definitely influenced the traditional hierarchy of power and authority within the family unit, weakening the claims parents can make for filial support. This trend is of course closely linked to the widening of differences between the goals of the two generations.[12] Cases of migrants or strawberry workers who make no contribution to family income where there is a clear need for such assistance spark criticism from parents and other family members. However, little pressure is placed on such offspring to comply with their perceived filial duties.

Yet, kinship ties have certainly not lost their significance. Many older siblings continue to ease the way for younger ones (e.g., by paying for their education) and to support parents who have no state-run system to turn to in old age. In this particular region of western Mexico, however, largely because of women's entry into salaried work, the web of obligations tying family members to each other (especially children and parents and brothers and sisters) is undergoing considerable strain, as new models clash with old in the lengthy process of redefinition.

Conclusions

This case study has illustrated the crucial role played by rural women wage earners in assuring family livelihood in difficult times and in raising the standard of living for peasants in the region. Yet, despite their key role in building and expanding peasant family holdings, female contributions tend to be underestimated by the community at large, overshadowed by male income in the form of migrant remittances and cash crop earnings.

In distinguishing female work experience by marital status, I have stressed that while daughters have accounted for the majority of salaried workers, increasingly, both wives and other categories of women without men (such as widows, spinsters, and the abandoned) have also participated in the wage economy. I have highlighted the differential impact of events experienced by different cohorts at various points in time.

As in other times and places, this instance of female labor force participation implied crossing a number of boundaries which Halperin (1990: 139) labels as spatial, institutional, and cultural. As they commuted daily from rural to urban areas, moving in and out of agroindustrial wage labor while residing in households dependent on agriculture and belonging to a peasant society unevenly involved in capitalist relations, these women also experienced new cultural meanings. Some of the far-reaching implications of the resulting sociocultural change for women's place in the family and in the community have been suggested here. Future research on women's struggles for livelihood must consider both the economic and sociocultural impacts of their income-generating activities, for the two are inextricably linked.

As Teresa, one of the first freseras and now a mother of freseras, aptly sums up:

> Things have changed since women started to work in the plants. The village has progressed. Before we didn't have enough to eat. Now families can buy food and clothing. The girls have changed, too: they are not afraid to go out alone; they go wherever they want. It used to be that we didn't even know what the nearby town was like and we didn't talk to anyone who wasn't from the village. Now the girls have girlfriends and boyfriends—why, some even marry boys from other places who they met in the packing plants![13]

ENDNOTES

1. This study presents findings of my research project at El Colegio de Michoacán on "Changing Household Organization in a Setting of Male Emigration and Female Salaried Labor." Fieldwork (involving a village population census, household survey, and in-depth interviews) was conducted from March to August 1991 with a grant from the Asociación Mexicana de Población. The paper was written while the author held a Visiting Research Fellowship from the Center for U.S-Mexican Studies of the University of California, San Diego.

2. Arizpe and Aranda (1986) have pointed out the comparative advantages for the employers of hiring women. Smaller numbers of men (about twenty from Quiringiucharo) have also worked in the plants—in maintenance, in the freezers, or doing the more strenuous tasks such as transporting and loading raw materials and finished products.

3. Such concern is obviously not new, as Alter (1988) shows for a nineteenth-century European industrial city.

4. One father vividly expressed this threat to his virility by saying to his male counterparts that he would rather cut off his sexual organs than allow his daughters to work in the packing plants.

5. Other freseras channeled resources directly to the family's greatest needs by bringing home food, in some cases conscientiously circumventing the siphoning of hard-earned resources into male vices (such as alcoholism).

6. Rosado (1990:65–66) found a similar trend toward an increasingly personal use of income among strawberry plant workers living in a semiurban area in the Zamora-Jacona region of Michoacán.

7. In Mummert (1988), I discuss these new roles for migrants' wives (as well as for women migrants) in greater detail.

8. One father recounted his discomfort with the following incident: upon seeing his daughter with her boyfriend at the front gate of their house, he opted to continue walking about the village so as to avoid confronting the situation.

9. According to clinic records, in February 1991, 53 percent were using some form of contraception, mostly pills.

10. Wilson (1990) also found a trend toward neo-locality in another Michoacán town where women have been salaried workers in textile workshops for several decades.

11. The swiftness of the change can be appreciated in the fact that younger daughters were allowed to work in the packing plants, while their older sisters were denied this permission only a few years earlier.

12. In his study of another migrant community, Rouse (1989: Chapter 4) found such a generational divergence of life projects: migrant sons were not willing to sacrifice their ambitions in obedience to parents' wishes.

13. Interview, Quiringuicharo, April 20, 1991.

BIBLIOGRAPHY

Alter, George (1988). *Family and the Female Life Course: The Women of Verviers, Belgium, 1849–1990*. Life Course Studies. Madison: University of Wisconsin Press.

Arias, Patricia, and Gail Mummert (1987). "Familia, mercados de trabajo y migración en el Centro-Occidente de Mexico." *Nueva Antropología* 9:32 (November), 105–127.

Arizpe, Lourdes, and Josefina Aranda (1986). "Women Workers in the Strawberry Agribusiness in Mexico." In Helen I. Safa et al., eds., *Women's Work: Development and the Division of Labor by Gender*. South Hadley, MA: Bergin and Garvey.

Halperin, Rhoda (1990). *The Livelihood of Kin: Making Ends Meet "The Kentucky Way."* Austin: University of Texas Press.

Mummert, Gail (1988). "Mujeres de migrantes y mujeres migrantes de Michoacán: Nuevos papeles para las que se quedan y las que se van." In Thomas Calvo and Gustavo López, coords., *Movimientos de población en el Occidente de México*. Mexico: Centre d'Etudes Mexicaines et Centramericaines/El Colegio de Michoacán. Pp. 281–295.

Rosado, Georgina (1990). "De campesinas inmigrantes a obreras de la fresa en el Valle de Zamora, Michoacán." In Gail Mummert, ed., *Población y trabajo en contextos regionales*. Zamora: El Colegio de Michoacán. Pp. 45–71.

Rouse, Roger C. (1989). "Mexican Migration to the United States: Family Relations in the Development of a Transnational Migrant Circuit." Ph.D. dissertation, Stanford University.

Wilson, Fiona (1990). *De las casas al taller: Mujeres, trabajo y clase social en la industria textil y del vestido. Santiago Tangamandapio*. Zamora: El Colegio de Michoacán.

Part III. Political Practice

4

Women, Collective Kitchens, and the Crisis of the State in Peru

MARUJA BARRIG

As in many other Latin American countries, the role of the state in Peru as a provider of social services has progressively diminished over the past decade. This contraction in public spending, which in practice transfers almost the entire responsibility for social reproduction onto families, proceeded at the same pace as the structural adjustment program designed to eliminate inflation, fiscal deficit, and other economic indicators of crisis.

While this general situation applies to almost all of Latin America, its special characteristics in Peru can be seen in the broad scope and permanence of collective consumption activities involving tens of thousands of poor women, in the weighty presence of the Catholic Church as a channel for assistance to this population, and in the institutional deterioration of the state. The Peruvian case is also distinguished by the ironic observation that plummeting purchasing power and other important indicators of social crisis since the end of the 1980s originated not under an administration that bowed to the recommendations of the International Monetary Fund (IMF), but in the context of a heterodox experiment in economic policy.

The opening of the decade of the 1990s presents an even more complex scenario for the country. The current administration (1990–1995) is applying a structural adjustment program which, in addition to its economic implications (in a period of only a few months, the population living in poverty practically doubled), raises questions regarding the disappearance of the state as the principal agent of social inclusion. At the same time, Peru is facing a situation of internal war owing to the presence of the terrorist movement, Sendero Luminoso (Shining Path)—a war that has cost some 25,000 lives over the past twelve years.

Editors' Note: Translated by Lilian Autler.

When It Rains, Does Everyone Get Wet?

The "Good Times" of the Crisis: 1980–1985

The Peruvian military regime of the 1970s differed from other South American dictatorships of that period by expanding the role of the state and taking an active part in both distribution and production. The political discourse of the government, in addition to its nationalist emphasis, sowed the seeds of contempt for traditional political institutions through its deliberate promotion of new social organizations at a time when they were not widespread and strengthening of existing ones, such as labor unions. When the first signs of the economic crisis appeared toward the end of the 1970s, the popular struggle against the dictatorship was first and foremost in defense of the household economy, rather than a demand for representative democracy and civil liberties. This point is key because the emergence of the notion of citizenship among a certain sector of the population—especially from the 1960s on—took as its reference point a state which, though far from conforming to the classic model of a welfare state, played a far more important role as an agent of social inclusion than as a guarantor of civil or political rights (Barrig 1989).

The 1980s opened with a new national constitution that incorporated several of the military government's populist reforms and the election to the presidency of Fernando Belaúnde of the National Action Party, who had been overthrown twelve years earlier. Faced with an overgrown state that acted as an agent of production and the principal regulator of the market, the new regime moved half-heartedly toward the implementation of a neoliberal model. Its initial economic measures depleted foreign currency reserves, provoked the first signs of industrial recession, and caused annual inflation rates to rise from 60 percent in 1980 to 125 percent in 1983. The emergence of political terrorism during the decade along with the government's scrupulous repayment of the foreign debt explain why almost 50 percent of the national budget was spent on debt service and defense.

At the first signs of discontent among the population, the government's response was to organize housewives in Lima's poor neighborhoods for the operation of "Family Kitchens" (Cocinas Familiares). Infrastructure and donated food were initially provided to poor women who supported the governing political party. The pervasive national rhetoric of "creating virtue out of need" relied on the doctrinal mainstay of the National Action Party—the population's ancestral collectivist spirit and Andean networks of solidarity—in order to exhort women to voluntarily undertake all of the work involved in running the collective kitchens: shopping, preparing the food, cleaning, accounting, distributing the rations, and so on.

Family Kitchens marked the beginning of an official practice that continued throughout the 1980s and was based on the coordination of a particular form of action (voluntary organizations) and social subject (poor urban women) for the purpose of distributing food donations. Nevertheless, this type of organization already existed among women outside of the official sphere. A study conducted in Lima at the beginning of the decade detected about 200 collective kitchens, or *comedores*, promoted by CARITAS, a philanthropic organization of the Catholic Church which was one of the principal channels for food donations from the Agency for International Development (USAID) (Lafosse 1984). The extensive network of parishes in poor neighborhoods and the multiplicity of church-based and NGO advisors made it possible to replicate this experience throughout the city. A similar model was used in most districts: an assembly composed of between 20 and 40 women members who, in weekly rotations, performed the tasks of receiving the food, cooking, keeping the books, and so on. The rations were sold at a minimal price among the members, and the revenues were used to buy food items not included in the donations.

The government, however, did not take into account the existence of these other comedores in designing and implementing its own Family Kitchens program. This lack of coordination resulted in segmented organizations with different modes of operation. Nor was there coordination with other government food assistance programs or private food donor organizations. If there was no effort on the part of the state to coordinate even the various food assistance programs, much less did the will exist to integrate these programs into food and agriculture policies at the national level. No attempt was made to construct the bridge which could have linked the state and civil society, nor to articulate these "emergency" welfare measures with medium-term development projects.

By 1985 there were 600 collective kitchens in Lima, and a Coordinating Committee had been formed to represent dozens of these organizations located in the poorest neighborhoods of the city. In discussing these types of organizations, I should also mention the municipal "Glass of Milk" program, created in 1984 by Lima's socialist mayor, Alfonso Barrantes. While guided by a doctrine different from that of the central government party, the municipal government also discovered the effectiveness of women's organizations in preparing and distributing a daily glass of milk as a means of counteracting the effects of poverty on children's health and nutritional intake. The program draws upon the tradition in the Peruvian Left of organization as the basis of self-help practices. According to the municipal government, in 1986, 100,000 women were organized to serve one million beneficiaries.

Monetary Income, Yes, But Food as Well: 1985–1990

During the first two years of its administration, the APRA (Alianza Popular Revolucionaria de América) government led by Alan García (1985–1990) instituted a set of economic policy measures which increased purchasing power and revitalized the manufacturing sector. Women were direct or indirect targets of some government programs such as the Direct Assistance Program (PAD) and the Temporary Income Support Program (PAIT). Statistics indicate that women's labor force participation in the Lima metropolitan area reached nearly 50 percent in 1986, largely as a result of these programs.

A few months after assuming office, President Alan García created PAD, which promoted the formation of mothers' clubs for food preparation, as well as skills training workshops for poor women. These collective kitchens were regulated by a statute which, in practice, placed them under the auspices of the government; they had access to infrastructure in the form of government "loans," and cooks were paid a salary by the state. The PAD comedores were the official version of the *comedores del pueblo*, a form of subsidized restaurant which the APRA, now in power, had formed to gain voter support in the months before the presidential elections. The Family Kitchens of the previous regime were dismantled, regardless of the fact that these new organizations perpetuated the same pattern of instrumentalizing women's work, government control, and dispersion of efforts. It was, however, a different party in power.

Once again, the autonomous comedores were marginalized. Their leaders protested, petitioned the government, and demanded a share of the benefits in the form of kitchen facilities, pots, and utensils which were bestowed upon the PAD clubs amid great displays of publicity. Their marginalization reinforced the autonomous stance of these organizations, but it did not erase the bad taste left by the spectacle of "the poor competing against the poor." The APRA government showed no interest in cooperating with these groups—some 500 in Lima alone—which had emerged under the auspices of the Catholic Church. Nor was there any attempt to establish a relationship with the women's committees of the Glass of Milk program, thereby contributing to the social fragmentation which is the other side of diversity and recognition of the other (Vega 1987).

The government-sponsored collective kitchens and workshops were not the only official options for poor women during this period. In an attempt to increase internal demand, the government created the Temporary Income Support Program (PAIT), which paid the minimum wage (the equivalent of 50 dollars per month at the time) to workers involved in community improvement projects in their neighborhoods. Almost 80 percent of those who signed up for the program, which initially created 50,000 jobs nationwide, were women living in poor neighborhoods.

The effect of the PAIT on employment levels has been extensively analyzed in other studies. First, it is important to mention here that while many of the women who were members of collective kitchens also performed income-generating work, the types of work they did (self-employment, hourly domestic service, etc.) afforded them the necessary flexibility in their schedules to also fulfill their weekly responsibilities in the comedor. In 1986, however, the number of women members who enrolled in the PAIT, which involved 45 hours of work per week, was so great that collective kitchens began to lose their staffs. Facing the risk of having to close down the kitchens because of women's desertion, the comedor leadership was forced to relax the commitments required of members. Even so, according to a study by Huamán (1989), the reason given in more than a third of the cases for the women's abandonment of the collective kitchen is that they "found a job." This finding clearly indicates that economic need is the principal motivation behind women's incorporation in this type of organization.

The level of female unemployment in Lima, estimated at about 10 percent, does not reflect the real dimensions of the problem. For different reasons, many women fail to have access to economic resources for starting a business or, lacking child care, are unable to seek work and thus are not counted among the economically active population. I hypothesize that this hidden unemployment is higher among women than among men: the rapid response of women in poor neighborhoods to the opportunity offered by the PAIT cannot be explained otherwise. On PAIT projects, women would bring their young children with them and would improvise on-site child care arrangements. Tasks required no special training, and work was generally carried out in the women's own neighborhood, which saved time and transportation costs and allowed them to remain within easy reach of their homes in case of an emergency.

A second important point is the apparent mobility of poor women, their flexibility in simultaneously adopting diverse livelihood strategies in response to the adverse effects of economic policies and the shifts in income and consumption levels within their households. As Boggio (1989) correctly asserts, more than collective kitchens impacting families, the inverse is true: families influence the dynamics of the collective kitchens according to modifications in household composition, income, and employment. No studies exist regarding the number of collective kitchen members who also perform remunerative work, whether that number has increased—though it is easy to deduce that it has—or the type of employment in which they are engaged. This type of information would facilitate a more refined analysis of the impact of the economic crisis on the ways in which poor women invest their time and energy in alleviating the impacts of falling incomes and inadequate public services.

The PAIT began to decline at the same time that the government's heterodox experiment was failing. By 1988 real wages had dropped 50 percent since 1980, and per capita spending on social services had fallen from $48 (U.S.) in 1981 to $26 in 1988 (Instituto CUANTO 1991). Investment and GNP showed negative growth rates, while the inflation rate reached 1,722 percent.

In September 1988, a harsh set of economic measures, which aimed at achieving stabilization without abandoning the heterodox framework, mobilized the members of the collective kitchens which by that time numbered more than 1,500 in the Lima metropolitan area. With the assistance of NGOs, they elaborated a proposal for the state to subsidize 58 percent of the cost of the food rations prepared in the comedores. The subsidy was based on the minimum nutritional requirements provided by a basic food basket which incorporated local agricultural products so as to eliminate dependence on food imports. The government disregarded the proposal.

Nevertheless, that moment was a milestone in the process of consolidating the women's movement around struggles for subsistence to the extent that, for the first time in the almost ten years since the first comedores had been formed, the members recognized the state and its policies as the direct source of their problems. In the past, these organizations had had an almost exclusive relationship with the Catholic Church as food donor and organizational advisor. In the meantime, however, many other self-managed comedores had emerged outside of CARITAS and even the government. A more independent network of comedores with a centralized leadership was thus coming into being, and this broadened the projection of their actions.

It was also in 1988 that the concept of social "emergency" came into use in reference to the purportedly short-term measures—which eventually become permanent—directed at the poorest segments of the population. However, the continually growing number of the poor overwhelmed any possibility of short-term, targeted intervention. This period was characterized by what Franco (1991b) calls semantic "operations": the definition of social policies as emergency programs and, consequently, a shift of resources and attention away from the improvement of living conditions for the population as a whole, to the battle against extreme poverty. The ultimate outcome is the state's renunciation of its role as a provider of universal services, focusing instead on programs or projects for targeted groups.

How Do Families Reproduce Themselves?

Not all household reproduction activities are under the control of households themselves; many other agents intervene in the circuits of needs satisfaction. The specific role of each agent and its relative importance varies according to social class and the particular historical period or conjuncture. I would argue that since 1988, despite the fact that the government food program has remained in place and even expanded, there has been a virtual withdrawal of the Peruvian state as an agent in the circuit of needs satisfaction of poor urban households. This tendency has become accentuated under the current administration (1990–1995). In other words, in the set of practices, processes, exchanges, and networks which compose a circuit of needs satisfaction, the transfer of resources between poor women and other poor people has virtually replaced the withering social function of the state.

By 1990 social spending represented 13 percent of all public expenditures, whereas between 1970 and 1976 it had reached 25 percent. As government investment in infrastructure contracted, the salaries of employees in the health care and education sectors fell, and government credit for housing construction dropped from 5,000 loans in 1989 to only 53 in 1990. At the same time, the number of comedores operated by mothers' clubs and by the official PAD rose from 784 in 1989 to 5,822 in 1990 nationwide. The channeling of food supplies to poor women became practically the only social program of the APRA government's feeble mechanism of social legitimation.

The new government which took office in July 1990 initiated a new economic program based on IMF guidelines. The social cost of these new policy measures was enormous. Whereas in June 1990 a third of Peru's population lived in poverty, the number of poor skyrocketed to 12 million, or over 50 percent of the total population, after structural adjustment. Between June and November 1990, the number of children among the economically active population of Lima increased by 133 percent, and the number of women by 21 percent, according to a survey of 400 households.

At the same time, food service organizations multiplied. The National Commission of Comedores (CNC) informally calculated the existence in July 1991 of 7,200 comedores in the Lima metropolitan area alone. This calculation includes some comedores of the disactivated PAD of the previous government as well as many other collective kitchens supported by various private organizations. Preliminary statistics from this period suggested that the comedores prepared and distributed approximately one million food rations daily.

The heterogeneity in the organization of the comedores makes it difficult to calculate precisely the number of women involved in them. But if we use as an average the figure given by the CNC in July 1991, we are talking about 250,000 women, or a third of the poor female population over 15 years old in the Lima metropolitan area (Reyes 1991).

Social policy analyses that refer to family reproduction strategies and their supposed rationality tend to overlook the fact that women carry the major burden of household responsibilities. Consequently, economic policies which disproportionately affect the poor will also differentially impact poor women. As we have seen, in the past decade in Peru, women's time, energy, and labor became the "instrument of choice" for executing emergency programs, both government-sponsored and private. The tendency of international organizations to promote projects which, in their very design and methodology, place the responsibility for their implementation on women who are also its supposed beneficiaries frequently creates counterproductive effects. The structural adjustment policies and emergency programs which accompany these projects contain a hidden gender bias to the extent that they rely on the transfer of economic activities to the so-called private realm of women's unremunerated and more elastic labor time (Elson 1987).

The previous summary has become virtually rhetorical. Organizations of collective consumption have been the research subject of a plethora of studies, conferences, and seminars. In reviewing the past decade, however, I would like to point out some of the gaps in our knowledge about these types of organizations, and especially about the women who compose them. While it is clear that the question of food provisioning to the poor encouraged the organization of the popular sectors, it has become more and more difficult over the past ten years to sort out the relationships between the set of institutions involved in these collective actions and the relative importance of the state within this range of configurations. This knowledge would be useful in order to understand the forces that support state-run assistance and emergency programs, in the context of adjustment policies (also applied by the state) that increase poverty and aggravate inequality and income concentration.

The state, as I have suggested, has begun to disappear as a provider of social services and to transfer the responsibility for reproduction to families—more specifically, to the women of poor families. The expansion of state-sponsored collective kitchens and the contraction of public spending on other social services are clear evidence of this trend. Furthermore, in the food programs, the state acted fundamentally as an intermediary for channeling foreign donations between outside agencies and the receiving population. In other words, the state withdrew from its role as a provider, but maintained control and the power to determine who would be the beneficiaries of the food donations by regulating the distribution channels according to political and partisan criteria.

Citizenship, I Am Looking for You

Social Policies and Citizens' Rights

The social policies of the state express, through their actions or omissions, the theoretical principles and the praxis which guide the reproduction and maintenance of a country's human resources. I refer not only to processes of family reproduction, but also to political interests and development models which promote particular mechanisms for the production and distribution of resources.

A historical overview of the conduct of the Peruvian state and its social policies over the past decades would be necessary in order to understand what took place during the 1980s without resorting to simplifications and schematic generalizations. Nevertheless, consensus appears to exist around the idea that state policies in Peru reflect complex processes of negotiation and compromise among diverse social forces, and any analysis of this process cannot overlook several factors: the fragile articulation of popular and national interests in Peruvian society, the large role of the state within this society, its limited capacity for pressure and representation, and the populist character of its successive governments.

The Peruvian state was the principal protagonist in offering a set of social services directed mainly at a small sector of the lower middle classes and at recent migrants to the cities. The Peruvian case is distinct from that of other countries of the region in at least three ways. First, the state has been highly selective in its attention to the demands of certain social groups based on their pressure tactics or the establishment of clientelist relations. As a result, social assistance policies, rather than being neutral and universal, were transformed into *asistencialismo,* that is, the selective application of policies in response to the dynamics of political pressure and clientelism.

A second distinguishing characteristic of Peruvian social policies has been the direct involvement of the supposed "beneficiaries" in the execution of the infrastructure required for services, basically by providing free labor. Thus, in the process of negotiation and confrontation with the state in order to obtain certain demands, the ingredient of *esfuerzo propio*—achieving gains through one's own efforts—became central for the low-income population, as is evident in the self-construction of their homes, schools, or medical clinics.

Finally, the government's distributionist programs did not imply an effective redistribution of social spending. For example, during the 1960s Peru spent a higher percentage of GNP on education than most other countries in the region. However, this increase in public spending on education, proposed by the executive branch, was only accepted by Congress after political negotiations with those members who represented landowning and business interests, to whom the state granted subsidies and tax exemptions which, in the end, generated a tremendous fiscal deficit (Cotler 1978). Almost thirty years later, President Alan García's unsuccessful attempts to stimulate private investment also entailed subsidies to capital, while at the same time the state implemented programs to increase internal demand and held down fees for public services, once again provoking an unmanageable fiscal deficit.

This third characteristic of the Peruvian state with respect to social policy—its distributionist zeal—has always culminated in drama, since the state has simultaneously attempted to leave capital benefits untouched and concede greater advantages to private enterprise, both domestic and foreign, at the cost of the state coffers. As a result, state-sponsored social inclusion has ultimately generated its own limits. Expansion of the educational system outpaced the quality of teaching and the necessary infrastructure. Or, more recently, the broadening of the Social Security system's medical coverage went hand in hand with a contraction in the salaries of doctors and nurses and a reduction in spending on maintenance of and investment in infrastructure.

These characteristics can in some ways be traced to the nature of the Peruvian state itself, which is, to use Adrianzén's (1990) label, a "perverted version of the modern liberal state." In other societies with market economies, the basic rights of liberty and equality, which are embedded in their constitutions and sustain liberal ideology, legitimated the practices and values of capitalism. By contrast, in Peru, not only was this ideology of equality not explicity expressed, but the state itself exuded the elitism of the dominant classes who were its tributaries within a system of ethnic and racial discrimination. (Implicit in this feature of the state is the concept of assisting the poor, in the sense of offering paternalistic charity. The notion of the *estado de compromiso*, where the state is an arena for negotiation and compromise, did not exist.) We have only to recall that illiterate people, who are mainly among Quechua-speaking groups of the rural Andean regions, have only had the right to vote since 1980.

On the other hand, populism—a twist which has characterized numerous administrations—also manifested itself in an authoritarian and hierarchical manner. By privileging the state as the arena of social inclusion, populism reinforced a notion of citizenship based more on social rights than civil rights. At the same time, populism has tended to block the expression of autonomous institutional interests by neutralizing or subordinating proposals which do not revolve around its own agenda or leader (Adrianzén 1990; Balbi 1991).

We are faced, then, with a paternalistic, elitist, occasionally populist state, in which the marginal space for maneuver in negotiating the inclusion or exclusion of popular demands shrank in the face of economic crisis, as occurred at the end of the 1980s. As Peru's fiscal crisis deepened, the state became more and more impermeable to social demands—which were increasing—and its traditional prebendalist traits were accentuated.

How did the response of the leadership of the collective kitchens reflect this tension? Faced with evidence that the government attended selectively to other similar organizations which were under its control, in their proposal for direct state subsidies covering 58 percent of the cost of a basic food basket (1988) they affirmed: "We as poor women have learned our lesson. We are citizens and as such we ask to be treated not with charity, nor paternalism, nor clientelism, but only with equality." This statement denotes, in the first place, their recognition and rejection of a political practice of the state (charity, paternalism, clientelism) which nonetheless became consolidated to the extent that the "pragmatism" and acquiescence of poor migrants (Franco 1990) in the face of such practices served to reinforce them.

On the other hand, for those who signed the manifesto, citizenship apparently means equality not in relation to all Peruvians, but in relation to other entities of collective consumption assisted directly by the government. This seems to corroborate the tendency toward segmentation in the process of forming units of political representation within popular society. Citizenship, as the standard of equality, should be the firm common foundation from which to advance specific claims based on class, gender, or ethnicity. In Peru, however, the process tends to be the inverse: the precarious notion of political citizenship is only a flimsy platform from which to appeal for the strengthening of group identities, making it difficult to construct an inclusive democratic order (Adrianzén 1990).

In addition, the context in which these popular leaders' identity and expectations of progress have germinated is one which articulates their experience as poor migrants and slum dwellers with their condition as organized consumers and members of the comedores. This position is key for understanding certain aspects of the women's peculiar notion of citizenship. The fact that food is the axis which articulates the action of these organizations constitutes one more "turn of the screw" in the displacement of citizen by consumer in the process of constituting identities, which Lechner (1982) identifies as a current tendency in many societies. Under certain regimes, citizenship does not refer to collectively recognized universal rights, but rather to a restricted identity revolving around consumption. This situation gives rise to a corporativist order which is difficult to mesh with a global project for integrating diverse interests.

Finally, a third element that allows us to trace the way in which the notion of citizenship has been constituted among the members of these organizations is the idea of sacrifice as the basis for merit, prevalent in poor neighborhoods. As Gonzalo Portocarrero (1990) has pointed out in his insightful analysis, among the popular sectors, "to suffer is to be worthy," and when it comes to defending hard-won spaces—from a land invasion in order to secure a plot on which to build a home to a mothers' club—people do not appeal to formal rights, the obligations of the state, or individual effort, but rather to the sacrifice and suffering invested in order to achieve these goals. This is even more clear-cut in the case of women, because in addition they appeal to the multitude of hardships and deprivations endured for the sake of their children. The banner of suffering replaces that of rights, and when it is ultimately in the name of children, this "worthiness" is transferred onto them, making the sacrifice all the more altruistic and genuine. Portocarrero's analysis elaborates on the speech we have heard dozens of times from poor women which usually begins: "After all the suffering I have been through. . . ."

Up to now, I have briefly outlined the relevant factors shaping the relationship among the state, social rights, and the notion of citizenship among women involved in collective consumption. As we shall see in the following section, this relationship is rendered even more complex by the impacts of the country's economic problems on the institutional dynamics of social organizations and political parties.

Political Parties and Social Institutions

As López (1990) accurately describes, the fiscal crisis has corroded and weakened the state over the past decade, pushing political parties and other institutions to the brink of illegitimacy. The institutional impact of the crisis, evidenced by the state's incapacity to meet basic social needs, is one of the factors which has led to the collapse of legitimacy which drags political parties down with it. In a society where interests are ever more fragmented and social relations more dispersed, the aggregation and representation of these interests becomes increasingly difficult.

Furthermore, political parties lose influence among social movements if they appear to be inefficient vehicles for resolving structural problems or meeting the urgent demands of citizens. This situation gives rise to the widespread sensation of the parties' "betrayal" of their constituency which, in turn, encourages the election of independent candidates from outside the partisan framework. The breakdown of institutionality and the consequent social disintegration is also experienced by the groups organized around subsistence.

After more than a decade of action and expansion by these organizations, it is valid to ask ourselves about the course of this movement and its internal dynamics. This need is underscored not only by the indisputable fact that its massive presence has converted the leaders of the comedores into visible public figures whose projection transcends the community setting, but also because the role played by these leaders is constantly highlighted by politicians in their discourse and their practice.

Let us first consider the articulation between social movements and political parties. The phenomenon of social movements has been extensively analyzed and conceptualized. The collective kitchens exhibit the recognizable pattern of groups which construct their identity on the basis of concrete needs and, through this process, present "non-negotiable" demands to the rest of society and to the institutions of the state.

The collective kitchens are functional organizations which tend to display corporativist forms of representation. To the extent that they do not adopt a territorial structure, they have expanded and grown stronger independent of neighborhood committees and even of local, municipal-level governments. They are distrustful of municipal political authority and respond intransigently to the attempts at co-optation which would serve the political interests of the mayors and other local elected officials. These are, in addition, "masculine" spheres of political power, in contrast with the essence of the organization of comedores whose mission—feeding families—imparts new political meaning to one of the activities carried out by women in private space.

In the case of the collective kitchens, this self-marginalization from the institutional political sphere is reinforced by the influence of outside agents (NGOs and especially the Catholic Church), which overvalue direct community action and spaces uncontaminated by the political parties. This has meant that the leaders of the comedores at the district or zone level operate in the contradictory situation that Cardoso (1984) calls a "perverse dialectic": revulsion toward politics and an emphasis on grassroots action prompted the leaders of these organizations to present concrete demands to government officials, who usually conceded to their claims. The leaders have found themselves alone, without broader political alliances, in the face of functionaries who have granted their specific, isolated requests without altering in the least the state's mechanisms of domination, indeed, legitimizing some of the state's actions in the process.

While the dynamic described above has evolved, political parties have been losing their representativity as their internal authoritarianism and closed top-level negotiations become increasingly rigid. Many analyses of the popular women's movement in Peru have remarked on its lack of confluence with broader projects for change and democratization. However, reluctance on the part of the organization of comedores to risk joining a project which may not in fact represent it is understandable in the atmosphere of social chaos which currently prevails.

Despite the general rejection of political parties, however, many of the leaders of the sixty or so central coordinating bodies of the CNC are militants or sympathizers of leftist or center-left parties or movements. The higher level leaders are undoubtedly heirs to the "golden legend" of the Peruvian popular movement of the 1970s, and are not ideologically susceptible to conservative rhetoric (Backhaus 1988). This does not automatically imply, however, their direct affiliation with a radical party.

The internal situation of the organization is also conflictive because of the many different varieties of comedores and their lack of institutionality. The CNC was elected "provisionally" in the mid-1980s, though it is not in fact national, but almost entirely Lima-based. The collective kitchens have multiplied so rapidly and assumed such diverse organizational forms that it is almost impossible to regulate them, provide statutes, or renew their leadership. Furthermore, since the confusion persists as to the nature of the collective kitchen—whether it is a community service or an organization—many registered "members" continue to exchange their shifts with others in return for payment in money or in kind, making it very difficult to keep track of the organizations and the number of participants in them. This, in turn, hinders the possibility of establishing criteria for legitimate representation.

Moreover, when one observes the countless tasks, the drudgery, and the hectic pace undertaken by the leaders of the kitchens, one wonders about the attraction of this position. The leaders tend to be women with higher educational levels than the rest of the members, and are usually about 35 to 40 years old, thus unlikely to have small children requiring their attention. Also, several studies conducted in Lima during the 1980s found that these women have a somewhat higher status relative to the others, manifested, for example, in the fact that they have spouses with steady jobs. The fact that many of the leaders have participated or continue to participate in other neighborhood organizations suggests that they have a certain amount of free time available for community-level activities. For these reasons, it is not surprising that the leaders see themselves as having "sacrificed" in order to direct organizations like the comedores, which help people poorer than they are (Stokes 1991).

Over the years, however, this initial motivation on the part of the leaders has been eclipsed by another, legitimate but less altruistic, interest. This more recent motivation arises from the division between, on the one hand, the members of the collective kitchens dedicated to the day to day delivery and administration of services and, on the other hand, the leaders who, in carrying out their public functions, have begun to broaden their network of relations beyond those of the immediate community and to acquire visibility and recognition (Boggio 1989). Given the rigid stratification of Peruvian society, and the evident deprivations they have experienced because of their social origins, these leaders—as well as those of the Glass of Milk programs—have discovered in the fulfillment of their responsibilities a vehicle for upward social mobility which gives them access to the offices of the mayor and the bishops, the corridors of the various ministries, and even the president of the Republic. In addition, they are interviewed and photographed by the alternative press as well as the mass media. Although no empirical evidence is available, there are signs of increased self-esteem among the leaders, and even of changes in their relationships with their husbands and partners.

The distance between the leaders who represent the organization and those who play a role more directly tied to community service has also become evident in the claims on the part of the latter that their time and labor—including the management and administrative skills they have acquired—are worthy of remuneration.

The organization's history of diversity, which, nonetheless, does not undermine its efficiency, along with the cooperation between its most important leaders and NGOs, paved the way for the elaboration in 1990 of a legislative bill which would grant legal status to social organizations, including those which provide food support. This law (No. 25307) was unanimously approved by the Parliament despite the fact that, among other provisions, it indicates that the state must subsidize 65 percent of the food rations offered by these organizations, in blatant contradiction of the current policy of cutting subsidies. In fact, the law was never implemented, and the accelerated decline which the organization is currently experiencing has not allowed it to mobilize in order to demand compliance.

Looking Forward into the 1990s

As already mentioned, the government elected in July 1990 proposes and is carrying out a structural adjustment similar to that which has been applied in dozens of other Third World countries. This implies measures ranging from the deregulation of labor relations to cuts in social services which are even larger than those experienced in previous years.

The objective, we are assured, is to modernize the country and reduce the role of the state in all spheres. This raises several questions regarding the reactions and political behavior of the poor, whose notion of citizenship appears to have grown out of the struggle for social rights. In a situation where the state is no longer the guarantor of social inclusion and the domestic market is limited and depressed, it is not preposterous to wonder what will be the source of citizen identity in the future, particularly in a country with no tradition of defending individual freedoms and civil rights. This is the only explanation for why thousands of women will march in the streets to protest cuts in food subsidies, and yet there is only a weak turnout at demonstrations in defense of human rights, even given the fact that Peru has been the country with the highest number of people who were detained or who disappeared for four years in a row.

In addition, subsistence-related organizations must face the greater challenge of setting their sights beyond the immediate issues of food and associated services, in order to articulate a strategy for defending social spending. As Elson (1987) suggests, cuts in public services must be selective and must take into account the needs of women to the extent that, although cuts have a negative impact on everyone, it is the female population that assumes responsibility for the daily and generational reproduction in the household that will be particularly hard hit. If, in addition, we suppose that women's income-generating activities will also increase, their burden will be even greater.

Finally, there is still a long way to go in order to recover a degree of social institutionality within the movement. Obviously this depends not only on women's groups, but also on the political will of the representatives of state institutions. In any case, it is an urgent item on the agenda of women's subsistence organizations. They undoubtedly constitute the most dynamic urban social actor, and consequently many leaders have received death threats or been assassinated by Sendero Luminoso. The usual strategy followed by the terrorists in the name of the people it claims to represent is, first, to spread rumors of corruption about a certain leader, in order to prepare the justification for their action; they then use threats and intimidation to convince her to abandon her position; and finally, they kill her. The effect of these deaths is traumatic for the national conscience in general, but especially for organized women of the popular sectors, and is aggravated by the savageness of Sendero Luminoso's actions. Any leader who does not submit to its political objectives is at risk of being assassinated. If the autonomy of the women's organization is firmly maintained, then there is a greater possibility that leaders with a long history of neighborhood activism will resist infiltration by Sendero Luminoso and refuse to comply with its orders. The women's organizations have been a wall of contention facing the authoritarianism of Sendero Luminoso in its attempts to advance into the cities. Nevertheless, murders and threats are rapidly having their effect: many leaders have abandoned their posts and gone into hiding, others have left the country and their families, others have died. The tens of thousands of women who remain do so by maintaining a low profile with an emphasis on service provision.

In this case, once again, recognizing the isolation of these leaders, who are left without political alliances and economic resources, is another urgent element in the task of articulating national interests and strategies for peace.

BIBLIOGRAPHY

Adrianzén, Alberto (1990). "Estado y sociedad: Señores, masas y ciudadanos." In *Estado y sociedad: Relaciones peligrosas*. Lima: Centro de Estudios y Promoción del Desarrollo.

Balbi, Carmen Rosa (1991). "Modernidad y progreso en el mundo informal." *Pretextos* (Lima), no. 2.
Backhaus, Annette (1988). "La dimensión de género en los proyectos de promoción de la mujer: Necesidad y retos." Lima: Fundación Naumann.
Barrig, Maruja (1989). "The Difficult Equilibrium between Bread and Roses: Women's Organizations and the Transition from Dictatorship to Democracy in Peru." In Jane Jaquette, ed., *The Women's Movement in Latin America: Feminism and the Transition to Democracy*. Boston: Unwin Hyman.
———. "Quejas y contenamientos: Historia de una política social, los municipios y la organización femenina en Lima." In Carmen Rosa Balbi et al., eds., *Movimientos sociales: Elementos para una relectura*. Lima: Centro de Estudios y Promoción del Desarrollo.
———. (1991). "Mujer, cooperación y desarrollo: Repensando estrategias." In *Mujer y desarrollo: Una nueva mirada*. Lima: Flora Tristan (en prensa).
Boggio, Ana (1989). "Estrategias de promoción y comedores." In Nora Galer M. and Pilar Núñez C., eds., *Mujer y comedores populares*. San Antonio, Lima: Servicios para el Desarrollo (SEPADE).
Borsotti, Carlos (1984). "Circuitos de satisfacción de necesidades, selección y educación." In *Desarrollo social en los 80*. Santiago: CEPAL, ILPES and UNICEF.
Cardoso, Fernando Henrique (1984). "Las políticas sociales en crisis: Nuevas opciones." In *Desarrollo social en los 80*. Santiago: CEPAL, ILPES and UNICEF.
Cotler, Julio (1978). *Estado y nación en el Perú*. Lima: Instituto de Estudios Peruanos.
Elson, Diane (1987). "The Impact of Structural Adjustment on Women: Concepts and Issues." Wid Programme, Commonwealth Secretarial, ms. Manchester University.
Franco, Carlos (1991a). "Exploraciones en otra modernidad: De la migración a la plebe urbana." In Henrique Urbano, comp., *Modernidad en los Andes*. Cuzco: Centro de Estudios Regionales Andinos, "Bartolomé de las Cases."
———. (1991b). "De la política social en el Perú: 1976–1990." Ms. Lima: CEDEP.
Huamán, Josefina (1989). "Economía y organización de comedores." In Nora Galer M. and Pilar Núñez C., eds., *Mujer y comedores populares*. Lima: Servicios para el Desarrollo (SEPADE).
Instituto CUANTO (1991). "Ajuste y economía familiar 1985–1990." Lima.
Lechner, Norbert (1982). "Qué significa hacer política?" In Norbert Lechner, ed., *¿Qué significa hacer política?* Lima: DESCO, Centro de Estudios y Promoción del Desarrollo.
López, Sinesio (1990). "El Perú de los 80: Sociedad y estado en el fin de una época." In *Estado y sociedad: Relaciones peligrosas*. Lima: Centro de Estudios y Promoción del Desarrollo.
Moser, Caroline (1989). "The Impact of Recession and Adjustment Policies at the Microlevel: Low Income Women and Their Households in Guayaquil, Ecuador." In *The Invisible Adjustment, Poor Women and the Economic Crisis*. UNICEF.
Portocarrero, Gonzalo (1990). "El silencio, la queja y la acción: Respuestas al sufrimiento en la cultura peruana." In Carlos Iván Degregori et al., eds., *Tiempos de ira y amor: Nuevos actores para viejos problemas*. Lima: Centro de Estudios y Promoción del Desarrollo.
Reyes, José (1991). "La pobreza en Lima: El impacto de la crisis en la calidad de vida." Ms. Lima: ADEC-ATC.
Sara-Lafosse, Violeta (1984). "Comedores comunales: La mujer frenta a la crisis." Ms. Lima: SUMBI.

Stokes, Susan (1991). "Politics and Latin America's Urban Poor: Reflections from a Lima Shanty Town." *Latin American Research Review* 26(2), 75–101.

Vega, Jorge Enrique (1987). "Entre la fragmentación y la política." Paper presented at the seminar "Modernidad, post-modernidad e identidad en América Latina." Buenos Aires: CLASCO.

5

In No-Man's Land: Poor Women's Organizations and Political Violence in Lima's Neighborhoods

CECILIA BLONDET

In February 1992 María Elena Moyano, an Afro-Peruvian leader and a very special friend, was murdered in the midst of Peru's violent civil war against Sendero Luminoso. When we first heard the news of her death, we were angry and indignant; but we were also scared and felt powerless because, at that point, the murderous Maoist guerrillas seemed to be stronger than we were. We were losing the war: it was as if we were trapped in a Greek tragedy with no end in sight.

Today, we have reconstructed a María Elena in each of us, and perhaps this more personal, new black woman within threatens us less, makes us all a little less uneasy. Through her daring, her irony, her marked presence, her irreverent laughter, María Elena generated admiration and envy, jealousy and love, rivalry and solidarity. She was both astute and dangerous as a politician, and, aware of this, Sendero killed her. They found her unbearable and assumed that, through their tears, women would share with them the same calm her death undoubtedly brought them. What they did not count on was the strength of a movement built from a reality rooted in the collective projects it engendered and which were woven together and sustained by the women's personal goals. They did not consider that the women had never aimed to conquer a perfect and idealized paradise; that they had instead united for a very concrete reason—namely, to achieve higher standards of living for their families. Similarly, they had no way of knowing that through their struggle, the women had gradually learned to affirm themselves as women.

Author's Note: I want to thank Susana Oboler for her excellent editorial work and translation of this essay.

Why were the women's organizations so important to Sendero's strategies? Indeed, what was Sendero's relationship to the women's organizations in the poor neighborhoods of Lima? Why did they target their leaders and how did these women respond? Certainly, much has been written about Sendero Luminoso—about the 12-year war it waged against Peruvian society as a whole, and the strategic importance it placed on the poor neighborhoods surrounding Lima after its first Congress in 1989. Yet little is known about the specific violent strategies it developed against the women's organizations and the latter's forms of resistance.

This essay discusses the war waged by Sendero against the women's organizations to suggest that both Sendero's strategies and the responses of the women's leaders stemmed from deeply rooted and long-standing ideologies that depict women as harmless and irrelevant in Peru's public sphere. Confronted by the obvious political strength of the women's organizations, Sendero was forced to modify its ideological perception of women and, consequently, to change its strategy toward them. At the same time, while the leaders of the women's organizations were also embedded in the society's prevailing gender ideologies, their confrontation with Sendero's terrorist tactics necessarily led some of them to develop new strategies that both invoked and challenged traditional gender roles. Grounded in the particular ways they positioned themselves both as women and as leaders, individual leaders organized their responses to terrorism according to the particular strategy Sendero adopted toward them and their neighborhood. Nevertheless, as I argue below, in spite of the political strength and resilience of the women's organizations—at that point almost unique among Peru's political institutions—their precariousness ensured that they were no match for the Senderistas, who ultimately murdered several of their leaders and destroyed their organizations through violence and terrorism.

What Did Sendero Luminoso Want?

Sendero sought to destabilize society's political and social institutions, murdering officials, leaders of the popular sectors, and labor organizers, and creating what they referred to as a "power vacuum." According to various declarations shortly before the capture of their leader and patriarch, Abimael Guzmán, in September 1992, the party had reached what it defined as a "strategic balance" and was thus ready to force the state into a full-fledged open confrontation over both military and political power. This "balance" assumed that the Armed Forces and "Yanqui imperialism" would jointly develop and intensify a counterinsurgent war which would inevitably result in a "genocide," and a large defection of the disenfranchised population to the ranks of the guerrillas.

It is difficult to assess the realism of their prediction, given the extent to which the nation's various institutions had disintegrated by the early 1990s. Certainly, the assaults on the capital and different parts of the country in the days preceding Guzmán's capture had led many to believe that while Sendero's evaluation might be exaggerated, the general paralysis with which their indiscriminate and criminal offensives were met by established institutions could indeed ultimately lead to a national breakdown in the not-too-distant future. What is clear, however, is that if Sendero insisted on taking power and destroying the country's "traditional and obsolete power," the city of Lima invariably played a fundamental role in achieving that aim: in Peru power is concentrated in Lima and Sendero chose its most precarious sites—the poor neighborhood organizations, which were primarily run by and for women and their families—as both their point of entry into the city and the target of their attack.

Why the Women's Organizations? The Background

In the early 1980s, when Peru was entering a new democratic period and Sendero was simultaneously launching its strategy to destroy the state and take power, thousands of women began to participate at an unprecedented level in social movements and, indirectly, to support the notion of democracy. Although the scope of their actions was clearly defined, poor women shunned violence and sought instead to develop alternative means to improve the conditions in which they and their families lived. From the beginning, women's organizations focused on family-based demands, their members' roles as mothers, access to food, and collective strategies to lower their expenses as means of contributing to their families' survival. This approach both required and coincided with offers of support from such entities as the Catholic Church and private and public institutions and became part of the state's policy to "attend to the needs" of the poor sectors of the population.

Grounded in a welfare-styled structure, by the mid-1980s the organizations had expanded to include a growing sector of the population, thus increasing the base of organized women. The movement's membership and leadership reflected the social heterogeneity of poor women, including their different educational and organizational backgrounds. In time, the organizations became more diverse and included mothers' clubs, glass-of-milk committees, people's kitchens, skills-training workshops, landscaping and literacy groups, and the like. At the same time, the interests and proposals of various supporting agencies added to each neighborhood's particular practices, engendering several new kinds of organizations.

The development of the neighborhood movements prompted the creation of networks that centralized the vast movement on the basis of territoriality and type of organization. As the movement's internal structures became more complex, they simultaneously shaped the women as both subjects and legitimate interlocutors of the political parties, private institutions, and the state. In short, then, there was a trend toward consolidating a process which, although conflict-ridden, had the vitality necessary to resolve contradictions in a positive way.

After 1989, however, the economic and political context began to deteriorate significantly. Pauperization among the poor sectors increased and the channels of political representation gradually lost their legitimacy, affecting the women's organizations in various ways: the relatively well established and regular procedure for food donations changed; neglecting many of the existing organizations, the state implemented a welfare-styled policy aimed at attenuating the impact of the crisis on poorer sectors and resorted to concentrating and redirecting the distribution of food donations.

In 1989 this interventionist structure began to collapse. For a variety of reasons—among them corruption, the government's lack of interest in improving living conditions, and the NGOs' budget cuts—donations to women's organizations declined and, worse, the distribution of subsistence items became irregular. Although the women continued to cook collectively, many organizations also began to combine different strategies to replace the subsidies that, until then, had come from above.

These kinds of collective survival organizations, based on subsidies and donations, could exist only as long as the state maintained its welfare-styled policy. Toward the end of the 1980s, many of the organizations faced an overwhelming number of demands: for food, education, political work, and family health. For example, besides preparing and distributing milk, the glass-of-milk committees were also called upon to establish networks to produce and sell their by-products. Through their neighborhood organizations, women began to learn about cholera and diarrhea; they attended literacy classes, read the Bible, formed human rights commissions, and reacted against the violence perpetrated by Sendero. They attended workshops on sex education and adolescent psychology; on how to make clothes, dolls, and decorated cakes. They grew vegetables, raised guinea pigs, and weighed the pros and cons of starting a bread shop or a school uniform factory. As a result, the organizations found themselves further pressured by both the women participants themselves and outside institutions (NGOs, churches, and cooperating agencies) to whom they were accountable: they had to respond to the requests of international agencies by participating in vaccination campaigns; to comply with the interests of the Catholic Church by forming catechism groups; to placate the feminists by learning about abortion and the need to take control of their bodies; and to satisfy the concerns of the political parties by attending marches and demonstrations.

They did all of this to guarantee access to the food, training, and information that ensured their economic and social support, and hence reinforced their relationship to the institutions. In this respect, the outside agencies were particularly at fault, for they did not notice the effect that carrying out their projects was having on the organizations. In fact, rather than meeting the needs of the organizations and thus strengthening them, these additional tasks instead fueled the exhaustion and inefficiency of the organizations and their leaders.

Charged with organizing and overseeing a growing number of activities, women leaders were forced to change long-established practices within their organizations, in their relations with the various outside supporting institutions, and with the state. As a result of the economic crisis and the state's retreat from its social responsibility, they found themselves under growing pressure to satisfy the membership's needs, and less able to achieve their goals under these new conditions. Not surprisingly, questions began to arise about the extent to which these organizations and their leaders were indeed representative of their constituencies. At the same time, the organizations were being forced into new structures which effectively undermined their quest for organizational autonomy. Internally, relations among the leaders and between them and the membership were also affected: the previously efficient distribution of donations was now pitted against the principles of democratic practice. In some cases, loyalties were fractured, as internal relations and dynamics began to disintegrate, uncovering the more conflict-ridden aspects of institutional life. As a result, the tenuous channels of representation and for constructing poor women's identity risked being blocked: the network of women's organizations became more fragile and their leadership's increasing delegitimization began to threaten the continuity of the organizations' role as mediators between the neighborhood populations and a state which had little if any interest in acknowledging, much less satisfying, their needs.

In 1990, under the guidance of the International Monetary Fund

(IMF), President Alberto Fujimori enacted the harshest structural readjustment measures in Peru's history, unaccompanied by any policies to deal with the hardships created by the sudden rise in unemployment, poverty, and hunger, and the declining health conditions among large sectors of the population. As a result of Fujimori's tactics, aimed at reducing the hyperinflation and reinserting Peru into the international market, the rate of inflation declined from 7,650 percent in 1990 to 139 percent in 1991. The number of poor people, though, rose to approximately 15 million, or 68 percent of the population. Faced with the gradual collapse of political and social institutions, women's organizations remained the only viable political channel of representation for poor women and the disenfranchised sectors of the city's population.

Left to their own devices, and lacking an adequate emergency program to minimize the impact of what came to be known as the "fuji-shock", the women's organizations began to build a popular safety net, redoubling their efforts to provide food and support to the ever-growing number of poor families.

Precisely because of the skill with which they organized the struggle against hunger and the astuteness with which their grassroots organizations found new ways to survive, the leaders of the women's movements became targets of Sendero's violent assaults. Indeed, these women were the visible and acknowledged heads of a movement which did not serve the terrorists' interests. Yet, abandoned by the state and caught in the infighting among the largely delegitimized political parties, they lacked the necessary support from society's political and social institutions and were besieged by their networks' internal conflicts and the delegitimization of their leadership. As Sendero gradually became aware of the powerful obstacle these leaders and their organizations posed to the fulfillment of their goals, it subjected them to acts of violence and death threats.

Fatal Attraction: Sendero Luminoso's Attack on Women's Organizations

During the 1980s, Sendero's interests had primarily focused on peasants, local officials, and teachers in the rural areas. As they penetrated urban areas toward the end of the decade, however, they began to target leaders of the neighborhood organizations, youth groups, and labor movements. Rooted in traditional gender ideologies that view women as harmless and ineffective second-class citizens, they—like the neighborhood male leaders—did not recognize the political relevance nor organizational potential of the public kitchens or glass-of-milk committees, and allowed them to organize and grow undisturbed. It was only in 1991 that the "party" began to perceive the strategic relevance of the women's organizations and hence to attempt to co-opt or destroy them. Indeed, by then, the organizations were clearly a threat to Sendero because of their ability to mobilize the population because they provided food for the resident families through collective food programs—from which the guerrillas, incidentally, also benefited. But above all, Sendero came to perceive the women as a threat because they realized that they organized daily family life and thus articulated neighborhood residents around very concrete interests. In other words, they nourished the very social fabric which Sendero sought to destroy. Moreover, the terrorists reacted violently against the organizations because of the latter's links with what they called the "revisionist" left, as well as with the NGOs, churches, and municipal governments. As they stated in their graffiti, "We must remove these organizations from the claws of imperialism." In short, then, insofar as Sendero wanted to disconnect the different neighborhoods around the city and disarticulate any effort by the organizations of the poor to unite, to organize, and to resist, the women's organizations clearly threatened the guerrillas' objectives. This prompted Sendero to develop a strategy aimed at dismantling and/or controlling these organizations for their own benefit.

Using terror, boycott, and persuasion, Sendero Luminoso implemented a divide-and-conquer strategy in the poor neighborhoods. It sought to deepen the existing conflict between the leadership and the masses, pit the various organizations against one another, feed old rivalries and power struggles among all the participants, and thus destabilize the very fragile organizational bases through which the country's poor populations had, until then, constructed strategies to resist hunger and combat growing pauperization.

The basis of the Senderistas' strategies to destroy the women's movements was its systematic assault on their leaders, which varied according to the position each occupied in her organization and the strategic importance of her particular neighborhood. Attacking the most important leaders it deepened the internal conflicts among them, exacerbating existing petty jealousies, envy, and power struggles. By spreading rumors about the leaders' corruption, theft, and opportunism, Sendero sought to undermine their prestige and create distrust within the neighborhood, thus planting the seeds that would later serve to justify their murder to the neighborhood populations.

Once they had tainted, divided, and crippled the top leadership, the

Senderistas moved on to the middle-level leadership. Many of these women had themselves once hoped to enter the top leadership ranks. But their efforts had been frustrated by the deepening of the crisis which undermined the mechanisms that previously allowed leadership to rotate, reinforcing instead the authority of the few who were best known in the neighborhood. The scene was thus set for Sendero to exploit old rivalries and long-festering resentments between these women and those in the higher leadership ranks. But in this case, the party adopted a different strategy, one based primarily on co-opting many of the leaders in the lower ranks. Isolating their targets from the other women, the Senderistas set out to cultivate an individual relationship with each woman, helping her to deal with the various problems that plagued her personal life, whether related to children, health, or food concerns. They pretended to care for the individual herself, showering her with personal attention and showing concern about her and her individual problems. What might have felt like affection was, in fact, a trap. Need and the precarious economic circumstances in which these women lived again played a role in their gradual involvement with the guerrillas. Caught between terror and the need for attention, they gradually fell into the party's clutches. Clearly, not all leaders in the middle ranks complied: those who resisted, however, met threats, blackmail, beatings, and even death. Yet, whether through paying attention or causing terror, the Senderistas were bent on achieving their goal, either by winning them over or by neutralizing them.

Sendero's actions were also brutal, although more subtle, at the grassroots level, spreading both terror and confusion in the ranks. This sector had a number of unresolved demands and doubts, ranging, for example, from the amount of donations that arrived and who was supposed to receive them, to whether the entire donation was actually distributed—in short, a set of fantasies fed and magnified by the lack of resources and the deepening crisis. With the masses increasingly distrustful of their leaders, some of whom had been tainted, trapped, or openly converted by the party, all Sendero now had to do was spread further confusion among them. If, for example, the masses decided to hold a march or demonstration on a particular date, leaflets appeared announcing a different date; if an agreement was reached, rumors were spread to disavow it; if people decided to attend some activity, warnings were sounded that the Sendero or the police would be there to attack them. This strategy is extremely effective—almost perfect—when people live in fear. Nobody has to appear, no one shows his or her face. Actions, comings and goings, rumors and gossip simply materialize without anyone claiming responsibility: they surface merely as voices, whispers, shouts that feed bewilderment, exhaustion, fear, insecurity, distrust—feelings that all Peruvians, male and female, experienced at that time.

Finally, new leaders and grassroots sectors also existed among the poorest of the poor. These included primarily migrant women, widows, single mothers, or abandoned women, new arrivees from the emergency zones in the Andes. They were part of the large contingent of marginal and displaced women who did not take part in the public kitchens, who were not yet familiar with the workings of the various institutions of the city and neighborhoods, and who, in general, neither spoke the language nor understood the customs of urban life. From them, Sendero essentially sought unconditional support when they needed lodging or refuge. If the women shunned them, the Senderistas would appeal to their shared memories of life in the Andean villages. These women were also condemned to silence and isolation.

Thus, although Senderistas penetrated all levels of the neighborhood populations, they did not attack their organizations directly, but instead developed a strategy of assaults on individual women, particularly the leaders. As stated in graffiti and flyers prior to murdering María Elena Moyano:

> . . . They say that the COMMUNIST PARTY OF PERU has launched an offensive against the "collective kitchens," against the "popular organizations," "destroying offices, burning the food in storage facilities as in Villa El Salvador," WHICH IS COMPLETELY FALSE. Therefore, we indignantly reject this vile charge against the PCP and we denounce it as a SUICIDAL ACT, carried out by revisionist and opportunist leaders, headed by María Elena Moyano, made as a cover-up of their thefts, precisely when they had to present the accounts, and used as a smokescreen to generate public opinion in her favor and launch herself as a candidate for deputy; this is why she wants to appear as a victim and defender of the people. . . .

Caught between the general distrust and petty jealousies invariably magnified by Sendero's presence, the women leaders responded according to a variety of personal and political factors, ranging from individual bravery and political convictions to the symbolic or real importance of their particular neighborhood. Ultimately, the reality of Lima's poor neighborhoods was their forced coexistence with Sendero. Recognizing this fact is fundamental for understanding the varying behaviors of the women leaders. In the midst of the uncertain conditions in which they lived, each developed her own means of daily negotiation that allowed her to continue to live in the neighborhood. Not surprisingly, their reactions to Sendero's war against them varied, and many of them developed ambiguous ways of responding to the terrorist assaults. Most of the women leaders, for example, were evasive, a result of a combination of fear, lethargy, tolerance, and even excuses, and thus preferred not to say anything either in favor of or against the Senderistas. Although they totally rejected the bloody violence, they had to coexist with it, to exorcise the nostalgic remnants of their own leftist pasts, ultimately finding themselves unable to clearly identify Sendero as the enemy. Others made guarded references to the "compañeros" for, as they put it, "my children could be like them: how can I denounce them?" Hence, a sense of ethnic identification also played a key role in neutralizing many of the women leaders.

Others were fearful but, nevertheless, more forthcoming in their opposition. For example, those targeted by Sendero waited until they received several death threats before telling anyone about them. They did not dare confront them publicly, but were willing to participate in mass demonstrations. In these cases, distrust played an important role in explaining their attitude: no one knew who was who, even among the closest leaders.

Indeed, Sendero's various tactics ultimately paralyzed most of the women leaders, tainting them as possible terrorists, either by spreading rumor, innuendo, and distrust, or by placing them in situations that invariably tainted them in the eyes of their constituencies. For the individual leader, it was a no-win situation: once tainted, who would protect her? What options were open to her? What was best for her? Who, for example, would believe that she had been tainted by the Senderistas, that she had inadvertently fallen into their trap, that she was not one of them?

The few, more politicized leaders who were fully legitimized by their organizations recognized the severity of the situation created by the terrorists. They were the first to publicly communicate the death threats they received and bravely confronted Sendero through the media at mass meetings and in the neighborhood assemblies. As in the early days of the neighborhood women's organizations, they went out of their way to seek support and coordinate the movement—aware that once again, they could not do it alone, that they needed to join together to prevent the spread of terrorism. The women confronted considerable risks in both their public and private lives. Highly vulnerable to Sendero and lacking the necessary security forces to protect them, they had no option but to go about their daily routines. After all, although they were important leaders in their neighborhoods, they were also mothers, and, as such, they still had to take their children from one place to another, go to the market for food for their families, and wait in lines to get water for their homes.

These women clearly identified the Senderistas as the enemy and thus, despite their differences and disagreements, did not shy away from cooperating with local governments and institutions in the neighborhood, including the security forces, in order to at least meet the terrorists on more equal grounds. Unfortunately, however, their attitude invariably led to the murder of important leaders, such as María Elena Moyano.

Unlike most of the other leaders, María Elena publicly grounded her sense of self in a deeply feminist perspective which strongly reinforced her position of leadership. She constantly called on others to join her in the public sphere, insisting that women unite in the struggle against Sendero, that they march and demonstrate, that they insist that the state acknowledge their right to its protection, that they make demands based on their needs as women, mothers, and citizens. Yet while her feminist stance led her to base her public rejection of Sendero on the strength of the women's movement she led, it also created enormous ambivalence toward her on the part of the other women leaders. The latter both admired and hated her and were forced to take positions that entailed both personal and political risks, even while they acknowledged the validity of her strategies and offered few if any alternatives to their constituencies.

It is not suprising, then, that Sendero considered María Elena a dangerous enemy. She consistently strove to create a movement against them that simultaneously raised women's consciousness of themselves as women and that refused to accept Sendero's disruptive presence, its political, cultural, and personal seductions, or, for that matter, women's relegation to a subordinate position in society's public sphere and traditions.

In this respect, María Elena's behavior and approach toward Sendero also bring to light the discrepancies between her progressive reputation in relation to women and Sendero's obviously recalcitrant strategies toward the women's organizations during the war years. Some, for example, have pointed to the number of women who held important leadership positions among the Senderistas; others have suggested that Sendero Luminoso was the only political organization to take women seriously, to treat them as equal to men, and that the Senderistas in this sense were better than the traditional parties in sustaining the idea of the equality of women. Yet for the most part, the women in the party's leadership ranks were called on to surround and protect their leader, Guzmán, and were primarily charged with ensuring that his decisions were implemented. Moreover, as noted above, Sendero's strategy toward women's organizations showed their disdain for women—visible in their earlier misguided assumptions about women as harmless, their misjudgment about the political relevance of the latter's organizations, or in the ways they later drew on traditional patterns of male-female relations as part of their strategy to co-opt individual neighborhood leaders.

Unlike the other women leaders, María Elena's approach was neither submissive nor reflective of traditional gendered behavior attributed to other non-white women on Peru's political scene. Instead, perhaps because of her Afro-Peruvian background, which distinguished her from "real" Peruvians, she was able to establish a strong presence in the public sphere, one which was more easily accepted than might otherwise have been the case. Certainly, María Elena had a stronger public will and ambition than the other women leaders, and again, unlike them, she publicly confronted the Senderistas, demanding and challenging them to identify themselves and openly confront the neighborhood populations. Thus, conscious of herself as a woman, she publicly defined herself in those terms and openly grounded her actions on the support of other women. Through her fearless public posture, she effectively challenged both Sendero's disdain and prejudices against women and the traditional image of poor women as unassuming, fearful, and irrelevant to the larger society.

While women's organizations today are gradually regrouping and the pain of Peru's violent civil war is slowly subsiding, María Elena's memory lives on. She is considered an important heroine in the struggle against Sendero. Her murder was one more example of the atrocities that today force the government and the politicians to recognize their continued neglect of the rights of all Peruvians.

6

Power and Patriarchy: The Long Struggle to Forge a Coordinated Women's Movement in Nicaragua

MALENA DE MONTÍS

Several structural and historical contradictions have impeded the formation of a strong, united women's movement in Nicaragua capable of designing strategies for the sustained promotion of women's struggle for power. These have limited the development of a movement with the capacity to advance processes of organization and consciousness-raising for women both personally and collectively, both "in themselves" and "for themselves,"[1] that would allow them to proceed with greater commitment in their struggle for emancipation.

Here, I focus on some of the challenges and problems that have arisen in the construction of a coordinated women's movement in Nicaragua. For that purpose, I will draw on the specific experience of the Luisa Amanda Espinoza Women's Association (AMNLAE), which until February 1990, when the Sandinista National Liberation Front (FSLN) lost the national elections, defined itself as the coordinator of the various women's organizations in the country. Specifically, I will refer to certain contradictions related to its agenda and its methods of organizing, both of which limited its coordination effort.[2]

Historical Antecedents

The history of the women's movement in Nicaragua reaches back to the years before the triumph of the Sandinista Revolution in July 1979.[3] Some of its roots can be found in the Women's Patriotic Alliance, created

Editors' Note: Translated by Lilian Autler.

in 1967 by the Socialist Party; in the incorporation of women's demands into the Historic Program of the FSLN; and in the creation of the Women's Association to Confront the National Problematic (AMPRONAC), founded in 1977 on the initiative of several women who were militants and cadres of the Sandinista Front. The churches' efforts to organize women also form part of that history. For example, the "Feminine Societies" promoted by the Baptist Church have been organizing women since the 1950s for the purpose of promoting literacy, providing theological instruction and interpretation of the Bible, or simply for women to socialize with one another.

AMPRONAC was the first broad-based women's organization in the country. Female professionals, students, housewives, and shopkeepers united to protest as mothers, wives, daughters, and sisters. They joined together mainly to denounce the horrendous human rights violations that were being committed during the Somoza dictatorship, but also to push for the recognition of certain problems specific to women. They demanded equal pay for equal work and the elimination of prostitution, among other things, thus introducing a feminist perspective to women's organized struggles.

In September 1979, with the Sandinistas' seizure of governmental power, AMNLAE was founded, replacing AMPRONAC, and becoming the most extensive women's organization in the country during the early years of Sandinista rule. The association emerged thanks to the militancy of women who managed to integrate themselves into the popular movement and become an important social and political force during the insurrection and throughout the decade of Sandinista government despite the structural limitations of underdevelopment, war, and the dominant patriarchal ideology.

From the outset, AMNLAE maintained that only through its political coordination would women succeed in changing their historically inferior status and gain an equal space in the new society. The slogan that the association adopted during the early years—"Construyendo la Patria Nueva forjaremos a la Mujer Nueva" (In constructing the New Country we will forge the New Woman)—accurately expressed its emphasis on women's insertion into the revolutionary process as the means for achieving changes in their social condition (Murguíalday 1990).

The gains made by women during the period of Sandinista government were undeniably significant. Women achieved legal and social rights, struggling from their diverse organizational spaces and conducting various broad demonstrations. Some obtained employment in positions traditionally reserved for men; preschools and child care centers were created; and important laws were enacted, though there was much resistance to their actual implementation. In the majority of cases, they were not enforced, either because women themselves were not aware of their existence, or because the mechanisms needed to put them into practice were lacking. Examples of these were laws requiring equal pay for equal work; the prohibition of the commercial use of women's bodies as sexual objects; agrarian reform legislation that recognized women as legal subjects capable of holding land titles regardless of their marital status; and finally, the laws regarding family relations and alimony which required men to take responsibility for their children. Women even managed to introduce gender-based claims in revolutionary documents as important as the Women's Proclamation and the Constitution of the Republic in 1987.[4] Women who held leadership positions in the various FSLN political organizations, most of whom were from the middle and upper classes, played an important role in this achievement.

This social force composed of women was in some cases formally identified with AMNLAE and in other cases not. Other more autonomous women's groups also emerged. Within some institutions, both governmental and nongovernmental, research teams were formed to study issues affecting women. Free legal assistance clinics were created to attend to women who came with all types of problems related to rape, divorce, child support payments, and the like. Autonomous groups were also formed to promote health care, education, and productive projects locally, many of them financed by nongovernmental organizations or international solidarity committees composed mainly of women.

Some of these groups were initially sympathetic toward AMNLAE, although little by little they came to reject its role as the central coordinating body. Many of the groups moved toward feminist perspectives as they sought to resolve strategic gender needs, even while operating in a cultural context where the concept of feminism still produced uneasiness and conflict. Among the contradictions that explain AMNLAE's loss of legitimacy as coordinator of the various women's groups, two of the more important are its agenda and its organizing techniques. Both themes figure in the current debates within the movement.

AMNLAE'S Agenda

When the Sandinista Front came to power, it facilitated and promoted the expansion of popular women's organizations so that they could participate in the general tasks of the state, and thus defend the revolution and improve living conditions. At the same time, women struggled to resolve their own specific demands. They participated on a massive scale in the various mobilizations during the decade of Sandinista government. Contrary to the commonly held image of the Nicaraguan women's movement,[5] however, only 14.6 percent of all women over 16 years of age participated in women's organizations in 1989.[6]

Women who participated exhibit the following general characteristics. Income levels in all sectors are very low, and the drop in purchasing power in recent years has provoked a high rate of job turnover, especially in the service sectors. The majority live in urban areas and work outside the home, meaning a triple work day for many.[7] There are high percentages of illiteracy among female peasants and agricultural workers, low levels of schooling among industrial workers, and only moderate levels of educational attainment among health care workers and teachers.

The revolution opened political, economic, and social spaces to women so that they could struggle for the resolution of their specific claims as women at least as much as possible in the context of U.S. military aggression, its economic boycott, and a *machista* culture. However, "the Sandinista Front rarely managed to go beyond its homogeneous discourse regarding the entire *pueblo*, as if the *pueblo* were not composed of individuals with distinct identities and interests. They privileged what the Sandinista leadership considered to be the general or overall interests of the country. The specific demands of different sectors or social groups, especially those of women and of the ethnic groups of the Atlantic Coast, were for a long time considered diversionist or, at best, secondary to the strategic interests of the Revolution" (Criquillón 1989). The objective conditions imposed by the national struggle against foreign military aggression, which demanded a range of pragmatic solutions in the face of shifting and complex sets of circumstances, demanded immediate attention, it was argued.

AMNLAE was built up by the FSLN and therefore depended on the directives of the party, as did all the other Sandinista mass organizations during the period of revolutionary government. Consequently, it mainly promoted the development of women's consciousness regarding the national sociopolitical situation. Problems of gender subordination and women's need to struggle for emancipation were approached in a limited and timid manner, thus impeding a greater development of gender consciousness among women.

AMNLAE's specific demands focused fundamentally on the resolution of women's practical needs.[8] Women were mainly mobilized to participate in health campaigns, neighborhood cleanups, the collection of bottles needed in factories which did not have the currency to import them, the establishment of family gardens, and the like. The high-priority task assigned to AMNLAE by the FSLN as a consequence of the war was to support the implementation of the Patriotic Military Service (SPM) by attending to the needs of the mothers of combatants. The Association arranged for visits to the encampments, provided news about their relatives, delivered mail, and so on. As a result, AMNLAE was often seen as an organization of mothers of combatants, or "heroes and martyrs," an image which isolated it from many young women who did not identify with that role.

In the context of the 1980s, and as a consequence of the war, the possibilities for introducing a deeper analysis of strategic gender needs were severely limited, as was the possibility of promoting a strong women's movement with a greater capacity for reflection and action to transform the patriarchal structures of society. The ideological and political struggle unfolded only partially, with taboo strategic topics only very timidly introduced into the public debate and only at particular moments. Examples of these topics were sexual harassment, abortion, the repression of sexuality, shared child care responsibilities, the sexual division of labor, domestic violence, and women's right to participate in the military. Moreover, by missing important opportunities, AMNLAE did not manage to shape a strategy for action which articulated the resolution of the practical needs felt by the majority of women with the strategic, emancipatory claims presented in certain declarations of the FSLN itself, such as the Women's Proclamation. This sharply limited women's ability to open up important new spaces of power.

There was a lack of knowledge and analysis within AMNLAE about the multiple forms of subordination which women experience, and especially about the underlying cultural factors. The Association hardly recognized the heterogeneity of oppression according to sector, geographic region, age, religious creed, myths, forms of economic insertion, private and public spheres, and so on. This limited the ability to elaborate particular strategies derived from women's specificities yet encompassing the global objectives of the revolution. If women had felt implicated in the struggle based on their own particular identities and circumstances, rather than feeling that they were in competition with one another, it might have been easier to achieve the cohesion and broad participation necessary to create a more effective women's movement.

The low level of awareness was exacerbated by the failure to systematize the experiences of women's groups, hampering the theorization of these complex experiences full of lessons. Missing were debate and conceptual development regarding feminism, gender, the sexual division of labor, and other topics that AMNLAE could have advanced based precisely on that experience. These themes were surfacing in various women's spaces, mainly in groups which little by little came to define themselves as feminist and were rejected by AMNLAE. The Association lent priority to pragmatism and activism over this type of reflection. It advocated the need to respond to immediate tasks demanded by the war—which did impose a rhythm of life in the country—and argued that such ideas and categories were imported and thus generated confusion and diversionism among women. AMNLAE's resistance to systematization and theorization was in turn reinforced by the predominance of oral culture in Nicaragua and by a certain generalized rejection of "intellectual work" by the majority of Sandinista leaders. Theoretical readings and the complexities inherent in reflective analysis were generally perceived as unnecessary. There was a need to act immediately and time could not be wasted on such "abstractions."

In addition, the lack of an agenda for struggle which aimed for the resolution of women's strategic needs was due, to a great extent, to the fact that equality between men and women was not a fundamental postulate of the revolution. The lack of equity, which defines patriarchal forms, was not considered a structural element of society to be overcome. Despite its progressive position, the FSLN's Women's Proclamation did not holistically integrate the element of gender, with its many dimensions and implications, along with class-based and democratic objectives. As in most parts of the world, discussions of politics and democracy in Nicaragua have been restricted to the public arena of individuals, while the relations of domination within the private, untouchable realm of the home have remained hidden.

Two assumptions underlie these positions. First is the belief that the integration of women into public life will automatically lead to their emancipation and that gender inequality disappears to the extent that women are incorporated into production.[9] According to the erroneous evolutionist way of thinking which prevailed, women's subordination would be overcome following, or as a result of, the elimination of other inequities. In other words, women's emancipation was foreseen as an evolutionary consequence of social and economic development, assuming that economic backwardness and class differences were at the root of oppressive relations between men and women. A second assumption has been that the vanguard party, and particularly its leaders, all men, are the "enlightened ones" who hold the truth and the responsibility to guide the oppressed masses in their struggle for liberation. As a result, from the pinnacle of party power, the

FSLN's "orientations" were "passed down" to AMNLAE to guide its political action.

Though the revolutionary political system significantly democratized certain dimensions of public power,[10] the notions and exercise of power which prevailed still attributed it exclusively to the members of the vanguard and to the mass organizations serving as "transmission channels" for the implementation of orders from the top. The slogan "dirección nacional ordene" (national leadership commands), widely used during the Sandinista government, clearly reflected these positions. According to this notion, the "vanguard" holds an integral knowledge of all the particular realities of the oppressed, a knowledge which is gradually disseminated among the "masses" so that they will actively participate in those tasks defined as priorities.

This conception of power obviously negates the possibility of using organizing methods based on mutual learning between leaders and the rest of the population, and by ruling out processes that recognize the diversity of existing realities and types of knowledge, it prevents historically oppressed groups from developing the capacity to make their own decisions. In this manner, the political system reproduced the wide differences in access to power characteristic of patriarchy, thus further obscuring the question of gender. It maintained elitist and authoritarian patterns of "power over others," imposing a hierarchical vision which justified manipulation and took away autonomy. This obstructed not only the development of human creativity in general, but also AMNLAE's ability to combine and coordinate the particular creativities of the various women's groups which expressed new ideas, new visions, and more democratic and inclusionary organizational and work methods.

AMNLAE'S Work Methods

Early in the Sandinista government, AMNLAE activists sought to integrate people into the various tasks that "came down" from the leadership, such as the militias, cleanup brigades, and so on. Meanwhile, AMNLAE's role was not entirely clear, causing tensions with other organizations whose members were involved in the same tasks. As a result, AMNLAE modified its organizational structure so as to operate within the different popular organizations.

Thus they gradually created the Women's Secretariat of the Agricultural Workers' Association (ATC), the Women's Section within the

National Farmers' and Ranchers' Union (UNAG), and the National Women's Commission within the Nicaraguan Confederation of Professionals (CONAPRO). These internal bodies began to articulate more concretely women's interests with the specificities of social class or occupation, and the resulting dynamism within the organizations enabled them to achieve certain gains. The National Committee of AMNLAE, composed of representatives from these various groups along with AMNLAE's leadership, attempted in this way to represent the different sectors and popular organizations. However, AMNLAE itself maintained its own national and regional structures headed by activists who were strongly rejected by the women who worked with other popular organizations. Immersed in power struggles among themselves and against the majority male leadership of each organization, the female grassroots activists and leaders divided and exhausted themselves as they lost opportunities to unite and become a true force in their own right.

Each sector followed its own ways of implementing the "lines" of work drawn up by the FSLN, resulting in a great dispersion of effort and reproducing within each organization the verticalism and centralization that characterized the FSLN's political practice. Similarly, the women's organizations independent of party or government structures which emerged and grew stronger throughout the period lost confidence in AMNLAE's capacity to mobilize and coordinate, even though many of these organizations had initially maintained a rather close relationship with AMNLAE, such as the Collective of Matagalpa, the Collective of Masaya, some of the Casas de la Mujer (Women's Houses) in Managua, various NGOs, among others.

AMNLAE thus lost credibility as the official expression of the women's movement—credibility which could not be restored even by its final efforts, shortly before the defeat of the FSLN, to hold its own internal elections. Like the other popular organizations, AMNLAE remained subordinate to the party that appointed its leadership. The vertical and sectorally fragmented mode of operation undoubtedly hindered the construction of a popular power which would allow for women's transformation from oppressed objects, dictated by the values of traditional Nicaraguan political culture, into social subjects with their own voices. The great majority of women mobilized by AMNLAE remained subordinate to decisions made by men, with only limited opportunities to influence these decisions and achieve positive solutions to their problems. Moreover, given women's enormous difficulties in identifying with each other and their lack of experience in exercising power, many identified with men and ended up reproducing the vertical, authoritarian, and competitive work methods of the patriarchal system.

As a result of these internal and external contradictions during the last decade, AMNLAE paradoxically became something of an elite without privileges. Separated from women at the grass roots by an ideology of integration with the Sandinista economic and political line, it could not act as a mechanism for uniting women as a social force in Nicaragua, and much less as its power instrument, although it was in many senses the spearhead for the diffusion of some emancipating ideas among the popular sectors. Let us examine what has happened to AMNLAE and the women's movement since the 1990 elections.

Current Coordination Efforts of the Movement and New Challenges

> Having given birth 12 times, Paula Pérez, now 8 months pregnant and determined not to have any more children, explained in a mixture of Miskito, Creole English and Spanish: "I wanted to know what was going to be said in this meeting. In Río Grande, we don't know what's going on in other places, and nobody knows about our problems. We are very poor and I've come to get help." (*Gente*, January 31, 1992)

Between the 24th and 26th of January, 1992, the "Conference of Nicaraguan Women for Unity in Diversity" took place in Managua. About 900 women gathered from different parts of the country, social strata, political and ideological inclinations, ethnic groups, ages, occupations, and organizational experiences. During the three days, they conversed about politics, sexuality, education, pleasure, violence, reproductive policies, the environment, the impact of the structural adjustment measures being applied by the new government led by Violeta de Chamorro, and their struggles for livelihood and survival.

In the context of the democratic spaces which the Sandinista government opened up, and the profound tensions and changes occurring across Nicaragua, this conference represented an important step in the struggle to forge a strong, coordinated, and militant women's movement. It has helped to reinterpret how society works, and what it means for civil society to engage in a politics which promotes new forms of consensus—as well as mechanisms and styles of organization and leadership—that allow women's voices to be heard in government independently of the political parties.

The event was organized by a committee of women who came together voluntarily, without the sponsorship of any political party or social organization. Unlike most conferences organized by AMNLAE or the FSLN, women did not have to participate as part of a delegation; any woman could attend in an individual capacity. By using a methodology based on questions which tapped the women's own creativity and initiative, rather than relying on documents or prepared position statements, a new working style was promoted. It encouraged self-affirmation and individual autonomy, and managed to break through the paralysis, conformism, and sense of victimization experienced by many women (Montenegro 1989).

This meeting among women of diverse organizations was the culmination of the desire expressed by many to "revitalize" the women's movement after the FSLN lost the national elections in February 1990. Until then, as has been mentioned, AMNLAE had constituted the central axis of the women's movement and defined itself as its leading organization.

As a forum led by and for women to defend their interests and expose their struggles for survival, the meeting tested the viability of more democratic relations. It demonstrated a new way of exercising power in which women participate as social subjects and agents of change, and contribute to the construction of a new social order by questioning the values, norms, everyday relations, and subordinated identities which currently shape women's lives in Nicaragua. Nevertheless, various problems emerged during the process which constitute new challenges for women in their efforts toward coordination.

AMNLAE decided not to participate in the conference despite the efforts that were made to secure their presence. This deepened the first formal internal split that had occurred on March 8, 1991, when the existence of multiple autonomous women's groups became publicly evident.[11] Among the women who did attend the conference, there were different concepts and definitions of feminism and different strategies for the construction of the movement (Criquillón 1989). In addition, strong rivalries, complaints over impositions, and alternative interpretations of hegemony were expressed among the organizers, which impeded the emergence of a "new type" of coordination. The old and new conflicts which arose between the organizers limited the possibilities for discussing precisely those conceptual differences and strategic visions. Such a discussion could have allowed women to move toward a collective definition of an alternative system of broad-based coordination, grounded in the experience at the conference and other events: autonomous of political parties, possibly with rotating leadership, and which could truly reflect the conference's theme, "unity in diversity."

The efforts following the conference have had little impact. At the event, seven networks of activity were formed: Sexuality, Health, Education, Violence, Economy and Environment, Political Organization, and Communications. Each network was supposed to follow up on the proposals related to its particular theme. However, very few of these networks have been active. A formal strategy and coordination among the different groups does not exist, nor does the level of dynamism necessary to protect the gains made during the past decade and to launch new global demands vis-à-vis the government.

In the new national context of structural adjustment, the challenges facing women are enormous. They are the first to be laid off from their jobs; the budget for social services such as health care and education is insignificant; child care centers are now almost nonexistent; and the media constantly send out messages which reinforce women's traditional roles of obedience to the husband and absolute responsibility for the children. The National Assembly has approved a new article for the Penal Code which sentences any person "who induces, promotes, advertises or practices copulation between people of the same sex in a scandalous manner" to between one and three years in prison. At the same time, the efforts to bring together and promote solidarity between the networks formed at the conference have been minimal. For example, the Sexuality Network issued a call to protest in front of the government offices against the new Penal Code article, but received only a very feeble response and meager attendance.

These circumstances underscore the urgent need to discuss the possibility of forming a coordinating body for the movement that is capable of forging coalitions and articulating particular strategies with global ones for the purpose of fighting back within the new national context, where many achievements of the past decade have already been lost and there is the clear danger of losing many more.

In order to advance in these coordination efforts it is necessary to include new challenges. Women must analyze the lessons derived from their own experiences in the light of the "pending" theoretical themes—what feminism is understood to be, the coordination of the movement, and so on—but they must also reflect on the exercise of patriarchal power, what type of power women want, and the competitiveness and animosity that arise among them in their efforts to obtain it.

The exclusion of "pending" themes from discussions during the conference within the work commissions, despite the fact that participants showed interest in them, was the source of much frustration and conflict at the event. Paradoxically, just as there used to be a reluctance to debate the issue of strategic gender interests within AMNLAE's leadership and include them in its agenda, there is now resistance—on the part of precisely the same intellectual leaders who were promoting those discussions, and some of whom were organizers of the conference—against debating certain equally strategic issues within the movement.

Drawing on earlier strategies, which promoted recognition of the importance of women's work and participation in the public sphere and began to demystify the private sphere by exposing it, women's current challenge is to encourage reflection regarding even more intimate and personal spheres. Women must not only develop an empowering consciousness of the issues mentioned above and their relationship to immediate survival needs; above all, and precisely in order to survive, women must become aware of how their psychological identity is constructed in ways that prevent them from working together. They must create a new sense of relationship and collectivity—one of cooperation among different women who come together and truly recognize one another—so that by living life in a profoundly liberating way, they can change the world.

Only by continuing to deconstruct their subordinated identities, by overcoming the personal insecurities and fears which hinder the development of mutual trust and undermine the sense of sisterhood indispensable for working together, will women manage to transform the patriarchal system which has pitted them as enemies. To the extent that this is achieved, women will be able to generate new coordination and work methods, and become the unimaginable force needed to transform the world.

ENDNOTES

1. Based on the conceptualization of Antonio Gramsci (1957) with regard to the proletariat, consciousness "in itself" refers, in this case, to women's achievement of consciousness regarding their condition of subordination, while consciousness "for itself" refers to women's awareness of the necessity to act collectively for their transformation.

2. There are several magnificent recent analyses of AMNLAE and other expressions of the women's movement in Nicaragua which give a more exhaustive account of these activities. See, among others, the excellent works of Ana Criquillón, Amalia Chamorro, Clara Murguíalday, and Norma Stoltz Chinchilla.

3. The "movement" or "movements" refers broadly to the different organizational expressions of women in the country. They include spaces in which women come together to struggle or obtain some type of benefit.

4. On March 8, 1987, the FSLN publicly announced its Proclamation titled "Women and the Sandinista Revolution." This identified AMNLAE as the official mechanism for organizing women, with the fundamental objective of promoting women's incorporation into all the different revolutionary projects. The new Constitution, which is considered to be one

of the more advanced in Latin America with respect to women's rights, was ratified in the same year.

5. On this subject, Clara Murguíalday (1990) has written: ". . . after the debates in 1986, it was impossible to move backwards. Women's nameless problems emerged from clandestinity and appeared on the front page of the newpapers, in parliamentary sessions, in the demands and platforms of AMNLAE, in the meetings of the Sandinista leadership, in the streets, markets, buses, and bedrooms. Since then, not a single corner of daily life or public space has escaped the effects of the 'feminist explosion.'"

6. According to the survey conducted by CENZONTLE in 1989, the distribution of organized women is the following: Luisa Amanda Espinoza Women's Association (AMNLAE), 12 percent; Sandinista National Liberation Front (FSLN), 8 percent; Sandinista Youth (JS19J), 13 percent; National Association of Nicaraguan Educators (ANDEN), 20 percent; Federation of Health Care Workers (FETSALUD), 2 percent; Sandinista Workers (CST), 2 percent; religious organizations, 43 percent.

7. Of the 14 percent of organized women, 68 percent work outside the home, 18 percent are housewives, and 11 percent are students. Thirty-eight percent are between 26 and 35 years old, 31 percent are between 16 and 25 years old, and 30 percent are over 35. Seventy-six percent live in urban areas and 24 percent live in rural areas. The majority belongs to the generation of young people that participated in the revolutionary war to overthrow the Somoza dicatorship (Cenzontle 1989).

8. Maxine Molyneux's (1984) conceptualization of strategic and practical gender interests is very useful for this analysis. Strategic interests refer to those which emerge from an analysis of women's subordination to men, and vary according to the sociopolitical context in which they arise. They could include the total or partial abolition of the sexual division of labor; the reduction of the burden of domestic work and child rearing; the elimination of institutionalized forms of discrimination in the area of property rights or access to credit; the establishment of political equity between women and men; freedom of choice in reproduction; the adoption of adequate measures against male violence and control over women, etc. Practical interests refer to those which arise from the immediate and concrete conditions in which women live owing to their gender position within the given sexual division of labor. They do not challenge existing forms of subordination, although they derive directly from them. This is the case, for example, of the need for basic services, better housing, and higher salaries.

9. For their part, the majority of the productive projects launched by the various organizations under the Sandinista government reproduced household labor, thus reaffirming the "domestic destiny" of women. For example, almost all of the projects AMNLAE developed revolved around traditionally feminine activities such as sewing collectives, raising chickens and pigs, communal kitchens, beauty salons, etc. These projects implied a double or triple workday for women, deepening the inequity between men and women. Moreover, most of them failed financially, provoking a sense of incompetence and weakness among women themselves and reinforcing their subordination.

10. Regarding the political dimension within the public sphere, we can point to the implementation of the system of representation, the displacement of oligarchic groups, popular participation in carrying out the tasks of the state, the general armament of the people, etc. With respect to the economic dimension, it is important to mention the agrarian reform, access to credit, and the formation of production cooperatives, among others.

11. On March 8, 1991, AMNLAE decided not to participate in the planning process

of the conference, which took almost a year to take shape. On that date, AMNLAE also chose to organize its own assembly to celebrate International Women's Day, instead of joining the many other autonomous organizations in the country which celebrated the occasion with a three-day "Festival of the 52 Percent," an allusion to the percentage of the Nicaraguan population that is female.

BIBLIOGRAPHY

AMNLAE (1980). *La mujer nicaragüense: La participación de la mujer en el proceso de lucha por el derrocamiento de la dictadura*. Managua.

———. (1989*a*). "Mujeres: Profundizar la Revolución." *Diario Barricada*, 17 de septiembre.

———. (1989*b*). *Primer Encuentro Nacional de Mujeres de las Fuerzas Fundamentales, "Nora Astorga."* Managua.

ASDI (1986). *Situación de los proyectos para la mujer en Nicaragua*. Managua. Mimeographed.

ATC (1988). *Acuerdos de la Asamblea Nacional de Obreras Agrícolas*. Managua. Mimeographed.

ATC-CIERA-MITRAB (1984). *Las mujeres en las cooperativas agropecuarias en Nicaragua*. Managua. Mimeographed.

Baumeister, Eduardo (1991). "El ajuste y sus efectos en el agro centroamericano." En *Acción Concertada* (Costa Rica), August.

CENZONTLE (1990). *Mujeres: Panorámica de su participación en Nicaragua*. Managua. June.

———. (1991*a*). *Un marco conceptual para el análisis del poder de las mujeres*. Managua. September.

———. (1991*b*). *Subordinación de género en las organizaciones populares nicaragüenses: Un estudio sobre la participación política de las mujeres*. Managua.

Chamorro, Amalia (1989). "La mujer, logros y límites en 10 años de revolución." *Cuadernos de Sociología* (Universidad Centroamericana), no. 9–10 (January–June).

Chinchilla, Norma Stoltz (1986). *Mujeres en movimientos revolucionarios: El caso de Nicaragua*. Managua.

CIERA (1989). *La mujer en la vida cotidiana*.

Comité Feminista de Solidaridad con las Mujeres Centroamericanas (1987). *Memorias del taller: Mujer centroamericana, violencia y guerra. IV Encuentro Feminista Latinamericano y del Caribe*. Taxco, Guerrero, Mexico.

Criquillón, Ana (1989). "La rebeldía de las mujeres nicaragüenses: Semillero de una nueva democracia." In *Construcción de la democracia en Nicaragua*. Managua: Escuela de Sociología, Universidad Centroamericana.

Downs, Cynthia (1986). "La representación de la mujer en los puestos de dirección." In *La situación socioeconómica de la mujer en la zona especial II: Avance de investigación*. Managua: CIDCA.

Frente Sandinista de Liberación Nacional (FSLN) (1987). *El FSLN y la mujer en la revolución popular sandinista*. Managua.

———. (1989). *Plataforma de lucha: 1990–95*. Managua.

Gramsci, Antonio (1957). *The Modern Prince and Other Writings*. New York: International Publishers.

Guido, Lea (1989). "Diez años de lucha por la emancipación de la mujer." In *Revista Revolución y Desarrollo* (CIERA, Managua), no. 5 (July).

Molyneux, Maxine (1984). "Movilización sin emancipación? Los intereses de la mujer, estado y revolución en Nicaragua." *Desarrollo y Sociedad*, no. 13, pp. 179–195.

Montenegro, Sofía (1989). "Entre una mujer desnuda y yo." *Semana Cómica*, no. 425.

Murguíalday, Clara (1990). *Nicaragua, revolución y feminismo*. Madrid: Ed. Revolución.

Pasos, Mayra, and Malena de Montís (1990). *Evaluación la sección de la mujer de la UNAG*. Managua. September.

Soja, Ana (1985). *Mujer y política*. Departamento Ecuménico de Investigación. San José, Costa Rica.

UNICEF (1989). *Análisis económico social*. Managua.

7

The Difficult Path toward Organizing Household Workers: A Dialogue

AÍDA MORENO VALENZUELA
AND ELSA M. CHANEY

Introduction

Elsa: In this discussion, Aída and I will focus on two main themes. First, we would like to give you an idea of household workers' struggles for livelihood and the ways in which they have organized themselves to confront their situation. Second, we will outline the ways in which academics and feminist-activists are collaborating with domestic workers both in research and in other types of support.

Aída will represent the point of view of the household workers, and I the perspective of the academics. We do not claim that our model of exchange between workers and researchers is the only one. However, because our experience has been positive (with its difficult moments, of course), perhaps we can give you a sense of the extent to which such a collaboration can be useful, and of its limits once the group receiving support is able to continue functioning independently.

To begin, Aída briefly outlines her background, a story similar to that of many other domestic workers in Latin America.

Aída: I was born in a small town in Chile, Graneros, 82 kilometers from Santiago. I am from a poor *campesina* (peasant) family. During my childhood, I was surrounded by very strong women. My grandmother was a campesina who worked all her life milking cows and cooking for the other campesinos. She had important skills; she was a midwife and "meica," or traditional healer. I often accompanied her on the noble mission of delivering a baby or curing a child of the evil eye.

Editors' Note: Translated by Lilian Autler.

My mother also began her working life as an adolescent, milking cows on the farm. I was a product of deception, born out of her ignorance and innocence. I was born sick and did not begin to walk and talk until I was three years old. Despite being sickly, when I was ten years old, I had to get up at three o'clock in the morning to help my mother milk the cows so that we could earn more money.

I was the oldest of four sisters. Two died because of a lack of medical attention. I went to the rural school which was very far away from where we lived. My father was an alcoholic, and the little time he spent at home was only to abuse my mother and us.

When I was fourteen, I left my home to work in Santiago. That was in 1954. I was taken to the house of a foreign family, where I was well received. They were concerned about my health and gave me vitamins, and thanks to the good nourishment, I recovered. I was very comfortable; it was a house with a beautiful garden and many dogs, and I like animals a lot. I worked there nine years, until I found out about the organizations of domestic workers.

In those days I was not aware of the great suffering of many of my sister household workers, and if I had not encountered the Juventud Obrera Católica—JOC (Young Catholic Workers), I would have spent the rest of my life in that house, unaware of what was happening in the rest of the world. The JOC, based in Belgium, was part of the international movement of the "lay apostolate" of the Catholic Church.

My first experience organizing domestic workers was with the Hogar de la Empleada (Center for Household Workers), today the Asociación Nacional de Empleadas de Casa Particular—ANECAP (National Association of Workers in Private Homes). In 1958 I began to take basic education courses there and then first aid courses because I wanted to work as a nurse. In this Center, there were groups of domestic workers who were militants of the JOC, and they began to invite me to their weekly Sunday meetings. One of our activities was the organization of the First Conference of Household Workers in 1962. Since I showed a great deal of motivation, the JOC asked me to work full-time in the Center. In the JOC, they told us that a good militant was one who was committed to and participated actively in organizing his or her worker group. I spoke with my employer. We were both very sad about my leaving, but I felt the desire to serve the God whom I was getting to know through my *compañeras*. I could only visit my mother, grandmother, and sister every two months. But my family never prevented me from doing the work I wanted to do; they just asked that I take care of myself.

Thereafter, I began to work actively with the domestic worker organizations that had emerged in the 1920s during the ferment that gave rise to the strong labor movement in Chile. I was working once again as a live-in domestic worker, but devoting all of my free time to the movement. Later I found a situation that was not live-in. A friend and I rented a room together, and that's how the time passed. Over the years I have held various positions in our Sindicato de Trabajadoras de Casa Particular—SINCATRAP (Union of Workers in Private Homes); in our Savings and Loan Cooperative; and in ANECAP.

The military coup changed everything. We lost everything we had worked for. Few unions were able to remain active, and ours, which had 3,000 members in 1973, dropped to 300. Nevertheless, SINCATRAP continued to meet every Sunday in two rooms rented to us by the Construction Workers Federation. We had to get permission from the mayor's office, and with the police present, the few members who remained continued to meet. We went on like that until the premises were broken into and searched, and for months we were unable to recover the union's property. ANECAP took us in and offered us a room, and that is how we continued to work, adapting ourselves to the military government's new labor laws regarding unions and fulfilling all legal requirements.

We are now recovering, and many prospects are opening up for us at both the national level in Chile, and at the international level as the headquarters of the new Confederación Latinoamericana y del Caribe de Trabajadoras del Hogar—CONLACTRAHO (Confederation of Latin American and Caribbean Household Workers) which today links the associations and unions of 13 countries.

In the course of my collaboration in the domestic worker organizations, I have worked not only with women from poor neighborhoods, but also with professional women. This allowed me to meet two women from the Centro de Estudios de la Mujer—CEM (Center of Women's Studies) in Chile, Thelma Gálvez and Rosalba Todaro, who have done research on domestic service. Through them I met Elsa Chaney, a North American political scientist with whom we began the work of forming our Confederation.

Elsa: This marks the tenth year of collaboration between Aída and me, and for many of those years we have been in contact at least two or three times a month. I have always been a researcher, and since the beginning of the 1970s I have been very interested in domestic workers. To this day, I find it hard to understand why we social scientists have ignored domestic workers in our research, despite the fact that they make up at least 20 percent of the counted female labor force in Latin America, and in some countries, a much higher proportion.

A personal note may help explain my attraction to this topic. My mother was the daughter of a Swedish woman who left her village with her two sisters to work as a domestic servant in Oslo. One of the sisters stayed in Norway; another returned to her village in Sweden to get married; and the third, my grandmother, migrated to the United States with her three small children in 1907.

In 1982 I met Aída Moreno and Adelinda Díaz, the two leaders who later (along with Yenny del Carmen Hurtado of Colombia) became the architects of the Confederation of Domestic Workers. On a trip to Chile in that year, Thelma and Rosalba gave me Aída's address and I stopped by SINCATRAP's small office, housed in the same building as the ANECAP, as Aída explained. I found Aída to be a very serious, level-headed, and thoughtful woman—she has always been this way. I believe it was on that occasion that Aída told me that the union's only goal during those years was to survive.

The same year, I met Adelinda Díaz, the president of the Coordinadora Sindical de Trabajadoras del Hogar de Lima Metropolitana—COSINTRAHOL (Coordinating Office of Household Worker Unions of Metropolitan Lima), at a workshop of Perú-Mujer, a center for study and action on behalf of women, located in Lima. I remember that we were in a long narrow room, and at one end this impressive woman began to speak with striking clarity about the problems facing domestic workers. When she finished her presentation, I had to run to catch her before she left, since I was at the opposite end of the room. She very graciously invited me to visit her union's office, which it shared with a male union. It was not yet clear at that time what type of collaboration could be initiated either with her or with Aída, but we remained in contact. This is an opportune place for Aída to tell about the characteristics of domestic work in the various countries of Latin America and the Caribbean.

Characteristics of Domestic Work

Aída: March 1992 marks the fourth anniversary of the founding of CONLACTRAHO. This achievement is of extraordinary importance to the enormous number of women who do this type of work in the developing countries of Latin America. I will now speak about the long path leading up to the constitution of our Confederation.

In earlier times, domestic service was performed by black slaves brought from Africa or by the colonized indigenous peoples of our continent. Consequently, the people who did this work were considered part of an inferior social class, capable only of such labor. In the case of black slaves, the workers were bought, while the indigenous people were taken by the colonizers as part of their expected reward for the sacrifice of coming to colonize the new lands.

These customs changed with time. Later it was the sons and daughters of campesinos who were taken as servants in the homes of the landowners, and eventually transferred to their houses in the city. Often they received no salary; their only payment was the used clothing of their employers and other types of assistance for their families, who lived in very humble circumstances. Even today there are still very poor families whose desperate situation leads them to the extreme of handing over their daughters in exchange for a farm animal, or sending them away to live with their godparents so that they can at least have the chance to attend elementary school.

This tendency to migrate from place to place continues to characterize our *gremio*, which is composed mainly of women. What few statistics we have indicate that about 95 percent of domestic workers are women, the majority of campesino origin and a considerable number from indigenous communities. Their pilgrimages begin from the time they leave their poverty-stricken homes for the houses of wealthier families; they move from their villages to the city, and once there, they move from house to house, since this work is very unstable.

We migrate because we want to study, to find a different kind of work, to realize our potential as human beings and as women. But often we find ourselves marginalized, with no protection as workers. Many of us come to accept our situation, and once we get used to it, conformism and fatalism set in. When we lose our jobs, we have to wander around homeless until we find another position. Sometimes the employer doesn't pay us for the time we have worked, and we are left without any savings or social security benefits. The situation is worse when we have to migrate to other countries without the required working papers.

In addition, trying to get ahead through education is difficult, since the little free time we have does not allow us to attend school during regular hours, and the handful of educational programs provided by domestic worker organizations is very small compared to the number of workers.

Elsa: Aída has broadly outlined the situation of domestic workers in terms of migration, education, and family. Now it is my turn to give you an idea of the ways in which academics working in research centers, women's organizations, and other entities have supported domestic workers since the late 1960s.

Despite the importance of domestic workers in the economically active female population, only a few works on the subject existed at the end of the

1960s. A 1966 article about Ecuador by the sociologist Emily Nett was the first published study of domestic service. In 1978, Heleieth I.B. Saffioti published her book *Emprego doméstico e capitalismo*, but since it was never translated from Portuguese into Spanish or English, it remained inaccessible to most researchers interested in this sector. Margo L. Smith's doctoral dissertation (1971) and subsequent publications have been very influential (1973; 1975; 1977; 1989). In Peru, two small books also awakened interest in the topic: *Simplemente explotadas* (1973) by Rutté García, which contained the life stories of five domestic workers; and *Llamados de ser libres* (Cussiánovich 1974), a JOC training manual. Curiously, however, this latter work was written by a priest in completely masculine terms, without any acknowledgment of the high percentage of women in the profession or of their special problems as single mothers. In 1975 Blanca Figueroa very generously passed on to me the results of her own survey conducted in the early 1970s, which was not published until 1983 (*La trabajadora doméstica* [Lima, Peru]).

My first encounter with the domestic service sector was in Lima in 1959, when I attended a training session with a group of domestic workers that was receiving guidance from priests of the JOC. As Aída mentioned, the JOC has been very important in the efforts to organize domestic workers throughout Latin America, and played a strategic role in the formation of the early leaders. In my interaction with the domestic workers, I realized that many of these young women had recently migrated to the city, and that their lives were very difficult, particularly during the first few years as they learned to manage in a strange and hostile environment.

Thus, as I believe was the case for many researchers, my interest in the phenomenon of migration led me to learn more about domestic workers. In the 1970s I read some studies about migration to Lima and noticed the high percentage of women between the ages of 15 and 29 who were arriving and continue to arrive in the metropolitan area today (Martínez, Prado, and Quintanilla 1973; Macisco 1975). Some data suggest that women have not simply accompanied male migrants; a large number of (middle-aged and older) women interviewed by Macisco (ibid., pp. 65–66) arrived in Lima with children and without husbands. The question was, How were they surviving? It did not take long to learn that many were working in private homes as domestic servants.

The emergence of migration and women as a central research theme can be dated to the mid-1970s with the appearance of two seminal studies by Latin American researchers that since have been widely cited. They are *Migración a las ciudades y participación en la fuerza de trabajo de las mujeres lati-*

noamericanas: El caso del servicio doméstico by Elizabeth Jelin (1976); and *Women in the Informal Labor Sector: The Case of Mexico City* by Lourdes Arizpe (1977).

Jelin's work reviews studies of the relationship between the work of women migrants and family relations in cities, and outlines a direction for future research. Although the book is not based on her own research and does not place the theme of women and migration within any particular theoretical framework, it has been extremely influential in opening up two new fields of research: women and migration, and women in domestic service. Jelin elaborates her ideas in a subsequent article (1978) which also explores theoretical approaches appropriate for the study of women who migrate to cities.

Up to this point, however, few academics had given due attention to this important sector of working women. Aída will now discuss the working conditions in the sector.

Working Conditions

Aída: Working conditions in the domestic service sector are similar in all of our countries: a form of modernized semi-slavery. Society does not value this work because it does not see it as productive or as contributing to the development of the country. Even sadder is the fact that in many cases it is not even valued by the household workers themselves, who feel inferior to people who do other kinds of work. What is not recognized is that domestic workers provide a service that allows *others* to produce goods and services that the society considers important. We never talk about the fact that those others—professionals, government employees, business people, and, yes, even militants of the feminist movement—could not carry out their work if we were not in their homes caring for their children and doing the essential domestic chores that keep their households functioning smoothly.

How, then, can our work be disparaged as unimportant? And why are we forced to work under conditions that are barely human? There is no country in which domestic service is accorded the same status as other types of work, or even in which a decent working schedule has been established for our vocation. We have to work 14 to 16 hours a day for a minimum wage that does not even cover half of the real cost of living. In many countries, social security benefits and maternity leave are not available to domestic workers. Nor do we have the right to an education; to think and develop as people; to have our own private home; to have respect for our own language and customs; to recreation, vacations, or pensions. In most cases work contracts do not even exist.

The existing labor laws are not favorable for domestic workers since they fail to protect our rights even in countries where the rest of the workers have achieved a minimum wage, an eight-hour workday, and so on. In some countries, domestic workers do not have the right to organize into unions because of the fear that they will unite and defend their labor rights.

The labor situation of household workers is very similar throughout Latin America and the Caribbean. In most countries, the current laws regulating working conditions for domestic service are contained in special articles in the labor code under "special contracts," with norms that diverge significantly from standard labor regulations. This exceptional legislation undeniably leads to discriminatory treatment that violates the human rights and responsibilities set forth in the Universal Declaration of Human Rights of 1968:

> All are equal before the law and are entitled without any discrimination to equal protection of the law. All are entitled to equal protection against any discrimination in violation of this Declaration and against any incitement to such discrimination (Article 7)

We are seen as inferior, as beings from another planet; it is as if we are invisible, as though we do not exist—but we had better get the work done! Many animals are treated better than we are. Yes, sometimes we count when there are elections. Some politicians remember us when they are running for office or when they have to gather a crowd for their rallies, but it's only momentary. Afterward we are forgotten and become anonymous once again. Sadly, not even our fellow workers in the big labor movements pay any attention to us.

Elsa: As occurs in all new fields of study, researchers' early attempts to write about domestic workers were mainly descriptive, focusing on the working conditions that Aída just outlined.

An extraordinarily important and influential effort to further document the sector—and one of the first to advance beyond the theories established by Saffioti in her first book—was the project undertaken in the early 1980s by Thelma Gálvez and Rosalba Todaro of the Center for the Study of Women (CEM) in Santiago. Their project is an excellent example of a successful collaboration between workers and academics, which produced three works. Two were popular, nonacademic publications: *Trabajadoras de casa particular* (1984) and *Yo trabajo así . . . En casa particular* (1985), the latter a collection of life stories. Later, the authors published an article directed at the academic community based on the research concluded in 1983–1984: *Trabajo doméstico remunerado: Conceptos, hechos, datos* (Todaro and Gálvez 1987).

The two researchers also presented one of the first efforts to move beyond descriptive aspects of domestic service with their article "Housework for Pay in Chile: Not Just Another Job" (Gálvez and Todaro 1989). Thelma Gálvez has since taken a position in the new government, but both women remain loyal friends to whom domestic workers can always turn for advice and support.

Others began to document the situation of domestic workers in Latin America in the early 1980s. Mary García Castro, a Brazilian sociologist contracted by the International Labour Office, designed and conducted several studies of the sector in Colombia along with Colombian colleagues that have appeared only in mimeographed form. Unfortunately, the government has not allowed them to be published (García Castro 1979 and 1982; García Castro, Quintero, and Jimeno 1981).

Mónica Gogna, with Elizabeth Jelin as her mentor, wrote her doctoral thesis and published several articles about domestic workers in Argentina (1981). Also during this period, a work was published by the domestic workers union (Sindicato Nacional de Trabajadores Domésticas) in Cuzco, Peru, *Basta: Testimonios* (1982), a collection of the life stories of 23 domestic workers. This book has perhaps had a greater impact than any other in arousing interest in the sector. The magazine *FEM* in Mexico also published a special issue on domestic workers (1980–1981).

One of the members of the *FEM* editorial board was Mary Goldsmith, a North American anthropologist living in Mexico who contributed a theoretical article to the special issue. In 1979 Mary and several colleagues created a link between academics and domestic workers through the Colectivo de Acción Solidaria con Empleadas Domésticas—CASED (Collective for Action in Solidarity with Domestic Workers). Inspired by the debate among feminists regarding housework, CASED advocated the economic and social importance of paid domestic work. However, because of a series of difficulties, the group disbanded (see Goldsmith 1989:232–236).

During those early years, Isis Duarte and her colleagues also conducted various studies of the domestic service sector in the Dominican Republic (1976 and 1983). Several other pioneering studies documenting the working conditions of domestic service appear in *Muchachas No More* (Chaney and García Castro 1989), including articles by Mohammed and Colen on the West Indies.

I will also mention, as part of this period, the work I did with Ximena

Bunster and other women in Peru in 1975–1976. We began a study of women who were mothers and who worked as street vendors, factory workers, market sellers, and domestic servants. Owing to circumstances beyond our control, we were unable to publish the results until 1985 in *Sellers and Servants: Working Women in Lima, Peru* (Bunster and Chaney 1985). Thus we benefited from the thinking and research done by others in the intervening years.

Aída will now discuss the social isolation and marginalization of domestic workers.

Social Marginalization

Aída: The fact that the majority of domestic workers are women from poor families who have little education leads many people to conclude that this is the only type of work they are good for. In general, domestic work is looked down upon, and the worker is seen as an inferior being without initiative who ought only to receive orders and work hard so she can learn to do her job efficiently.

The average worker leaves her home in search of self-improvement at the age of 12–14, so she doesn't have a normal adolescence like other girls her age. A whole stage of her life slips by, marked only by the demand to perform a specific task well.

These young migrant women suffer discrimination at the hands of the women who employ them, and from the rest of the family where they work. We are often isolated even from our own families. As migrants, we spend most of our lives far from our relatives, and in many cases lose all contact with them and end up alone.

This kind of social marginalization and loneliness helps explain why so many domestic workers are single mothers. These women are doubly marginalized; not only are they rejected by their own families, but it is also very difficult for them to find work since no one wants to hire a woman with children. The man generally abandons them, leaving them to confront their problem alone. Very few women in this situation manage to set up their own household.

In many cases the older domestic worker's life ends in an institution or in the home of someone who has been generous enough to offer her a place to stay. Our organization has never known of an employer concerned enough to make a donation for the creation of a home where aging domestic workers can end their days.

Unfortunately, it must be pointed out that among the employers are women who "fight for equality" and for "the value of women's roles," including feminists, leftists, and women active in the church. Often these women do not practice what they preach when it comes to the person who replaces them in caring for their children and their homes.

Domestic workers are also marginalized by the rest of the working class. We are seen as gullible women, and are taken advantage of and taunted as "the maids." Because of this, domestic workers often try to hide the kind of work they do, and they have to live with the constant insecurity and fear of being rejected when people discover what they really do. This isolation from our own class limits our personal development and the realization of our creative potential.

Organization

Aída: We believe that because of the social and economic situation in Latin America, domestic service will not disappear. Our concern, then, is that women be able to perform this work under more just and humane conditions in the future.

In order for this to happen, we must unite into organizations that represent the interests of the sector and fight for our progress as women and as workers. We know that live-in domestic service has almost disappeared in developed countries. Women come to the house only to perform specific functions, and are more respected. Nevertheless, there are still many Latina and Asian immigrants who are not protected by any legislation.

As we have mentioned, one of the institutions that has been most concerned with the plight of the large number of women who work as domestic employees is the JOC. In many countries, such as Brazil, Colombia, Chile, Paraguay, Peru, and Venezuela, the JOC in past years helped to form small groups for reflection and the development of self-esteem as daughters of God.

The organizations that have emerged are for the most part relatively new, except in Chile, where the first domestic workers union was founded 65 years ago, and in Argentina where such organizations have existed for about 30 years. The organizations in the rest of the countries are only about 15 to 20 years old. Our organizations are small and have serious financial problems because of the constant turnover of the members and the instability of their work. Membership dues are generally minimal since the workers' incomes are low.

In some countries, domestic worker organizations have been formed, in particular by the Opus Dei movement, whose goals are very different from ours. In some cases, these other organizations have generated divisions and competition within the sector that in the end only inhibit the growth of the organizations and of the domestic workers as people.

In addition, not all countries allow domestic workers to organize into unions, and there always are obstacles imposed by government bureaucracies. Unions have been formed in Argentina, Bolivia, Brazil, Colombia, Chile, Paraguay, Uruguay, and Venezuela. In the rest of the countries, only social or religious associations are allowed.

Argentina: There are several domestic worker organizations in Argentina, some quite old, others relatively new. Three years ago workers formed the Federación Nacional de Sindicatos (National Federation of Unions). CONLACTRAHO maintains ties with this federation and with individual unions in the cities of Córdoba, Catamarca, and La Rioja.

Bolivia: There are now three legally constituted unions in Bolivia—in La Paz, Cochabamba, and Santa Cruz—as well as groups in formation to become unions in Sucre, Oruro, Potosí, Tarija, Beni, and Pando. In general, they face severe financial difficulties and problems finding space in which to operate. Several conferences have taken place among the organizations, and they recently formed the Federación de Trabajadoras del Hogar de Bolivia—FENATRAHOB (Federation of Bolivian Household Workers).

Brazil: Brazil has a 35-year history of organization. Until 1989, domestic workers could organize only into associations, but since the constitutional reforms that allow for unions, many associations have taken the step of transforming themselves into unions. There are currently about 33 official unions, with some 60 associations and other groups in formation. They have done important work, managing to bring about changes in the law through active mobilization supported by women's organizations and the black women's movement. They also have formed a federation.

Chile: As I already mentioned, Chile is the country with the longest organizational trajectory. The first domestic workers union was created in 1926. It dissolved in 1945 and was reborn in 1947 as the Sindicato de Trabajadoras de Casa Particular del Area Metropolitana—SINCATRAP (Metropolitan Union of Workers in Private Homes). The Asociación Nacional de Empleadas de Casa Particular—ANECAP (National Association of Workers in Private Homes) was created in 1949 especially to provide education and training, and has affiliates throughout the country and many ties with the Church. In 1954 the Savings and Loan Cooperative was formed, and since 1962 a housing cooperative has provided about 2,000 homes for domestic workers in Chile. Over the years, these organizations have continued to provide the services for which they were originally created. They have never been large organizations, but they have had enough members to meet legal requirements. More recently, two other organizations have been added: Servicios Quillay, "a cooperative cleaning service" employing 40 ex-household workers. Funded for its first three years by the Inter-American Foundation, the cooperative is now on its own and in the black. The other new organization is Caminando Juntas (Journeying Together), to which members contribute a monthly quota toward the purchase of a house that will be available to older members who do not have a pension or who have nowhere else to go.

Colombia: Of the several groups of domestic workers in Colombia, the best known is the Sindicato Nacional de Trabajadoras del Servicio Doméstico (National Domestic Workers Union), which gained legal status in 1988. CONLACTRAHO recently provided the Bogotá organization with a loan that enabled it to complete payment on the house that serves as its center. There is another union in Cali. In Colombia, domestic workers have fought for and achieved some important improvements in labor conditions.

Dominican Republic: The domestic workers in the Dominican Republic started out as a group within a women's organization until they decided to become independent. As a result of their persistent efforts, the group has gained legal status as the Asociación de Trabajadoras del Hogar (Association of Domestic Workers). They are members of the Coordination of Women's Groups, and collaborate in many activities jointly sponsored by other women's organizations.

Costa Rica: A new association was formed just before Christmas in 1991, in collaboration with a women's organization in San José. We have been in regular contact with this group and are working to strengthen the connection.

Guatemala: A group was formed quite recently in Guatemala, and two years ago it established a center. Several professional women working with the household workers had to withdraw because of threats, and one worker leader was detained after attending an international household workers meeting. Because of the political repression, until recently the members have been working secretly and meeting on street corners and in tea shops; while they now have a gathering place, they cannot establish a formal association, much less a union.

Paraguay: As in most cases, the first group to emerge in Paraguay was linked to the JOC. This group gave rise to an association which, through the Catholic Church, established a home for domestic workers. Since the fall of the Stroessner government, a legal union has been formed that has established a child care center for domestic workers who are single mothers and cannot take their children with them to their workplace. This legally constituted union is one of the few with a positive link to the Labor Central (central labor body) in Asunción.

Peru: The only official union in Peru is the one in Cuzco, which has existed for 25 years; it gained union status before the govenment decided that household workers should not be allowed to organize into labor unions, and this privilege was never withdrawn. There are two associations in Lima. The Centro de Capacitación para Trabajadoras del Hogar—CCTH (Training Center for Household Workers) has its center in downtown Lima and sponsors Sunday get-togethers, seminars, and classes on such topics as first aid, nutrition, and traditional dance. It also has a daily radio program that has just celebrated its first two years. The CCTH participates actively in the Vaso de Leche (Glass of Milk) program for the children of household workers. The Instituto de Promoción y Formación de Trabajadoras del Hogar (Institute of Promotion and Formation of Household Workers), still affiliated with the JOC, sponsors leadership training courses, has a day care center, a medical dispensary, an *hogar de paso* (where unemployed household workers can sleep), and an employment service.

Uruguay: The national union as yet has not received official recognition. There is also an older domestic workers association supported by the Catholic Church. For internal reasons, organizing work in Uruguay is currently suspended, although existing members have been very active in the international Confederation.

Venezuela: The first group of domestic workers in Venezuela was also supported by the JOC, but did not last very long. Another group formed which has been working for several years in Caracas to gain legal status as a union. The difficulty is lack of a meeting place; a feminist group has offered a locale, but many times forgets to have someone on hand on Sundays to open the door. When that happens, the household workers must meet on the street.

CONLACTRAHO also has contacts in Ecuador, El Salvador, Honduras, Panama, and Nicaragua, and we believe that the working conditions of domestic servants in these countries are not very different from those elsewhere in Latin America. Just last year, CONLACTRAHO made contact with professional women in Panama, and we sent materials so that they can help to create a domestic workers organization.

Elsa will now say something more about research carried on in the affiliated countries.

Elsa: Several studies shed light on the situation of domestic workers in the countries mentioned by Aída. Of particular importance are the following: the first book written by domestic workers themselves in Peru, *Así, ando, ando como empleada* (Loza et al. 1990); the monograph by Graham (1988) about the world of domestic workers in Brazil; a study by Ortiz and Joffre (1991) of domestic workers in Cuernavaca, Mexico; Lesley Gill's monograph (1994) on gender and class in domestic service in Bolivia; and a collective work on household workers worldwide (Heyzer et al. 1994).

Articles analyzing the sector in the various countries include those by Bossen (1988) about employers and domestic workers in Guatemala City; by Radcliffe (1989 and 1990) about the incorporation of women migrants as domestic workers in Peru; and by Young (1987).

Several authors also explore the situation of Latin American immigrants employed in domestic service in the United States: West Indian women in New York (Colen 1990); Brazilians in New York (Margolis 1990); Mexican women in El Paso (Ruiz 1987). Romero writes about Chicana domestic workers (1988*a*; 1988*b*; and 1990). In addition, Anderson (1989) has studied domestic service in Jamaica. Household workers themselves are anxious to carry out their own research projects (see below). Chaney-García Castro (1989) contains 23 articles, 5 of them by household worker leaders. There are several historical pieces, as well as country studies, a section on "questions for feminism," and another on organizations and the state. The volume, including a 30-page bibliography, was recently published in Spanish by the Editorial Nueva Sociedad in Caracas.

Aída will now talk about the creation of the Confederation CONLACTRAHO.

Aída: As Elsa has indicated, feminist organizations in Latin America have until now rarely included domestic workers. Nevertheless, some researchers within women's groups and universities were interested in studying various aspects of our sector. As a result, the XI Congress of the Latin American Studies Association for the first time included a panel on domestic workers at its 1983 meeting in Mexico City. Adelinda Díaz, from Peru, and I were invited to comment on the research presented.

We took advantage of our stay in Mexico City to organize a small "encounter" which was attended by domestic workers from Cuernavaca, representatives of Mexican women's organizations, and the researchers who had presented their work at the Congress. As a result, we launched a network among the existing domestic worker organizations with the goal of preparing for our first international congress in Colombia in 1988.

The creation of CONLACTRAHO has enabled us to make progress in several areas: we have increased union participation and supported the creation of new organizations in several countries; we publish a small newsletter that allows us to share information about the work of affiliated organizations; we have provided materials to all the countries for International Domestic Workers' Day activities; and we have carried out our first regional training workshops in union organizing (in January 1993 in Colombia for affiliates from the Caribbean, Central America, and the northern half of South America, and in August 1993 in Paraguay for affiliates from the southern half of the continent). By now almost all of our affiliates have proposed new legislation, demanded better wages and work schedules, and so on. The fact that we have remained active in spite of all our limitations over the past years is a great achievement in itself, as was our ability to obtain funding for our second congress in August 1991 in Chile.

The task ahead of us now is to strengthen our Confederation with new affiliates and to make sure that it continues to meet its primary objective: supporting domestic worker organizations in countries where they are struggling to promote a new respect for the profession.

Future Plans

Elsa: In discussing their goals for the future during their second congress in 1991, the delegates agreed to direct support services to CONLACTRAHO's affiliated organizations in the following areas (in order of priority):

- offering training in union organizing (in three regional seminars);
- undertaking their own research on the situation of domestic workers in each country, collecting essential data for CONLACTRAHO and for the individual organizations;
- sharing the experiences of member organizations and exchanging personnel with expertise in the creation of services such as child care centers and retirement homes for older domestic workers;
- encouraging and assisting in the formation of savings and loan and housing cooperatives;
- assisting affiliates to improve conditions for household workers through professional cleaning services.

There are leaders among the domestic workers who have experience in all of these activities, and the idea is that they should travel to other regions to help initiate projects that have shown positive results in their own countries.

Training for Leadership

The first training workshop took place in January 1993 in Silvania, Colombia, for leaders from the northern countries of South America, Central America, and the Caribbean. The workshop was planned by SINTRASEDOM and drew on trainers from Colombian unions and community participation groups. Twenty attended the week-long workshop, with sessions on strengthening union organizations, leadership formation, fund raising and finances, labor legislation, communication (including publicity and public relations), how to participate in radio and television interviews), and public speaking. Reflecting on the first experience, the Secretariat has decided, however, that CONLACTRAHO should not count entirely on outsiders, but that domestic worker leaders should begin to participate as trainers in future workshops.

Studies of Domestic Workers in Various Countries

The Planning Committee for the II Congress agreed that in order to convince governments that domestic workers should have the right to organize, and in order to better inform the public about the situation of domestic workers, studies of the sector were needed in each country.

To begin the process of self-study, CONLACTRAHO invited Thelma Gálvez of the Chilean National Statistical Institute and Teresa Valdez of the Latin American Social Science Research Faculty (FLACSO) to give a day-long workshop on how to design studies based on surveys at the II Congress in Santiago. In addition, the Planning Committee asked Rosa Bravo, a feminist researcher at the Centro Latinoamericano de Demografía—CELADE (Latin American Center for Demography) to begin disaggregating statistical data on the sector in order to create a database. Statistics for the twelve countries with affiliated organizations were presented in preliminary form by Rosa Bravo at the II Congress. For the first time the household workers have statistics on domestic workers at the national level disaggregated from the category of "general services" where they have always been buried. This is yet another example of how researchers and workers can collaborate.

Following the workshop, the participants asked the Confederation to seek funds so that the affiliates could carry out studies in their own countries. They agreed to find academics with experience in survey-based research who could provide assistance and training for those organizations that want to learn how to conduct their own studies. Based on the twelve studies, a comparative study of the region will be published.

In Peru, the CCTH had already carried out a pilot study in 1990 of the night schools commonly attended by domestic workers. The Peruvian delegate suggested that it would have been helpful if her organization had received some assistance in constructing questionnaires, selecting survey samples, and analyzing data.

In 1992 the SINTRACAP of Santiago commissioned a study with some funds it had raised, and a systematic sample of 300 household workers, divided between live-in and live-out workers, was interviewed. The study was carried out by a research team headed by a sociologist, with questions provided by the household workers union. There was no further participation by the *domésticas;* although the research team used ten interviewers, it proved impossible to include household workers among them because a sufficient number could not take the required two to three weeks off from their work. The Secretariat agreed that the Chilean study will serve as the model for surveys in other countries with the proviso that at least two domestic workers will be included in the design, planning, execution, and analysis of the data. However, as the first four studies (in Mexico, Guatemala, Peru, and Bolivia) have developed, the household workers have assumed (each with a professional contracted by them) nearly total control of their studies: recruiting the interviewers from among their own *gremio*, and carrying out the training, fieldwork, coding, and data entry themselves. Since the funding is given to the household workers association, the control of the project remains in their hands.

A final interesting project: the delegates at the II Congress spent an afternoon working with a feminist labor lawyer who works for the unions in Santiago on a plan for a study that will compare legislation on domestic service in all the countries with affiliated organizations.

Child Care Facilities

Finding a safe place to leave their children is also a crucial issue for domestic workers. For live-in workers, the problem of what to do with their children before they reach school age is especially critical. Some opt to send their young children to be raised by their grandparents in rural areas.

Domestic worker organizations are seeking solutions to this problem. In Rio de Janeiro, the union itself runs a child care center in Copacabana, where many of its members work, and other unions are determined to open more centers in other cities. To have child care facilities near their workplaces is much more convenient for domestic workers than services in the neighborhoods where they live. Even where such services exist, the centers may be far from their homes, necessitating a bus trip to the day care center plus one or more additional buses to reach their work—with the reverse journeys to be faced in the evenings after work.

In Paraguay, the domestic workers union opened a center in 1991 where workers can bring their children on Sunday night or Monday morning and pick them up the following Saturday, on their day off. There is space for 20 children.

The members of CONLACTRAHO's Secretariat decided that each child care model should be studied, and the countries that want to establish centers would be able either to send a representative to Brazil, Paraguay, or Peru to observe the operation of the particular type of child care arrangement that interests them, or ask CONLACTRAHO to finance the trip of an advisor from one of the countries that has successfully established child care services.

Housing Cooperatives

Perhaps one of the strongest wishes of domestic workers in Latin America—and of poor people in general—is to have a home of their own. The two principal domestic worker organizations in Chile (SINCATRAP and ANECAP) addressed this need by founding a very successful housing cooperative in 1966 that is financed by the members themselves.

Each member makes a commitment to contribute a fixed amount of money to a common fund. When enough money has been saved, a group of workers collectively buys a piece of land and pays for the installation of urban services and infrastructure. They then apply for a loan from the National Bank of Chile to finance the construction of the houses, a loan that must be paid back over 15 to 20 years. CONLACTRAHO hopes to be able to fund leaders from the Chilean credit cooperative to go to work with affiliates in other countries to set up savings and loan associations.

Research and Activism: Past and Future

To complete the discussion, I will comment on Aída's points about collaboration between household workers and feminist researchers and activists who want to help strengthen the domestic worker movement. What have researchers and activists (and activist/researchers) contributed to the household workers movement? What are the limitations of our work, and what remains to be done for the future?

Efforts of feminists, activists, and researchers to "connect" with the *gremio* (sector) of household workers remain sporadic and isolated. When one considers that about 20 percent of the *counted* female labor force in

Latin America works in paid domestic service, this fact is all the more inexplicable. The Rio Association estimates that 10 million Brazilian women are engaged in paid household labor. Feminists and researchers have embraced enthusiastically the causes of *pobladoras* (poor women in the city slums) and *campesinas*, but not that of household workers. In four countries with affiliates to the Confederation, household worker organizations were launched with feminist encouragement and backing; however, the ties have been severed (by the household workers) in all of them. Why should this be so?

For one thing, household workers want to be autonomous, and in the cases above they felt that there was too much "maternalismo" and too little respect in the relationship. In one case at a Congress, I heard remarks such as "Here come . . . and . . . with their *pastoras*" (shepherdesses).

A second reason for the lack of connection, in my view, is the fact that members of the campesina and pobladora groups almost never arrive on the doorsteps of middle-class feminists and academic researchers, and only rarely are in an employer/employee relationship with them. Household workers, on the contrary, are present every day in the homes of professional and feminist-activist women, and their activities impinge on every aspect of the lives of their employers and family members. As an article in the Brazilian publication of the group "Agora e que são elas" (And now, who are they) puts it, some of the questions that feminist *patronas* agonize over are: "What proportion of the family budget does the salary of my *empregada* represent?" "What do I know of the affective and sexual life of my *empregada*?" "How long a workday does my *empregada* have?" The relationship between household worker and her employer is thus a great deal more complex than with poor people generally. Professional women and feminist organizers do not have to deal with the latter every day, and never on such a personal level as with their domestic workers.

There have been some concerted efforts by feminist organizations to bridge the gap. Perhaps the most interesting contemporary attempt is that of the Coordinadora de Organizaciones del Area de la Mujer (Coordination of Women's Organizations) of Santo Domingo which has successfully organized 39 member associations that collaborate on a range of issues, particularly those requiring rapid mobilization. Member associations include those devoted to civic participation and leadership, legal rights, credit for women in agriculture and microenterprise, women's health and reproductive rights, education and training, environment, and the like. Among Coordinadora members are autonomous organizations of campesinas and the

Association of Household Workers; the campesina organization forms part of the executive committee.

The president of the Coordinadora told me that "the household workers come to *everything*: the meetings, the training sessions, the marches, the demonstrations." The president of the household workers said, "We go to everything because although we have some difficulties with middle-class women, we believe that there are a lot of issues that all of us face as women. And we go because we are learning from the feminists: how to conduct meetings, workshops, and conferences, and how to raise funds."

The work of the Centro de Estudios de la Mujer—CEM (Women's Studies Center) in Argentina (no relation to the CEM in Santiago) deserves special attention. Cristina Zurutuza and Clelia Bercovich directed a project in 1985–1986 titled "Paid Domestic Service and the Problems of Unionization" (Zurutuza and Bercovich 1990). What is noteworthy is that Zurutuza and Bercovich did not stop at a study of the living conditions and organization of domestic workers, but went on to design a successful mobile food service program in conjunction with domestic workers of the neighborhood of Lomas de Zamora. Their customers are the shop owners and public sector employees in their neighborhood. They then started an office and housecleaning business as well as a laundry service. Their other efforts include a food cooperative, community organizing, protests, parties, summer camps for children, and the establishment of a medical clinic. The cooperative's membership grew from 27 to 70 women who participate in a wide range of activities. Twenty of those women hold paid positions, and the rest benefit from a variety of services.

The technical team of middle-class researchers, which has gradually withdrawn as the domestic workers themselves are able to take over the management of the project, characterized their collaboration as a "heartfelt commitment to a common objective" (Zurutuza and Bercovich 1990). This is an example of academic researchers who are not satisfied with simply completing a study that will be filed away, but who actually contribute directly to the fulfillment of a need. As Zurutuza puts it, her team wants to overcome the common complaint of grassroots groups: "The intellectuals, the academics, the technicians, they all come to study us and then leave without giving us anything in return."

Other efforts to unite research with action have taken place, such as the Perú-Mujer project in Lima. To complement the studies conducted by Blanca Figueroa, ten leaders chosen by the Coordinadora Sindical de Trabajadoras del Hogar de Lima Metropolitana received one-year scholarships equivalent to their salaries as domestic workers. Perú-Mujer designed a curriculum that enabled them to study theoretical and practical issues including union building, leadership training, publication and poster design, oratory techniques, the use of the media, and the management of an employment agency. There was also a recreational program that included outings to the theater and the cinema followed by critical discussions.

Perhaps the most ambitious effort, however, was a three-year program directed by Magdalena León in Bogotá under the auspices of the Asociación Colombiana para el Estudio de la Población—ACEP (Colombian Association for Population Studies). The project is described in Chaney-García Castro (1989), and I will not go into great detail here. León's project was undertaken to address the domestic workers' urgent need for consciousness-raising and training for community and political participation and leadership. The program also provided legal assistance to the organizations and to individual domestic workers, and assisted SINTRASEDOM in its efforts (eventually successful) to win the right for domestic workers to organize in official unions.

Domestic workers have maintained good relationships with the Coordinadora in Santo Domingo and the two CEMs in Santiago and Buenos Aires. However, serious disagreements arose between the domestic workers and those involved in the Peruvian and Colombian projects. It would be interesting to analyze why, despite good faith and hard work on the part of both domestic workers and activist-academics, misunderstandings can develop to the point of breaking off relations between the two groups.

What about research efforts? While the output so far is rather meager, as the bibliography at the end of this discussion shows, a start has been made. There is at least one study for most of the countries in the region, although several were written in the 1980s and need to be updated. Researchers have described the following general characteristics of household workers in the hemisphere:

1. Housework, whether done by the *patrona*, her household worker, or both, is everywhere a depreciated activity—and apparently one that demands no special training or skills. In a survey in Peru (Heyman 1974), women classified only two occupations as less desirable than domestic service: prostitution and begging.
2. Domestic workers are, for the most part, poor women with minimal education who migrate to the towns and cities. They are considered "inferior" not only because of their occupation, but also because of their culture, language, dress, and (frequently) race.
3. Because they do not work together in a plant or factory, but in iso-

lated workplaces, household workers remain "invisible" to themselves, to society, to governments, to other labor unions, to feminist organizers, to researchers.

4. Domestic worker organization is impeded by the fact that household workers are not considered bona fide "workers" and therefore are not governed by legislation affecting the working class. In many countries, this means that household workers do not have the right to organize.

While we now have a number of country studies, most are not comparative and they remain unconnected and uncoordinated with work in other places. Nor has there been much attempt to ground empirical work in theory. As Sanjak and Colen note in the introduction to their collective volume on household workers, "there is no broad, comprehensive, world systemic theory that accounts for the emergence of household work [as an issue] everywhere" (1990:10). Exceptions include the early work already cited of Arizpe, Jelin, and Saffioti, and the essays by Duarte, Gálvez and Todaro, Garcia, Castro, and León in Chaney-Garcia Castro (1989)

For the future, a series of questions remain unresolved and could form the basis for a research agenda. Mary García Castro and I elaborate on these questions in our introduction to the *Muchachas* collection mentioned above. They include the following:

1. the low status of household work in general, and in particular as a profession, and the search for recognition and dignity by household worker organizations;
2. whether there is occupational mobility among domestic workers, and the long-term social consequences when more than 20 percent of the female labor force is "locked" into this profession;
3. the relation of domestic worker availability to the deterioration of life in the rural areas, and implications of the (in some countries) apparently unlimited supplies of new immigrants to work in the domestic service sector—in their own countries and abroad;
4. the situation of the thousands and thousands of Latin American and Caribbean women who migrate northward to work as domestics—with and without documents;
5. the relationship of *patronas* who are feminists and professional women to those women who each day make it possible for them to carry out their professional and political work;
6. the heterogeneity of domestic service and its transformation over time; the potential for creating professional cleaning services and cooperatives by domestic workers themselves;

7. the lack of an affective life for many women who are in service, and alternatively, the increasing numbers of those who become female heads-of-household because of their search for affection;
8. the domestic workers' search for a class identity; the precapitalist work relations in domestic service that some theorists assert prevent it from being considered a productive occupation, and hence, those who carry it out as not belonging to the working class;
9. the domestic workers' own struggles to organize and their successes and failures in changing legislation (and its enforcement) to improve their working conditions; what *other* functions their unions can perform when they are most often not in a position to negotiate; the sindicato of household workers as surrogate family.

Afterword

Aída and Elsa: We hope that our dialog has informed you about a new field of action and research related to the situation of millions of women doing domestic work for pay in their own countries and in North America. Their efforts to organize, which we have highlighted here, offer perhaps the best hope for these women who are locked into an occupation that, at present, is low in status and dead end. If you are a paid domestic worker—whether in the North or South—we call on you to invite four or five colleagues to organize a group, with the eventual aim of affiliation to the Confederation of Household Workers of Latin America and the Caribbean. If you are a professional or feminist-activist patrona, we ask you to think about what you can do to improve the situation of the women who make it possible for you and others to do your professional or political work. If you are a researcher, we invite you to join in this challenging new field that still lacks so much basic information and analysis.

You can join the Friends of Household Workers and receive CONLACTRAHO's occasional bulletin; you can discuss your ideas about the kind of projects your group would like to propose to our organizations for possible collaboration; you can converse with us about your plans for research. We await your part in our dialog with much anticipation.

BIBLIOGRAPHY

Anderson, Patricia (1989). "Protection and Oppression: A Case-Study of Domestic Service in Jamaica." Second Disciplinary Seminar in the Social Sciences. St. Michael, Barbados: Women and Development Studies, University of the West Indies.

Arizpe, Lourdes (1977). "Women in the Informal Labor Sector: The Case of Mexico City." *Signs* 3:1 (Autumn), 25–37. Special issue on Women in Development.

Bossen, Laurel (1988). "Wives and Servants: Women in Middle-Class Households, Guatemala City." In George Gmelch and Walter P. Zenner, eds., *Urban Life: Readings in Urban Anthropology*. 2d ed. Prospect Heights, IL: Waveland Press. Pp. 265–275.

Bunster, Ximena, and Elsa M. Chaney (1985). *Sellers and Servants: Working Women in Lima, Peru*. Photography by Ellan Young. Granby, MA: Bergin & Garvey.

Chaney, Elsa M., and Mary García Castro (1989). *Muchachas No More: Household Workers in Latin America and the Caribbean*. Philadelphia, PA: Temple University Press. Spanish edition *Muchacha, cachifa, criada, empleada, embregadinha, servienta y . . . más nada: Trabajadoras del hogar en América Latina y el Caribe*. Caracas: Nueva Sociedad, 1993.

Colen, Shellee (1989). "'Just a Little Respect': West Indian Domestic Workers in New York City." In Elsa M. Chaney and Mary García Castro, eds., *Muchachas No More: Household Workers in Latin America and the Caribbean*. Philadelphia: Temple University Press. Pp. 171–194.

———. (1990). "'Housekeeping' for the Green Card: West Indian Household Workers, the State, and Stratified Reproduction in New York." In Roger Sanjek and Shellee Colen, eds., *At Work in Homes: Household Workers in World Perspective*. Washington, DC: American Anthropological Association. Pp. 89–118.

Cussiánovich, Alejandro (1974). *Llamados a ser libres*. Lima: Equipo JOC-Empleadas de Hogar; Centro de Estudios y Publicaciones.

de Oliveira, Anazir Maria ("Zica"), and Odete Maria de Conceiçao (1989). "Domestic Workers in Rio de Janeiro: Their Struggle to Organize." In Elsa M. Chaney and Mary García Castro, eds., *Muchachas No More: Household Workers in Latin America and the Caribbean*. Philadelphia: Temple University Press. Pp. 363–372.

Díaz Uriarte, Adelinda (1989). "The Autobiography of a Fighter (Peru)." In Elsa M. Chaney and Mary Garcia Castro, eds., *Muchachas No More: Household Workers in Latin America and the Caribbean*. Philadelphia: Temple University Press. Pp. 389–406.

Duarte, Isis (1983). "Condiciones de vida, ideología y socialización de los niños de las trabajadoras de hogar en Santo Domingo, R.D." Paper presented at the Congress of the Latin American Studies Association.

———. (1989). "Household Workers in the Dominican Republic: A Question for the Feminist Movement." In Elsa M. Chaney and Mary Garcia Castro, eds., *Muchachas No More: Household Workers in Latin America and the Caribbean*. Philadelphia: Temple University Press. Pp. 197–219.

Duarte, Isis, Estela Hernández, Aída Garden Bobea, and Francis Pou (1976). "Condiciones sociales del servicio doméstico en la República Dominicana." *Realidad Contemporánea* 1(3–4), 79–104.

FEM, Revista Femenina (1980–1981). Vol. 4, No. 16. México, D.F. Special issue on domestic service.

Figueroa Galup, Blanca (1983). *La trabajadora doméstica (Lima, Perú)* Lima: Perú-Mujer.

Flora, Cornelia Butler (1989). "Domestic Service in the Latin American *Fotonovela*." In Elsa M. Chaney and Mary Garcia Castro, eds., *Muchachas No More: Household Workers in Latin America and the Caribbean*. Philadelphia: Temple University Press. Pp. 143–159.

Gálvez, Thelma, and Rosalba Todaro (1984). *Las trabajadoras de casa particular en la década 1970–1980: Empleo y características*. Santiago: Centro de Estudios de la Mujer, Proyecto Trabajadoras de Casa Particular.

———. (1985). *Yo trabajo así . . . en casa particular*. Santiago: Centro de Estudios de la Mujer.

———. (1989). "Housework for Pay in Chile: Not Just Another Job." In Elsa M. Chaney and Mary García Castro, eds., *Muchachas No More: Household Workers in Latin America and the Caribbean*. Philadelphia: Temple University Press. Pp. 307–321.

García Castro, Mary (1979). "Migración laboral femenina." Programa de las Naciones Unidas, Proyecto Oficina Internacional de Trabajo sobre Migraciones Laborales. Bogotá. Mimeographed.

———. (1982). "¿Qué se compra y qué se paga en el servicio doméstico? El caso de Bogotá." In Magdalena León, ed., *La realidad colombiana*. Volume 1, *Debate sobre la mujer en América Latina y el Caribe: Discusión acerca de la unidad producción-reproducción*. Bogotá: Asociación Colombiana para el Estudio de la Población. Pp. 92–122.

———. (1989). "What Is Bought and What Is Sold in Domestic Service? The Case of Bogotá: A Critical Review." In Elsa M. Chaney and Mary Garcia Castro, eds., *Muchachas No More: Household Workers in Latin America and the Caribbean*. Philadelphia: Temple University Press. Pp. 105–126.

García Castro, Mary, Bertha Quintero, and Gladys Jimeno (1981). "Empleo doméstico, sector informal, migración y movilidad ocupacional en areas urbanas en Colombia." Programa de las Naciones Unidas, Proyecto Oficina Internacional de Trabajo sobre Migraciones Laborales. Bogotá: Final Report. Mimeographed.

Gil Izquierdo, Elena (1989). "Sharpening the Class Struggle: The Education of Domestic Workers in Cuba." In Elsa M. Chaney and Mary García Castro, eds., *Muchachas No More: Household Workers in Latin America and the Caribbean*. Philadelphia: Temple University Press. Pp. 351–372.

Gill, Lesley (1990). "Painted Faces: Conflict and Ambiguity in Domestic Servant-Employer Relations in La Paz, 1930–1988." *Latin American Research Review* 25(1), 119–136.

———. (1994). *Precarious Dependencies: Gender, Class and Domestic Service in Bolivia*. New York: Columbia University Press.

Gogna, Mónica L. (1981). *El servicio doméstico en Buenos Aires: Características de empleo y relación laboral*. Buenos Aires: Centro de Estudios e Investigaciones Laborales (CEIL).

———. (1989). "Domestic Workers in Buenos Aires." In Elsa M. Chaney and Mary García Castro, eds., *Muchachas No More: Household Workers in Latin America and the Caribbean*. Philadelphia: Temple University Press. Pp. 83–104.

Goldsmith, Mary (1980–1981). "Trabajo doméstico asalariado y desarrollo capitalista." *FEM* 4(16), 10–20.

———. (1989). "Politics and Programs of Domestic Workers' Organizations in Mexico." In Elsa M. Chaney and Mary Garcia Castro, eds., *Muchachas No More: Household Workers in Latin America and the Caribbean*. Philadelphia: Temple University Press. Pp. 221–244.

Graham, Sandra Lauderdale (1988). *House and Street: The Domestic World of Servants and Masters in Nineteenth-Century Rio de Janeiro*. New York: Cambridge University Press.

———. (1989). "Servants and Masters in Rio de Janeiro: Perceptions of House and Street in the 1870s." In Elsa M. Chaney and Mary Garcia Castro, eds., *Muchachas No More: Household Workers in Latin America and the Caribbean*. Philadelphia: Temple University Press. Pp. 67–80.

Heyzer, Noleen, Geertje Lycklama à Nijeholt, and Nedra Weerakoon (1994). *The Trade in Domestic Workers: Causes, Mechanisms and Consequences of International Migration*. London and New Jersey: Zed Books.

Higman, B.W. (1989). "Domestic Service in Jamaica since 1750." In Elsa M. Chaney and

Mary Garcia Castro, eds., *Muchachas No More: Household Workers in Latin America and the Caribbean*. Philadelphia: Temple University Press. Pp. 37–66.

Jelin, Elizabeth (1976). *Migración a las ciudades y participación en la fuerza de trabajo de las mujeres latinoamericanas: El caso del servicio doméstico*. Estudios Sociales No. 4. Buenos Aires: Centro de Estudios de Estado y Sociedad. Published in English as "Migration and Labor Force Participation of Latin American Women: The Domestic Servants in the Cities." *Signs* 3:1 (Autumn 1977), 129–141. Special Issue on Women and Development.

———. (1978). "La mujer y el mercado de trabajo urbano." *Estudios CEDES*, Vol. 1, No. 6. Buenos Aires: Centro de Estudios de Estado y Sociedad. Published in English as "Women and the Urban Labor Market." In Richard Anker, Mayra Buvinic, and Nadia H. Youssef, eds., *Women's Roles and Population Trends in the Third World*. London: Croom Helm, 1982. Pp. 239–267.

Kuznesof, Elizabeth (1989). "A History of Domestic Service in Spanish America, 1492–1980." In Elsa M. Chaney and Mary Garcia Castro, eds., *Muchachas No More: Household Workers in Latin America and the Caribbean*. Philadelphia: Temple University Press. Pp. 17–35.

León, Magdalena (1989). "Domestic Labor and Domestic Service in Colombia." In Elsa M. Chaney and Mary Garcia Castro, eds., *Muchachas No More: Household Workers in Latin America and the Caribbean*. Philadelphia: Temple University Press. Pp. 323–349.

Loza, Martha, Paulina Luza, Rosa Mendoza, and Flor Valverde (1990). *Así, ando, ando como empleada*. Lima: Instituto de Promoción y Formación de Trabajadoras del Hogar (IPROFORTH).

Macisco, John J., Jr. (1975). *Migrants to Metropolitan Lima: A Case Study*. Santiago: Centro Latinoamericano de Demografía.

Margolis, Maxine L. (1990). "From Mistress to Servant: Downward Mobility Among Brazilian Immigrants in New York City." *Urban Anthropology and Studies of Cultural Systems and World Economic Development* 19(3), 215–231.

Martínez, Héctor, William Prado, and Jorge Quintanilla (1973). *El éxodo rural en el Perú*. Lima: Centro de Estudios de Población y Desarrollo.

Mohammed, Patricia (1989). "Domestic Workers in the Caribbean." In Elsa M. Chaney and Mary Garcia Castro, eds., *Muchachas No More: Household Workers in Latin America and the Caribbean*. Philadelphia: Temple University Press. Pp. 161–169.

Moreno Valenzuela, Aída (1989). "History of the Household Workers' Movement in Chile: 1926–1983." In Elsa M. Chaney and Mary Garcia Castro, eds., *Muchachas No More: Household Workers in Latin America and the Caribbean*. Philadelphia: Temple University Press. Pp. 407–416.

Nett, Emily (1966). "The Servant Class in a Developing Society: Ecuador." *Journal of Inter-American Studies* 8:3 (July), 437–452.

Ortiz Pérez, Irene, and Ruth Joffre Lazarini (1991). *Así es, pues: Trabajadoras domésticas de Cuernavaca*. México, D.F.: Colectivo Atabal.

Pereira de Melo, Hildete (1989). "Feminists and Domestic Workers in Rio de Janeiro." In Elsa M. Chaney and Mary García Castro, eds., *Muchachas No More: Household Workers in Latin America and the Caribbean*. Philadelphia: Temple University Press. Pp. 245–267.

Prates, Suzana (1989). "Organizations for Domestic Workers in Montevideo: Reinforcing Marginality?" In Elsa M. Chaney and Mary García Castro, eds., *Muchachas No More:*

Household Workers in Latin America and the Caribbean. Philadelphia: Temple University Press. Pp. 271–290.

Radcliffe, Sarah A. (1989). "Ethnicity, Patriarchy, and Incorporation into the Nation: Female Migrants as Domestic Servants in Peru." *Environment and Planning. D, Society and Space* 8:379–393.

———. (1990). "Between Hearth and Labor Market: The Recruitment of Peasant Women in the Andes." *International Migration Review* 24(2), 229–249.

Romero, Mary (1988a). "Chicanas Modernize Domestic Service." *Qualitative Sociology* 11(4), 319–334.

———. (1988b). "Sisterhood and Domestic Service: Race, Class and Gender in the Mistress-Maid Relationship." *Humanity and Society* 12(4), 318–346.

———. (1990). "Not Just Like One of the Family: Chicana Domestics Establishing Professional Relationships with Employers." *Feminist Issues*, vol. 10, pp. 2–33.

Ruiz, Vicki L. (1987). "By the Day or Week: Mexicana Domestic Workers in El Paso." In Carol Groneman and Mary Beth Norton, eds., *To Toil the Livelong Day: America's Women at Work, 1780–1980.* Ithaca: Cornell University Press. Pp. 269–283.

Rutté García, Alberto (1973). *Simplemente explotadas: El mundo de las empleadas domésticas de Lima.* Lima: Centro de Estudios y Promoción del Desarrollo.

Saffioti, Heleieth I.B. (1978). *Emprego doméstico e capitalismo.* Petrópolis, Brazil: Editora Vozes.

Sanjek, Roger, and Shellee Colen, eds. (1990). *At Work in Homes: Household Workers in Third World Perspective.* Washington, DC: American Anthropological Association.

Schellekens, Thea, and Anja van der Schoot (1989). "Household Workers in Peru: The Difficult Road to Organization." In Elsa M. Chaney and Mary Garcia Castro, eds., *Muchachas No More: Household Workers in Latin America and the Caribbean.* Philadelphia: Temple University Press. Pp. 291–306.

Sindicato de Trabajadoras del Hogar-Cusco (1982). *Basta: Testimonios.* Cuzco: Centro de Estudios Rurales Andinos "Bartolomé de Las Casas."

Sindicato Nacional de Trabajadoras Domésticas (SINTRASEDOM) (1989). "The History of Our Struggle (Colombia)." In Elsa M. Chaney and Mary Garcia Castro, eds., *Muchachas No More: Household Workers in Latin America and the Caribbean.* Philadelphia: Temple University Press. Pp. 373–387.

Smith, Margo L. (1971). "Institutionalized Servitude: Female Domestic Service in Lima, Peru." Ph.D. dissertation, University of Indiana.

———. (1973). "Domestic Service as a Channel of Upward Mobility for the Lower-Class Woman: The Lima Case." In Ann Pescatello, ed., *Female and Male in Latin America: Essays.* Pittsburgh: University of Pittsburgh Press. Pp. 191–207.

———. (1975). "The Female Domestic Servant and Social Change: Lima, Peru." In Ruby Rohrlich-Leavitt, ed., *Women Cross-Culturally: Change and Challenge.* The Hague: Mouton. Pp. 163–180.

———. (1977). "El servicio doméstico como medio de movilidad ascendente para la mujer de clase baja: El caso de Lima." In Ann Pescatello, ed., *Hembra y macho en Latinoamérica.* México, D.F.: Editorial Diana. Pp. 233–252.

———. (1989). "Where Is María Now? Former Domestic Workers in Peru." In Elsa M. Chaney and Mary Garcia Castro, eds., *Muchachas No More: Household Workers in Latin America and the Caribbean.* Philadelphia: Temple University Press. Pp. 127–142.

Todaro, Rosalba, and Thelma Gálvez (1987). *Trabajo doméstico remunerado: Conceptos, hechos, datos*. Santiago: Centro de Estudios de la Mujer.

Young, Grace Esther (1987). "The Myth of Being 'Like a Daughter.'" *Latin American Perspectives* 54:14 (Summer), 365–380.

Zurutuza, Cristina, and Clelia Bercovich (1988). "Las sirvientas: Ellas, las otras y nosotras." *Revista UNIDAS* 2 (November), 91–118.

———. (1990). "De sirvientas a empresarias: Un camino hacia la autonomía: El papel de la capacitación sistemática en la autogestión de los emprendimientos de generación de ingresos." Buenos Aires: Centro de Estudios de la Mujer, Programa de Asesoramiento y Apoyo Técnico a la Cooperativa de Trabajo "Hijas de María Pueblo SRL" de Lomas de Zamora.

8

Concluding Reflections: "Redrawing" the Parameters of Gender Struggle

SONIA E. ALVAREZ

In reflecting upon the "lessons to be learned" from Latin American women's struggles, I will focus on three theoretical and strategic problematics addressed by Maruja Barrig in her compelling analysis of the changing relationship between women's movements and the state in Peru, since these issues also speak to many of the themes raised by other contributors to this volume. First, Barrig describes the growing *desdibujamiento* or "erasure" of the Peruvian state in its role as provider of social services. I highlight the Spanish term *desdibujamiento* because it quite vividly and graphically captures the rapid and dramatic erosion, if not erasure, of the state from the realms of social provision, redistribution, and social inclusion. Barrig documents the disastrous social and political consequences of this process in the Peruvian case. But, the erasure of the state from the realms of social welfare and inclusion is very much, indeed glaringly, in evidence in all corners of the globe today—South and North, East and West.

Second, Barrig points out that this *desdibujamiento* has resulted in a reprivatization or transfer of the responsibility for social reproduction from the state to the household, more specifically to poor women, and, even more specifically, to poor women's organizations. She shows conclusively that, in the Peruvian case at least, instead of "empowering" poor women, many of the community organizations of poor women have been *redibujadas*, redrawn or reconfigured, in ways that impose a triple or quadruple burden on women participants. That is, this reprivatization effectively reinforces poor and working-class women's dependence on an increasingly undependable state.

Third, Barrig takes up the often neglected question of women's citizenship and argues that, given the history of state-society relations in Peru (and, I would argue, in most Latin American countries that have experienced sustained periods of populist rule), gender-specific citizenship claims are couched almost exclusively within the discourse of social rights, while claims to broader or deeper civil or political rights for women are less often articulated.

I want to structure my concluding reflections around possible theoretical and political strategies that might help us redraw or *redibujar* the rather sobering, indeed somber, picture sketched out for us by Barrig and several other contributors. That is, I would like to take up Lourdes Benería's opening question—"Is there a way out?" Is there another picture, more optimistic though not necessarily utopian, that we could begin to paint collectively?

Undertaking this kind of revisioning or "redrawing" is an especially urgent task for feminist scholars and activists in the Americas today. In the North of the Americas, the erosion of the welfare state and the relentless economic recession have worked to further "feminize" poverty, especially among Latinas, African Americans, and other "minority" populations. In the South, the debt crisis and the egregious social costs of economic restructuring imposed by the North, and embraced and enforced by the Latin American state, have further abraded the already precarious life chances of the region's poor, especially its women and its indigenous and African populations. And, given the virtually unfettered mobility of global capital and the increasingly undisputed military, ideological, and geopolitical hegemony of the United States in the hemisphere at the dawn of this "post–Gulf War," unipolar, putatively "post-socialist" era, the fates of women and the poor throughout the Americas are ever more closely intertwined.

Developing forward-looking theoretical and political agendas for the 1990s and beyond is, moreover, all the more imperative if we are to avoid painting ourselves into two polarized, indeed schizophrenia-inducing and paralyzing, theoretical, and strategic corners. On the one hand, our analyses of what Lourdes Benería referred to as the "obscenities" of the "lost decade" in Latin America or of the Reagan-Bush era in the United States lead us inexorably toward doom-and-gloom prognoses about the fate of the Americas and of its women. We have extensively documented the multiple forms in which "development" and economic restructuring have placed an "unequal burden" on women and have reinforced gender power imbalances (Benería and Feldman 1992). Yet the vast literature on gender and the new international division of labor seldom indicates a strategic way out of this dire situation.

On the other hand, and this is especially true of much of the literature on women's involvement in the region's new social movements, we vest great hopes in the "resistance" everywhere in evidence in women's daily lives, household survival strategies, and collective struggles. Yet we too often ignore the less glorious, more contradictory, more paradoxical dimensions and sometimes ephemeral qualities of those struggles. More troubling still, while we rightly celebrate the resilience and innovative capacity of women's struggles and the democratizing potential they embody, we have not fully confronted the strategic question of how this potential might be realized at the level of the state and the economy.

How do we weave together these strands of feminist theorizing so as to devise viable feminist strategies that respond to the enormity of the crises confronting women in the Americas? In discerning how we might paint ourselves out of the proverbial theoretical corners I outlined above, the three problematics raised by Barrig must command our attention.

First, let us turn to the question of *desdibujamiento.* I suggest that the 1980s was not only the "lost decade" in terms of escalating economic crisis and rapid impoverishment, but also the decade that witnessed a rapid rise and decline of the hopes we vested in democratization; it was, in this sense, also the "decade of lost hopes."

Democratization in South America opened up new spaces for the expression and articulation of gendered demand-making—however restricted these might be. The increased visibility of women as political and social actors led to a growing—although often reluctant or opportunistic—recognition of women's rights by parties and the state.[1] Yet, this recognition of women's social and political rights came about precisely at a time when the national state's capacity and political will to create the conditions which would allow women effectively to enjoy those rights were rapidly eroding.

What To Do? Is There a Way Out of This Paradox?

Strategically, I think we need to look both beyond and beneath the nation-state for possible solutions. That is, we need to think about and experiment with both supra-national and sub-national feminist strategies.[2] This is especially true in light of the "bulldozing" of national economic and (even) political boundaries, described by Lourdes Benería, and in light of the growing "municipalization" or "provincialization" of the state which has been the concomitant, if less visible, consequence of the erosion or *desdibujamiento* of the national state.

At the supra-national level, there are many new arenas in which the articulation of feminist strategies could make a difference for women in all of the Americas.³ For example, new trade agreements—regional and global—are proliferating, such as NAFTA (North American Free Trade Agreement), MERCOSUR (Mercado Común del Sur), EEC (European Economic Community), and so on. These have triggered new policy debates and created a new set of international regulatory agencies and transnational arenas in which feminist intervention *might* make a difference. Groups like DAWN (Development Alternatives with Women for a New Era) are already engaged in efforts to influence such processes. Other feminists have similarly been working at the supra-national level to incorporate women's rights into new formulations of international human rights.

Recent trends toward decentralization have, moreover, redrawn parameters of the Latin American state and created local and regional instances of state power and policy making which also demand the attention of feminists and other progressive social forces. Since the late 1980s, in response not only to the neoliberal obsession with "shrinking the state" but also to the persistent demands of social movements for increased local autonomy, more efficient and responsive public administration reforms, and more meaningful citizen participation, aimed at decentralizing the state have been undertaken in many Latin American nations.⁴ In the case of unitary state systems, such as those of Colombia, Peru, Chile, and Bolivia, entirely new administrative instances of the state and new representative political arenas have been created at the local and regional levels. In federal state systems, such as that of Brazil, recent constitutional reforms have enhanced the (potential) scope of authority of existing local and state governments.

At the sub-national level, many innovative local and regional political experiments are already under way which may present feminists with new opportunities to influence policy closer to home. For example, the "popular democratic" municipal administrations of the Workers' Party in Brazil have undertaken a project of inverting local government priorities, more equitably distributing the burdens of structural adjustment so that they do not fall exclusively or disproportionately on the popular sectors.⁵ Similar social democratic or popular democratic experiments are under way elsewhere—for example, the Frente Amplio administration in Montevideo, the Acción Democrática-M-19 municipal governments in Colombia, local governments ruled by the Movimiento-al-Socialismo in Venezuela, Sandinista-opposition local and state governments in Nicaragua.⁶ These local democratic alternatives suggest that the "biases of restructuring" outlined by Lourdes Benería are indeed neither inevitable nor invariable. They also present new strategic possibilities and new political arenas in which feminist and other democratic struggles can now be waged.

The crisis of the national state, coupled with decentralizing reforms of the political system, unquestionably have devolved the responsibility, if not the resources, for redistribution and provision of social services from national to local and regional levels of the state. Whether or not we think this is a positive development, it nevertheless enhances the importance of local and regional political arenas in Latin America, both theoretically and politically. The local political arena is one in which women's movements might have a significant impact—it is closer to home and thus at least potentially more permeable, more vulnerable to citizen scrutiny and intervention.

Of course, the devolution of responsibility from the national to the local and regional levels, propelled in part by neoliberal economic restructuring, has not necessarily been accompanied by a devolution of state resources and revenues. Therefore, the struggle for effective decentralization of the state may become crucial for feminists and other progressive social forces in the Americas in the 1990s.

Moving from the level of local politics to community politics and women's neighborhood struggles, I believe we also need to do a better job of theorizing the consequences for poor and working-class women of the increasingly wide variety of interventions in the community struggles of the popular classes.[7] The interventions or mediations by the state, the church, political parties, NGOs, and international and national development and philanthropic agencies have many implications for women's "empowerment," as the essays by Maruja Barrig, María del Carmen Feijoó, and Malena de Montís show. These multiple actors hold agendas and stakes in poor women's survival struggles which can significantly reconfigure, redimension, and even redirect those struggles. For example, they can further discipline womanhood; they can promote "fideo-making" (Feijoó); or, less often perhaps, these interventions can provide women with new tools for gendered resistance.

Most prominent among the latter type of interventions are those of feminist scholars and activists—including, significantly, all of the Latin American women whose work is assembled in this volume and of Elisabeth Souza-Lobo, the Brazilian feminist scholar and activist to whose memory this collection is dedicated.[8] Feminist interventions have been critical in Brazil, Peru, Mexico, Chile, and other Latin American countries in "feminizing" poor women's survival struggles. Herein lie potentially rich theoretical and political lessons about women's gender-conscious empowerment. I am, in effect, entreating us all to study more systematically the way we study and work with women of popular sectors, to better theorize the interventions of feminists in grassroots women's struggles and to examine what difference those interventions have made or could make.[9]

Herein also lies one of the crucial lessons from Latin America still to be learned by North American feminists—for we, too, have our own "movimiento de mujeres." But unlike our Latin American feminist counterparts, we have hardly riveted our theoretical or political attention on the transformative, radical-democratic, and/or feminist potential it may represent. We in the United States have much to learn about how to promote and reinforce the process of empowerment and gender consciousness among low-income and minority women who are involved in welfare rights struggles, in our own growing numbers of *comedores populares*, in our own government make-work programs, permanent "emergency" relief programs, and so on. Learning these lessons and tapping into the potential of grassroots women's organizing in the United States today would also help us better confront our own increasingly disciplinary, subsidiary state.

Finally, feminist scholars and activists must delve more deeply into the question of how to engender citizenship and engage in a systematic exploration of what both the broadening and deepening of democratic citizenship might mean for women in the Americas.[10] Although feminist theorists in the North of the Americas have begun to explore the meaning of citizenship for women, I fully concur with Barrig. Given the increasingly conservative and restricted character of Latin America's much-celebrated processes of democratization, we urgently need a feminist rethinking and revisioning of citizenship, one that moves beyond the extension of gender-differentiated social rights to women to encompass more meaningful political and, especially, civil rights.

Latin American feminist scholars have begun to problematize prevailing liberal and corporatist conceptions of citizenship and to question the Latin American Left's historic association of individual or civil rights with "bourgeois democracy." In analyzing "the institutional delegitimation of women's movements" in post-authoritarian Brazil, for example, Teresa Caldeira argues persuasively that "conservative discourses which undermine individual rights have flourished at the same time that democratization was routinized at the level of the political system and perhaps might be considered as a reaction to the expansion of political citizenship" (Caldeira 1993:8), and this, therefore, seriously obstructs the extension and deepening of gendered and sexual citizenship for women in Brazil.[11] Drawing on

T.H. Marshall's now classic analysis of the expansion of citizenship in the West (Marshall 1950), Caldeira maintains that the order of progression from civil, to political, to social rights which he argued typified the development of citizenship in the British case is precisely reversed in the case of Brazil and other Latin American nations:

> Social rights expanded—mainly labor rights—even during dictatorships which suspended political rights. The latter have had a convoluted history of going back and forth, of being guaranteed and taken away until they arrived at the current stage in which they are largely legitimated and exercised. Individual and civil rights, however, have always remained underdeveloped, together with the justice system which is, in principle, the institution in charge of assuring them. (Caldeira 1993: 19–20)

Echoing Barrig's critique of the problematic strategic focus on social rights in Peru, Caldeira insists that whereas "equality rights" and efforts to secure "rights to difference" are central to feminist strategies in Western liberal democracies, "In Brazil . . . where justice exists as a privilege for the elites and for men and where individual and human rights are not only disrespected but also evaluated in a negative way . . . the themes of justice and individual rights seem to constitute at this moment the main arena in which both democratization and the expansion of women's rights have to be addressed" (Caldeira 1993:21).[12] In a provocative comparative treatment of gender and citizenship in Europe and Latin America, Antje Weiner argues that "While citizenship might be interpreted as 'reformist' or 'bourgeois' in some historical settings, in others it might cause significant sociopolitical change" (Weiner 1992:16). In countries like Mexico, she suggests, the claims of women and the urban poor to "Citizenship, as the right to evoke constitutional rights through political practice based on the use of existing constitutional rights . . . radically questioned the legitimacy of a populist regime" (Weiner 1992). Current efforts by Brazilian feminists to "reactivate" the Brazilian judiciary, to develop more effective litigation strategies, and to secure better prosecution and conviction rates for batterers and rapists, for example, may also be seen in the light of Latin American feminists' efforts to engender democratic citizenship.[13]

If progress on women's civil rights has been slight, democratizing regimes in Brazil and the Southern Cone arguably *have* expanded political citizenship for women. For example, in several of the formally democratic regimes that are today the norm in the South of the Americas, women and women's issues have been *integrated* into the state and political parties;

women have carved out new spaces in the state through which they can ostensibly pursue the expansion of citizenship for women. But those new spaces, such as special councils or sub-ministries on the status of women, most often tied to the executive branch, have proven quite contradictory. Although, as was the case in Brazil during the drafting of the new Constitution of 1988, women's councils can sometimes prove effective vehicles for the articulation of gender-based demands within the state, "women's spaces" can also readily be relegated to bureaucratic obscurity and become mired by the vicissitudes of masculinist "politics as usual."[14]

Is it possible or even desirable, then, to launch or sustain a feminist politics from the state?[15] If so, how might women's citizenship rights, especially those of indigenous and African American and poor and working-class women, be most effectively pursued or articulated in masculinist policy-making arenas—local, regional, national, and global? We must conduct further research into four strategies which have prevailed among feminists seeking to integrate women's rights into male-dominant political arenas in the Americas and Europe: (1) women's mass organizations tied to the dominant party or to the regime (described in the case of Nicaragua by Malena de Montís); (2) executive-based strategies centered on the creation of women's councils, ministries, sub-ministries, or special agencies (established in postauthoritarian Brazil, Argentina, and Chile); (3) judicial branch-centered or litigation strategies (such as those that prevailed in the pre-Hill-Thomas United States); and (4) parliamentary-based strategies (most common in European nations). Each of these needs to be further investigated in terms of their comparative effectiveness in promoting a gender-sensitive policy process and generating policy outcomes that redress gender-based inequities.

Each strategy is riddled by profound contradictions: the first two by problems of representativeness and accountability to movement constituencies; the second two by problems of conjuncture and access. Executive-centered and mass organization strategies have most often pursued a single "women's policy agenda" which is typically subject to the ideological and programmatic dictates of political incumbents and thus does not always reflect the multiplicity of gendered claims articulated by diverse sectors of the women's movement whose interests are shaped by party or ideological affiliations or sympathies as well as by class, race, ethnicity, sexual preference, and so on. Litigation strategies, though perhaps less than effective (indeed even dangerous) in the North of the Americas today, may prove more viable in the South if a strengthening of the judiciary accompanies democratic consolidation. Comparative evidence suggests that parliamentary-based strategies, deployed at the local, regional, national, and supra-national levels, have proven most effective, allowing for the articulation of a more ideological, more programmatic women's policy agenda which better captures and reflects the diversity of women's gender-based political claims. This strategy implies much more than promoting and backing "feminist candidates" for legislative office. It entails seeking progressive parliamentary allies (both female and male) who could be further sensitized to gender issues and weaving together electorally viable politico-partisan alliances. Clearly, given the tortured history of the relationship between women's movements and male-dominant political parties, especially in the Latin American context, this strategy represents a monumental challenge for feminists in the Americas.

Finally, a feminist revisioning of rights also compels us to move beyond liberal *integrationist* conceptions of citizenship, which merely entail the incorporation of women and other socially, culturally, economically, and/or politically disenfranchised groups into existing political-institutional arrangements designed for and by men of dominant ethnic groups and classes. That is, it cannot be enough for women to be selectively and marginally absorbed into Brazil's "New Republic" or Bill Clinton's "New Morning in America." As Elisabeth Souza-Lobo put it, the problem is that "women are not integrated [as citizens] into the nation in the same way if their integration rests, for example, on maternity and paid labor" (Souza-Lobo 1992:233). The challenge for feminists in the Americas, then, is to promote a *transformative* conception of citizenship, which, while grounded in the practices of civil society and daily life, would simultaneously strive to redraw the masculinist, racist, exploitative, and exclusionary parameters of politics and culture in the Americas.

ENDNOTES

1. The literature on women's movements and the politics of democratization in South America has explored the multiple opportunities and constraints for the transformation of gender power relations represented by transitions to civilian rule during the 1980s. See "As mulheres e os novos espaços democráticos na América Latina," *Revista de Ciencias Sociais* 1:2 (1987), special issue; ISIS Internacional, ed., *Transiciones: Mujeres en los procesos democráticos* (Santiago: ISIS Internacional, 1990); Jane Jaquette, ed., *The Women's Movement in Latin America: Feminism and the Transition to Democracy* (Boulder, CO: Westview Press, 1991); Elizabeth Jelin, ed., *Ciudadanía e identidad: Las mujeres en los movimientos sociales latinoamericanos* (Geneva: UNRISD, 1987); Patricia Chuchryk, "Protest, Politics and Personal Life: The Emergence of Feminism in a Military Dictatorship" (Ph.D. diss., York University, 1984); and Sonia E. Alvarez, *Engendering Democracy in Brazil: Women's Movements in Transition Politics* (Princeton, NJ: Princeton University Press, 1990). The new contradictions and

obstacles encountered by women's movements in the so-called "new democracies" of South America, however, have not been as thoroughly explored.

2. This is not to say that, over the course of the last century, Latin American feminists have engaged in both sub-national and supra-national movements. See, for example, Lynn Stoner, *From the House to the Streets: The Cuban Woman's Movement for Legal Reform, 1898–1940* (Durham: Duke University Press, 1991), and Francesca Miller, *Latin American Women and the Search for Social Justice* (Hanover: University Press of New England, 1991).

3. For an analysis of the articulation of feminist struggles in the North and South of the Americas, see, for example, Teresa Carrillo, "The Importance of International Solidarity for Mexican Women's Movements" (paper presented at the XVII International Congress of the Latin American Studies Association, September 24–27, 1992, Los Angeles, Calif.). See also Cynthia Enloe, *Bananas, Beaches & Bases: Making Feminist Sense of International Politics* (Berkeley: University of California Press, 1990).

4. On local government and the decentralization of the state in Latin America, see Alicia Zicardi, ed., *Ciudades y gobiernos locales en América Latina de los noventa* (Mexico, D.F.: FLACSO, Instituto Mora and Grupo Editorial Miguel Angel Porrúa, 1991); Dieter Nohlen, ed., *Descentralización política y consolidación democrática: Europa-América del Sur* (Madrid and Caracas: Síntesis and Editorial Nueva Sociedad, 1991); and Jordi Borja et al., eds., *Descentralización y democracia: Gobiernos locales en América Latina* (Santiago: CLACSO, 1989).

5. On the Workers' Party's efforts to construct "popular democratic" municipal administrations, see Margaret Keck, *The Workers' Party and Democratization in Brazil* (New Haven: Yale University Press, 1992); Sonia E. Alvarez, "'Deepening Democracy': Social Movement Networks, Constitutional Reform, and Radical Urban Regimes in Contemporary Brazil," in Robert Fischer and Joseph Kling, eds., *Mobilizing the Community: Local Politics in a Global Era* (Beverly Hills, CA: Sage Publications, 1993); Emir Sader, *Governar para todos: Uma avalição da gestão Luiza Erundina* (São Paulo: Editora Página Aberta, 1992); Jorge Bittar, ed., *O modo petista de governar* (São Paulo: Teoria & Debate, 1992); Lucio Kowarick and Andre Singer, "A experiencia do partido dos trabalhadores na prefeitura de São Paulo" (unpublished manuscript, 1992); and idem, "Democratizando a cidade: Iniciativa e participação popular começam a mudar a face autoritaria das prefeituras municipais no Brasil," *Proposata* 54 (August 1992), special issue.

6. See Steven Ellner, *Venezuela's Movimiento al Socialismo: From Guerrilla Defeat to Innovative Politics* (Durham, NC: Duke University Press, 1988); María Pilar García, "The Venezuelan Ecology Movement: Symbolic Effectiveness, Social Practices, and Political Strategies," Orlando Fals Borda, "Social Movements and Political Power in Latin America," and Eduardo Canel, "Democratization and the Decline of Urban Social Movements in Uruguay: A Political Institutional Account," in Arturo Escobar and Sonia E. Alvarez, eds., *The Making of Social Movements in Latin America: Identity, Strategy, and Democracy* (Boulder, CO: Westview Press, 1992); and Marta Harnecker et al., *Frente amplio: Los desafíos de una izquierda legal* (Montevideo: La República, 1991).

7. For an especially insightful and provocative reconceptualization of popular women's organizations and poor and working-class women's "interests" in Latin America, see Amy Conger Lind, "Power, Gender, and Development: Popular Women's Organizations and the Politics of Needs in Ecuador," in Arturo Escobar and Sonia E. Alvarez, eds., *The Making of Social Movements in Latin America: Identity, Strategy, and Democracy* (Boulder, CO: Westview Press, 1992). See also Teresa Caldeira, "Women, Daily Life and Politics," in Elizabeth Jelin, ed., *Women and Social Change in Latin America* (London: UNRISD and Zed Books,

1990); and Cecilia Blondet, *Las mujeres y el poder: Una historia de Villa El Salvador* (Lima: IEP, 1991). For a theoretical exploration of the multiple interventions and practices that shape women's interests and women's "needs," see Nancy Fraser, *Unruly Practices: Power, Discourse and Gender in Contemporary Social Theory* (Minneapolis: University of Minnesota Press, 1989). See also Caroline Moser, "Gender Planning in the Third World: Meeting Practical and Strategic Gender Needs," *World Development* 17:11 (1989), 1799–1825.

8. Many of Elisabeth Souza-Lobo's writings were collected and published posthumously in *A classe operária tem dois sexos: Trabalho, dominação e resistência* (São Paulo: Brasiliense, 1992).

9. Feminist ethnographers, of course, have been especially prominent in advancing a critical rethinking of fieldwork and the nature of feminist interventions in the lives of our research "subjects." See, for example, Sherna Berger Gluck and Daphne Patai, eds., *Women's Words: The Feminist Practice of Oral History* (New York: Routledge, 1991); Mary Margaret Fonow and Judith Cook, eds., *Beyond Methodology: Feminist Scholarship as Lived Research* (Bloomington: Indiana University Press, 1991); Chandra Mohanty, "Under Western Eyes: Feminist Scholarship and Colonial Discourse," in Chandra Talbpade Mohanty, Ann Russo, and Lourdes Torres, eds., *Third World Women and the Politics of Feminism* (Bloomington: Indiana University Press, 1991); Aihwa Ong, "Colonialism and Modernity: Feminist Representations of Women in Non-Western Societies," *Inscriptions* 3:4 (1988), 79–93; and, Diane L. Wolf, ed., *Feminist Dilemmas in Fieldwork* (forthcoming). In Latin America, however, we have yet to explore fully what *difference* the "interventions" of feminist scholars and activists makes in the lives and political consciousness of participants in the poor and working-class women's organizations with whom so many of us have worked. For suggestive analyses of the relationship between feminist groups and grassroots women's organizations in Latin America, see Norma Chinchilla, "Marxism, Feminism, and the Struggle for Democracy in Latin America," and Nancy Saporta Sternbach, Marysa Navarro-Aranguren, Patricia Chuchryk, and Sonia E. Alvarez, "Feminisms in Latin America: From Bogotá to San Bernardo," in Arturo Escobar and Sonia E. Alvarez, eds., *The Making of Social Movements in Latin America: Identity, Strategy, and Democracy* (Boulder, CO: Westview Press, 1992).

10. Feminist political theorists recently have taken up the question of how to rethink citizenship from the vantage point of women. For an incisive review and lucid critique of the principal strands of that debate, see especially Chantal Mouffe, "Feminism, Citizenship, and Radical Democratic Politics," in Judith Butler and Joan W. Scott, eds., *Feminists Theorize the Political* (New York: Routledge, 1992). See also Wendy Sarvasy, "Beyond the Difference vs. Equality Policy Debate: Postsuffrage Feminism, Citizenship and the Quest for a Feminist Welfare State," *Signs* 17:2 (Winter 1992), 329–362; Carole Pateman, *The Sexual Contract* (Stanford: Stanford University Press, 1988); Carole Pateman, *The Disorder of Women: Democracy, Feminism, and Political Theory* (London: Polity Press, 1989); Antje Weiner, "Citizenship: New Dynamics of an Old Concept. A Comparative Perspective" (paper presented at the XVII International Congress of the Latin American Studies Association, September 24–27, Los Angeles, Calif.); Teresita de Barbieri and Orlandina de Oliveira, "Nuevos sujetos sociales: La presencia política de las mujeres en América Latina," *Nueva Antropología* 8:3 (1986), 5–29; Mary G. Dietz, "Context Is All: Feminism and Theories of Citizenship," in Jill Conway et al., eds., *Learning About Women* (Ann Arbor: University of Michigan Press, 1989); Susan M. Okin, "Women, Equality, and Citizenship," *Queens Quarterly* 99:1 (1992), 56–71; and N. Yuval-Davis, "The Citizenship Debate: Women, Ethnic Processes and the State," *Feminist Review* 39 (1991), 58–68.

11. For a provocative analysis of the lack of "sexual citizenship" for women, especially poor, relatively uneducated heterosexual women, transvestites, and street children in Brazil in the context of the AIDS epidemic, see Donna Goldstein and Nancy Scheper-Hughes, "AIDS Activism, Women and Sexual Citizenship in Brazil" (paper presented at the conference on Women and the State in Brazil, University of California, Berkeley, February 19, 1993).

12. In post-South Central Los Angeles-U.S., one would have to insist that an antiracist feminist agenda aimed at the extension of meaningful civil rights to minority populations and especially women of color must still be at the forefront of our struggles to promote a "democratic transition" in the United States.

13. On violence against women in Brazil and feminist efforts to reform the criminal justice system, see especially Americas Watch, *Criminal Injustice: Violence Against Women in Brazil* (New York: Human Rights Watch, 1991); Mariza Correa, *Os crimes de paixão* (São Paulo: Brasiliense, 1981); and Danielle Ardaillon and Guita Derbert Grin, *Quando a vítima é mulher* (Brasília: Conselho Nacional dos Direitos da Mulher, 1987).

14. For an analysis of the multiple contradictions confronting the state and federal councils on the status of women in Brazil, see my "Contradictions of a 'Woman's Space' in a Male-Dominant State: The Political Role of the Commissions on the Status of Women in Postauthoritarian Brazil," in Kathleen Staudt, ed., *Women, International Development, and Politics: The Bureaucratic Mire* (Philadelphia: Temple University Press, 1990), and idem, *Engendering Democracy in Brazil: Women's Movements in Transition Politics* (Princeton: Princeton University Press, 1990), especially chapters nine and ten. See also Danielle Ardaillon, "Estado e mulher: Conselhos dos direitos da mulher e delegacias de defesa da mulher" (unpublished manuscript, 1989).

15. In the United States, feminist political theorists have undertaken a critical reexamination of this question. Linda Gordon's excellent anthology *Women, the State and Welfare* (Madison: University of Wisconsin Press, 1990) provides a comprehensive sampling of recent feminist historical and theoretical analysis of the welfare state. See also Catherine A. MacKinnon, *Toward a Feminist Theory of the State* (Cambridge: Harvard University Press, 1989); Kathy Ferguson, *The Feminist Case Against the Bureaucracy* (Philadelphia: Temple University Press, 1984); and Wendy Brown, "Finding the Man in the State," *Feminist Studies* 18:1 (Spring 1992), 7–34. These analyses are, however, centered on the gendered dimensions of the state in "advanced" capitalist societies. There are as yet few feminist theoretical treatments of the Latin American state, however. The relationship of women's movements to the state is the central theoretical question explored in my *Engendering Democracy in Brazil*.

BIBLIOGRAPHY

Alvarez, Sonia E. (1990*a*). *Engendering Democracy in Brazil: Women's Movements in Transition Politics*. Princeton, NJ: Princeton University Press.

———. (1990*b*). "Contradictions of a 'Women's Space' in a Male-Dominant State: The Political Role of the Commissions on the Status of Women in Postauthoritarian Brazil." In Kathleen Staudt, ed., *Women, International Development, and Politics: The Bureaucratic Mire*. Philadelphia: Temple University Press.

———. (1993). "'Deepening Democracy': Social Movement Networks, Constitutional Reform, and Radical Urban Regimes in Contemporary Brazil." In Robert Fischer and Joseph Kling, eds., *Mobilizing the Community: Local Politics in a Global Era*. Beverly Hills, CA: Sage Publications.

Americas Watch (1991). *Criminal Injustice: Violence Against Women in Brazil*. New York: Human Rights Watch.
Ardaillon, Danielle (1989). "Estado e mulher: Conselhos dos direitos da mulher e delegacias de defesa da mulher" (unpublished manuscript).
Ardaillon, Danielle, and Guita Derbert Grin (1987). *Quando a vítima é mulher*. Brasília: Conselho Nacional dos Direitos da Mulher.
Benería, Lourdes, and Shelley Feldman, eds. (1992). *Unequal Burden: Economic Crisis, Persistent Poverty and Women's Work*. Boulder, CO: Westview Press.
Bittar, Jorge, ed. (1992). *O modo petista de governar*. São Paulo: Teoria & Debate.
Blondet, Cecilia (1991). *Las mujeres y el poder: Una historia de Villa El Salvador*. Lima: Instituto de Estudios Peruanos.
Borda, Orlando Fals (1992). "Social Movements and Political Power in Latin America." In Arturo Escobar and Sonia E. Alvarez, eds., *The Making of Social Movements in Latin America: Identity, Strategy, and Democracy*. Boulder, CO: Westview Press.
Borja, Jordi et al., eds. (1989). *Descentralización y democracia: Gobiernos locales en América Latina*. Santiago: CLACSO.
Brown, Wendy (1992). "Finding the Man in the State." *Feminist Studies* 18:1 (Spring), 7–34.
Butler, Judith, and Joan W. Scott, eds. (1992). *Feminists Theorize the Political*. New York: Routledge.
Caldeira, Teresa (1990). "Women, Daily Life and Politics." In Elizabeth Jelin, ed., *Women and Social Change in Latin America*. London: United Nations Research Institute for Social Development (UNRISD) and Zed Books.
———. (1993). "Justice and Individual Rights: Challenges for Women's Movements and Democratization in Brazil." Paper presented at the conference on Women and the State in Brazil, University of California, Berkeley, February 19.
Canel, Eduardo (1992). "Democratization and the Decline of Urban Social Movements in Uruguay: A Political Institutional Account." In Arturo Escobar and Sonia E. Alvarez, eds., *The Making of Social Movements in Latin America: Identity, Strategy, and Democracy*. Boulder, CO: Westview Press.
Carrillo, Teresa (1992). "The Importance of International Solidarity for Mexican Women's Movements." Paper presented at the XVII International Congress of the Latin American Studies Association, Los Angeles, CA, September 24–27.
Chinchilla, Norma (1992). "Marxism, Feminism, and the Struggle for Democracy in Latin America." In Arturo Escobar and Sonia E. Alvarez, eds., *The Making of Social Movements in Latin America: Identity, Strategy, and Democracy*. Boulder, CO: Westview Press.
Chuchryk, Patricia (1984). "Protest, Politics and Personal Life: The Emergence of Feminism in a Military Dictatorship." Ph.D. dissertation, York University.
Conway, Jill et al., eds. (1989). *Learning About Women*. Ann Arbor: University of Michigan Press.
Correa, Mariza (1981). *Os crimes de paixão*. São Paulo: Brasiliense.
de Barbieri, Teresita, and Orlandina de Oliveira (1986). "Nuevos sujetos sociales: La presencia política de las mujeres en América Latina." *Nueva Antropología* 8(3), 5–29.
Dietz, Mary G. (1989). "Context Is All: Feminism and Theories of Citizenship." In Jill Conway et al., eds., *Learning About Women*. Ann Arbor: University of Michigan Press.
Ellner, Steven (1988). *Venezuela's Movimiento al Socialismo: From Guerrilla Defeat to Innovative Politics*. Durham, NC: Duke University Press.
Enloe, Cynthia (1990). *Bananas, Beaches & Bases: Making Feminist Sense of International Politics*. Berkeley: University of California Press.

Escobar, Arturo, and Sonia E. Alvarez, eds. (1992). *The Making of Social Movements in Latin America: Identity, Strategy, and Democracy*. Boulder, CO: Westview Press.

Ferguson, Kathy (1984). *The Feminist Case Against the Bureaucracy*. Philadelphia: Temple University Press.

Fischer, Robert, and Joseph Kling, eds. (1993). *Mobilizing the Community: Local Politics in a Global Era*. Beverly Hills, CA: Sage Publications.

Fonow, Mary Margaret, and Judith Cook, eds. (1991). *Beyond Methodology: Feminist Scholarship as Lived Research*. Bloomington: Indiana University Press.

Fraser, Nancy (1989). *Unruly Practices: Power, Discourse and Gender in Contemporary Social Theory*. Minneapolis: University of Minnesota Press.

García, María Pilar (1992). "The Venezuelan Ecology Movement: Symbolic Effectiveness, Social Practices, and Political Strategies." In Arturo Escobar and Sonia E. Alvarez, eds., *The Making of Social Movements in Latin America: Identity, Strategy, and Democracy*. Boulder, CO: Westview Press.

Gluck, Sherna Berger, and Daphne Patai, eds. (1991). *Women's Words: The Feminist Practice of Oral History*. New York: Routledge.

Goldstein, Donna, and Nancy Scheper-Hughes (1993). "AIDS Activism, Women and Sexual Citizenship in Brazil." Paper presented at the conference on Women and the State in Brazil, University of California, Berkeley, February 19.

Gordon, Linda (1990). *Women, the State and Welfare*. Madison: University of Wisconsin Press.

Harnecker, Marta et al. (1991). *Frente Amplio: Los desafíos de una izquierda legal*. Montevideo: La República.

ISIS Internacional, ed. (1990). *Transiciones: Mujeres en los procesos democráticos*. Santiago: ISIS Internacional.

Jaquette, Jane, ed. (1991). *The Women's Movement in Latin America: Feminism and the Transition to Democracy*. Boulder, CO: Westview Press.

Jelin, Elizabeth, ed. (1987). *Ciudadanía e identidad: Las mujeres en los movimientos sociales latinoamericanos*. Geneva: United Nations Research Institute for Social Development (UNRISD).

———. (1990). *Women and Social Change in Latin America*. London: United Nations Research Institute for Social Development (UNRISD) and Zed Books.

Keck, Margaret (1992). *The Workers' Party and Democratization in Brazil*. New Haven: Yale University Press.

Kowarick, Lucio, and Andre Singer (1992a). "Democratizando a cidade: Iniciativa e participação popular começam a mudar a face autoritaria das prefeituras municipais no Brasil." *Proposata* 54 (August), special issue.

Kowarick, Lucio, and Andre Singer (1992b). "A experiencia do partido dos trabalhadores na prefeitura de São Paulo" (unpublished manuscript).

Lind, Amy Conger (1992). "Power, Gender, and Development: Popular Women's Organizations and the Politics of Needs in Ecuador." In Arturo Escobar and Sonia E. Alvarez, eds., *The Making of Social Movements in Latin America: Identity, Strategy, and Democracy*. Boulder, CO: Westview Press.

MacKinnon, Catherine A. (1989). *Toward a Feminist Theory of the State*. Cambridge: Harvard University Press.

Marshall, T.H. (1950). *Citizenship and Social Class*. London: Cambridge University Press.

Miller, Francesca (1991). *Latin American Women and the Search for Social Justice*. Hanover: University Press of New England.

Mohanty, Chandra (1991). "Under Western Eyes: Feminist Scholarship and Colonial Discourse." In Chandra Talbpade Mohanty, Ann Russo, and Lourdes Torres, eds., *Third World Women and the Politics of Feminism*. Bloomington: Indiana University Press.
Mohanty, Chandra Talbpade, Ann Russo, and Lourdes Torres, eds. (1991). *Third World Women and the Politics of Feminism*. Bloomington: Indiana University Press.
Moser, Caroline (1989). "Gender Planning in the Third World: Meeting Practical and Strategic Gender Needs." *World Development* 17(11), 1799–1825.
Mouffe, Chantal (1992). "Feminism, Citizenship, and Radical Democratic Politics." In Judith Butler and Joan W. Scott, eds., *Feminists Theorize the Political*. New York: Routledge.
Nohlen, Dieter, ed. (1991). *Descentralización política y consolidación democrática: Europa-América del Sur*. Madrid and Caracas: Síntesis and Editorial Nueva Sociedad.
Okin, Susan M. (1992). "Women, Equality, and Citizenship." *Queens Quarterly* 99(1), 56–71.
Ong, Aihwa (1988). "Colonialism and Modernity: Feminist Representations of Women in Non-Western Societies." *Inscriptions* 3(4), 79–93.
Pateman, Carole (1988). *The Sexual Contract*. Stanford: Stanford University Press.
———. (1989). *The Disorder of Women*. London: Polity Press.
Revista de Ciencias Sociais (1987). "As mulheres e os novos espaços democráticos na América Latina." Vol. 1, no. 2, special issue.
Sader, Emir (1992). *Governar para todos: Uma avalição da gestão Luiza Erundina*. São Paulo: Editora Página Aberta.
Sarvasy, Wendy (1992). "Beyond the Difference vs. Equality Policy Debate: Postsuffrage Feminism, Citizenship and the Quest for a Feminist Welfare State." *Signs* 17:2 (Winter), 329–362.
Souza-Lobo, Elisabeth (1992). *A classe operária tem dois sexos: Trabalho, dominação e resistência*. São Paulo: Brasiliense.
Staudt, Kathleen, ed. (1990). *Women, International Development, and Politics: The Bureaucratic Mire*. Philadelphia: Temple University Press.
Sternbach, Nancy Saporta, Marysa Navarro-Aranguren, Patricia Chuchryk, and Sonia E. Alvarez (1992). "Feminisms in Latin America: From Bogotá to San Bernardo." In Arturo Escobar and Sonia E. Alvarez, eds., *The Making of Social Movements in Latin America: Identity, Strategy, and Democracy*. Boulder, CO: Westview Press.
Stoner, Lynn (1991). *From the House to the Streets: The Cuban Woman's Movement for Legal Reform, 1898–1940*. Durham: Duke University Press.
Weiner, Antje (1992). "Citizenship: New Dynamics of an Old Concept. A Comparative Perspective." Paper presented at the XVII International Congress of the Latin American Studies Association, September 24–27, Los Angeles, Calif.
Wolf, Diane L., ed. (Forthcoming). *Feminist Dilemmas in Fieldwork*.
Yuval-Davis, N. (1991). "The Citizenship Debate: Women, Ethnic Processes and the State." *Feminist Review* 39:58–68.
Zicardi, Alicia, ed. (1991). *Ciudades y gobiernos locales en América Latina de los noventa*. Mexico, D.F.: FLACSO, Instituto Mora and Grupo Editorial Miguel Angel Porrúa.

Part IV. Bibliography

Women's Struggles for Livelihood: An Annotated Bibliography, 1980–1992

REBECCA ABERS

Since the early 1980s, Latin America has been immersed in economic and political crisis. Out of this crisis, a vast democratization process emerged, fueled by grassroots sentiments. The rise of civil society has been articulated in diverse ways, ranging from the appearance of self-help organizations on the community level to national political movements. This rise has been coupled with the flowering of a new feminist consciousness in Latin America. Feminism is no longer considered an exclusively Northern or middle-class phenomenon, as countless locally based feminist groups and grassroots women's organizations have appeared. Concurrently, researchers from both North and South have shown a growing interest in Latin American women, especially poor women, and how they confront their own realities.

One major emphasis of this body of research has been what we call women's "struggles for livelihood": the ways in which women deal with often overwhelming social constraints in their everyday lives. The word "livelihood," on the one hand, is used to emphasize that poor women's actions are not necessarily limited to survival. Study after study shows that women attempt and often succeed in improving their lives. The word "struggle," on the other hand, connotes the extreme difficulty of these endeavors. Poor women are disadvantaged in so many ways that heroic efforts often meet with failure. Researchers studying women's livelihood struggles are ultimately concerned with "seeing through the eyes of the poor." Their work has common objectives: to discern how poor women define their own problems and to comprehend the actions they take in the effort to improve both their economic and their status positions.

This research reflects a new perspective on development in poor countries which rejects the mainstream, top-down, growth-maximizing paradigm. All too often, "successful" development policies emphasizing national economic growth have failed to significantly improve the economic and status positions of subaltern groups. Researchers have increasingly argued that economic growth must be accompanied by a restructuring of existing power relationships if meaningful development is to take place. This new emphasis on "empowerment" argues that as long as states and policy makers dogmatically impose development programs from above, power relations are reproduced. New research efforts concern how disadvantaged groups can obtain the materials that allow them to gain control of the development process.

Numerous studies from throughout Latin America show that mainstream development planning has been particularly damaging to the condition of poor women. Such planning rarely takes into account the specificities of local social relations, generally targets men, and often contributes to the breakdown of those few social mechanisms through which women maintain some control over their lives. Much recent research on women in Latin America has therefore attempted to shed light on the grassroots perspective and to study the ways in which women can and do empower themselves. The seeds of empowerment are in struggles for livelihood in the household, in the workplace, and in the local community as women address their everyday, practical needs. But gains at these scales can ultimately be articulated into larger scale political and social action which may strategically transform women's disadvantaged economic and status roles.

The annotated bibliography that follows contains a selection of references to this research. The bibliography is by no means comprehensive. Instead, it aims to provide the reader with an introduction to the literature, a general sense of the themes involved, and a preliminary step in the research process. In attempting to narrow the focus of this listing to *contemporary studies of poor women's attempts to cope with poverty,* many worthwhile works about Latin American women have been excluded, including histories that do not emphasize the recent period, cultural and literary studies, and general descriptive and statistical volumes. The bibliography contains only references to entire *books,* rather than articles, and only covers those works published since 1980. Furthermore, in making selections, I have given preference to works written in Spanish and Portuguese, so as to make accessible studies with which English-speaking audiences are less familiar. About two-thirds of the books included were published outside the United States.

The main body of the bibliography is divided into seven sections, each addressing different, although overlapping, aspects of women's livelihood struggles. The first section includes works which directly document poor women's perspectives on life through testimonies and narratives collected in interviews. A surprisingly large number of such works have been published in the last decade, suggesting an increased appreciation of the need to "see through the eyes of the poor."

Section II, works on the household economy and everyday life, addresses women's struggles for livelihood in the domestic sphere. Some repeated themes in this section concern women-headed households, time-budgeting, life cycles, attitudes about biological reproduction, the relationship between domestic and extra-domestic work, and the impact of economic crisis on household organization.

The following two sections refer to women's struggles for material well-being through income-generating work. Many of the early studies on "women in development" started from the premise that if women had greater economic participation, their livelihood conditions and status would improve. Over the course of the 1980s, however, countless studies have shown that women already participate extensively in the economy, both in terms of work that directly generates income and in terms of unpaid domestic and agricultural labor. Significantly, many of these studies have suggested that this participation in the workforce may be a burden rather than a benefit for poor women. Work outside the household can accentuate women's disadvantages unless domestic responsibilities are diminished.

The studies included in Section III refer to women's employment in urban areas. There are four subsections here including general studies, blue-collar work, informal work, and paid domestic labor. Section IV refers to women working in the countryside. This section includes studies of women's work in rural areas, ranging from unpaid peasant agriculture to wage labor in large-scale plantations.

While the works in the sections described above largely concern women struggling for livelihood in isolation, Section V considers women's attempts to improve their conditions through collective action. Some of the studies included in this section emphasize how women work to improve their practical conditions, forming self-help groups aimed at generating income or providing services to their families. Other references consider women's struggles on a larger scale, taking into account how women's political practice strives to reformulate the social and political institutions which structure their experience.

Section VI includes some general literature reviews, anthologies, and regional studies of Latin American women. Section VII lists other available bibliographies about Latin American women. Most of these bibliographies are limited to works published in a particular country of Latin America.

Two indexes are provided to facilitate the use of this bibliography. The **Country Index** lists citation numbers by country. The **Author Index** lists citation numbers by author. Where works were co-authored, the authors are indexed separately.

Works that apply to more than one category are cross-referenced. The annotation appears in the section most applicable to the work. A shorter form of the citation appears in the other applicable sections, with a cross-reference with the citation number where the complete reference and annotation can be found.

I. In Women's Voice: Testimonies and Narratives

1. **Alegría, Claribel, and D.J. Flakoll (1983).** *No me agarran viva: La mujer salvadoreña en lucha.* México, D.F.: Ediciones ERA. 146 p.

   This book, a collection of testimonies by those who knew "Eugenia," recounts her life story, her path to becoming a revolutionary, and her eventual assassination.

2. **Barrig, Maruja (1982).** *Convivir: La pareja en la pobreza.* Lima: Mosca Azul.

   The main body of this book provides detailed, first person accounts of the lives of three people living in the slums of Lima. The first two stories are independent accounts of the life histories of both members of a married couple. The third tells the story of a woman whose life in the slums of Lima could be considered an extreme example of marginality. The two women differ in that one has maintained a long-term marriage while the other has had mostly short-term relationships with men. Yet for each, coexistence with men is the prevailing theme of their stories. The book stems out of a larger research project, entailing interviews of 250 women. Several chapters are dedicated to analysis and discussion.

3. **Bronstein, Audrey (1982).** *The Triple Struggle: Latin American Peasant Women.* Boston, South End Press. 268 p.

   This collection of interviews aims at capturing the perceptions Latin American peasant women have of their "triple struggle" as citizens of underdeveloped countries, as peasants living in remote regions of those countries, and as women. Bronstein visited communities in Guatemala, El Salvador, Ecuador, Peru, and Bolivia. Most of the women interviewed worked in organized cooperatives or community development projects and were Spanish-speaking. Although the book's main theme concerns women's views of how the "development" experience has affected them, the interviews touch upon the most intimate details of everyday life and shed light on cultural and personal particularities of each woman's life experience. In addition to verbatim interviews, the book includes an overview of development in Latin America, descriptions of the five countries visited, as well as discussions of the issues raised by the women interviewed.

4. **Burgos-Debray, Elisabeth** (1984). *I, Rigoberta Menchú: An Indian Woman in Guatemala*. London: Verso. 251 p. Spanish edition: Burgos-Debray (1983). *Me llamo Rigoberta Menchú y así me nació la conciencia*. Barcelona: Editorial Vargos Vergara.

This book is based on interviews conducted by anthropologist Burgos-Debray with Rigoberta Menchú, an Indian peasant woman who became one of Guatemala's principal Indian rights activists and won the 1992 Nobel Peace Prize. Menchú's testimony provides insight into a variety of aspects of the life of native Guatemalans, ranging from a detailed description of culture and everyday life in a peasant village to a depiction of the political struggles faced by peasant groups, the process of consciousness raising, organization, and resistance.

5. **Centro de Investigación y Estudios de la Reforma Agraria** (1989). *La vida cotidiana de la mujer campesina*. Managua: CIERA. 239 p.

This work contains the life stories of eight peasant women, three household heads and five married women with children. A discussion section places the stories in the context of information collected through participant observation and interviews with other family members. This section discusses women's work, the role of female household heads, and relationships between couples. The political and social participation of peasant women is also examined, noting in particular that female heads of households were more active in political and social organizations. A comparison of the eight life stories are compared with respect to such topics as work and school during childhood, adolescence, love, relationships with men, reasons for marriage, and marital violence.

Chaney, Elsa M., and Mary García Castro, eds. (1989). *Muchachas No More: Household Workers in Latin America and the Caribbean*. See 36.

Conselho Estadual da Condição Feminina, Centro de Memória Sindical (1985). *Mulheres Operárias*. See 31.

6. **Fisher, Jo** (1993). *Out of the Shadows: Women, Resistance and Politics in South America*. London: Latin American Bureau. 228 p.

This book intersperses women's testimonies about their struggles to survive and organize during dictatorships in four Southern Cone countries with commentary by the author describing and analyzing the context of those testimonies. The work explores how, as authoritarian regimes in Argentina, Chile, Paraguay, and

Uruguay destroyed formal political structures, women's activism at the community level came to center stage. A chapter on the military coup in Chile recounts through women's voices the mass searches and arrests that occurred in poor neighborhoods and the slow rebuilding of community self-help and resistence movements. A chapter on union activism in Uruguay uses women's testimony to narrate the story of how women struggled to introduce their concerns into union discourse. The chapter on Paraguay deals with women's contribution to the Paraguayan Peasant Movement and describes the emergence of a separate women's commission. Two chapters on Argentina trace the evolution of the Las Madres de la Plaza de Mayo movement and describe how Argentine women have responded to unprecedented economic crisis with shopping strikes, a wages for household work campaign, and a variety of self-help groups. The book ends with testimonies by members of the Chilean Movimiento de Mujeres Pobladoras (MOMUPO) on how this movement—born in a Santiago shantytown—developed a "grassroots feminism" that differs in ideology from "middle-class" feminism.

7. **León, Kirai de (1986).** *Andar andando: Testimonio de mujeres del sector florestal.* Santiago: CEM; Pehuen. 190 p.

This book is about women and their impressions of life in the Chilean forestry sector. The first part discusses theoretical and methodological issues related to conducting life story research. This part considers the relationship between the interviewer and the interviewed, the biases motivating each, the process of analyzing life histories, and how the subordinate position of the women interviewed surfaces in the narratives. The second part contains the narratives of two women, in composite and edited form, which shed light on two different places where the wives of timber workers characteristically live: the forest encampment and the town. The third part contains four life stories, each accompanied by a short analysis. Though edited, the original order of these interviews was preserved, demonstrating the process through which the narrative was constructed.

8. **Mafei, Maristela (1985).** *Sangue na terra: A luta das mulheres.* São Paulo: Ícone Editora. 94 p.

This book contains testimonies of the widows of rural workers who were murdered in conflicts over land with large landowners in Brazil.

9. **O'Gorman, Frances, et al. (1984).** *Morro, mulher.* São Paulo: Edições Paulinas. English edition: *Hillside Women.* São Paulo: CEAR, 1985. 156 p.

This work collects thirty-five life stories of women from two favelas in Rio de Janeiro, Santa Marta and Rocinha. The stories are short and poignant tales of women of all ages and all walks of life within the favela. Most striking about the collection is the similarity of the stories told, each repeating variations of the same struggles against poverty, abandonment, and powerlessness.

10. **Patai, Daphne, ed. (1988).** *Brazilian Women Speak: Contemporary Life Stories.* New Brunswick, NJ: Rutgers University Press. 398 p.

This work contains twenty life stories as told by women from the cities of Northeastern Brazil and from Rio de Janeiro. They are divided into six sections. "Commitments" contains the stories of women who emphasized their dedication to some aspect of their lives. "Family Portrait" contains the stories of two sisters and their mother, each told separately. "Women's Work" focuses on poor women who emphasized the importance of their traditional, typically female occupations. "Revolutionaries" tells the stories of political activists and their experiences during the military dictatorship. "Good Girls" contains the stories of a twelve-year-old schoolgirl and a nineteen-year-old prostitute. "Entrepreneurs" tells the stories of three wealthy women: two white women who inherited their wealth and one black woman who worked her way up. Patai's introduction is as compelling as the life stories themselves, in particular her discussion of ethical issues surrounding field research and the problem of editing oral versions into prose.

11. **Raczynski, Dagmar, and Claudia Serrano (1985).** *Vivir la pobreza: Testimonios de mujeres.* Santiago: PISPAL; CIEPLAN. 337 p.

This book differs from the others in this section in that testimonies by women are accompanied by very detailed analysis. The work is based on interviews with poor urban women in the Conchalí neighborhood of Santiago, Chile. Each woman is both wife and mother in a family where the male household-head is frequently unemployed for long periods. Extended narratives transcribed from interviews and detailed descriptions of particular families are arranged for discussion around three basic themes: (1) the organization of the household, its "social trajectory," the domestic division of labor, and the relations among household members; (2) the specific condition of women, with emphasis on behavior with respect to biological reproduction and family planning; and (3) survival strategies of families faced with long-term unemployment. Chapters and appendixes cover the macro-social conditions of Chile at the time of the study, methodological approaches, and descriptions of each household investigated. In their conclusions, the authors note that the typical poor, urban Chilean woman is virtually relegated to work within the home, only entering into the external workforce in times of extreme economic necessity. As unemployment soared in Chile at the time of the study (1983), use-value production, a typically female task, became increasingly important for family welfare.

Randall, Margaret (1980). *No se puede hacer la revolución sin nosotras.* See 60.

12. **Randall, Margaret (1985).** *Women Brave in the Face of Danger: Photographs of and Writings by Latin and North American Women.* Trumansburg, NY: Crossing Press. 128 p.

This book includes photographs, short testimonies, poems, and narratives of women from North and South America. The women range from famous composers and writers to poor peasants and city dwellers.

13. **Valdés, Ximena, et al. (1983).** *Historias testimoniales de mujeres del campo.* Santiago: Programa de Estudios y Capacitación de la Mujer Campesina e Indígena, Círculo de Estudios de la Mujer, Academia de Humanismo Cristiano. 339 p.

This book presents fifteen testimonies of women in five different rural areas of Chile: (1) the indigenous peasant communities of the Andean highlands which have recently suffered the intrusion of the copper extraction industry; (2) Chile's central region, which is increasingly characterized by tenant farming; (3) forest encampments where the primary activity is wood extraction; (4) Mapuche communities under the constant threat of elimination by Chile's "national society"; and (5) the Chilote region. Each set of narratives is accompanied by descriptions of the region including maps and glossaries.

Valdés, Ximena, and Paulina Matta (1986). *Oficios y trabajos de las mujeres de Pomaire.* See 46.

II. The Household Economy and Everyday Life

Barrig, Maruja (1982). *Convivir: La pareja en la pobreza.* See 2.

Benería, Lourdes, and Martha Roldan (1987). *The Crossroads of Class and Gender.* See 30.

14. **Bourque, Susan C., and Kay Barbara Warren (1981).** *Women of the Andes: Patriarchy and Social Change in Two Peruvian Towns.* Ann Arbor: University of Michigan Press. 241 p.

This book, which combines ethnographic analysis with detailed theoretical discussion, is about sexual hierarchies and social change in Peru. The research is based on fieldwork in two small towns on the western slopes of the Andes, Mayobamba in the district of Checras and Chiuchin in the district of Santa Lenora. Major themes in the work are the relationship between institutional structures subordinating women and negotiation on the part of women toward the transformation of their social roles; men and women's differing perceptions of sexual subordination; the relationships between gender equality and the sexual division of labor; the relative importance of class and ethnicity with respect to gender; and the changes in women's status as urbanization and capitalist expansion take place.

The first chapter analyzes the biographical portraits of women with different class, marital status, and employment backgrounds. The next two chapters examine analytical approaches to women's subordination and social change, present key conceptual definitions, and review contemporary approaches to the cross-cultural study of women. The remaining chapters comprise a comparative analysis of women's lives in the two towns, considering life cycles, marriage, household organization, domestic life, attitudes toward fertility, the sexual division of labor within rural economic structures, the differing experiences of men and women within the class system, structures constraining women's political participation, and the impact of social change on men and women in rural communities.

Centro de Investigación y Estudios de la Reforma Agraria (1989). *La vida cotidiana de la mujer campesina.* See 5.

Chant, Sylvia (1991). *Women and Survival in Mexican Cities: Perspectives on Gender, Labour Markets, and Low-Income Households.* See 21.

Cisneros, Antonio C., et al. (1984). *La mujer trabajadora.* See 25.

Ehlers, Tracy Bachrach (1990). *Silent Looms: Women and Production in a Guatemalan Town.* See 27.

15. Jelin, Elizabeth, and María del Carmen Feijoó (1980). *Trabajo y familia en el ciclo de vida femenino: El caso de los sectores populares de Buenos Aires.* Estudios CEDES, vol. 3, no. 8/9. Buenos Aires: Centro de Estudios de Estado y Sociedad. 85 p.

This book, based on research into the biographies of poor women in Buenos Aires, emphasizes the type of work women do at different periods in their lives, domestic organization, and time management. The major theme is that transition stages in the family life cycle are of central importance in the lives of women. The first chapter compares the childhoods of women from a variety of backgrounds. The second chapter discusses marriage and the formation of the household, stressing the everyday problems faced by the "wife-housewife-mother" and the domestic strategies she uses to confront them. The concluding chapter places the issues raised in the historical-social context of Peru and considers the impact of the economic recession on everyday life.

16. Magendzo, Salomón, et al. (1983). *"Y así fue creciendo—": La vida de la mujer pobladora.* Santiago: Programa Interdisciplinario de Investigaciones en Educación, Academia de Humanismo Cristiano. 251 p.

This book discusses a project implemented in a poor area of Santiago aimed at improving women's participation in popular organizations and promoting reflection and consciousness raising about the condition of women in popular sectors. The main body of the book describes a workshop in which a group of women were urged to discuss their problems and preoccupations and consider possible solutions. In the concluding chapter, the authors compile a list of verbal expressions and manners of explanation that appeared repeatedly throughout the workshop.

These are categorized according to a series of themes: machismo, sexuality, isolation and loneliness, aging, work, children, women's rights, jealousy, and infidelity.

Raczynski, Dagmar, and Claudia Serrano (1985). *Vivir la pobreza.* See 11.

Rojas, Raquel (1986). *Kuña Paraguay: La mujer en la domesticidad rural.* See 43.

17. **Valdés, Teresa (1988).** *Veníd, benditas de mi padre: Las pobladoras, sus rutinas y sus sueños.* Santiago: FLACSO. 396 p.

This book addresses the worldview of poor, urban women in relation to reproductive behavior. The work is an analytical consideration of a collection of life stories obtained firsthand through interviews with women in Santiago, Chile. One chapter considers theoretical and methodological issues and another describes the women interviewed, placing them in historical context. The final two chapters outline two different, but not necessarily contradictory, readings of the data collected. The first reading is a "transversal" analysis, based on the life-cycle concept, where important transition stages or momentous decisions in women's lives (such as marriage, children, etc.) are identified. The common routines of everyday life that fill the gaps between transitions are also examined. The second reading is a "longitudinal" analysis, through which the trajectory of each woman's life is considered as a distinct process. The author formulates three ideal types of "reproductive behavior projects" which are to represent the total of life stories analyzed.

III. Urban Women's Work

General Studies

18. **Aguiar, Neuma, ed. (1984).** *Mulheres na força de trabalho na América Latina: Análises qualitativas.* Petrópolis, Rio de Janeiro: Editora Vozes. 284 p.

In the introduction to this collection of essays on women and work in Latin America, Neuma Aguiar explores the theoretical and methodological questions involved in studying women's work, considering problems in defining productive work, household heads, periods of reference, life cycles, and identifying household activities.

Beatriz M. Alasia de Heredia, Maria France Garcia, and Afrânio R. Garcia, Jr. write on the role of women in peasant households and intrahousehold relations among small producers linked to the sugar plantations of Northeastern Brazil. E. A. Cebotarev presents the results of a study of time budgeting by peasant women in Brazil, Venezuela, and Mexico, considering the relationship between social roles and both domestic and nondomestic activities and discussing the ideological basis for such relationships. Ruth Sautu discusses women's participation in industrial agriculture and seasonal migration in northeastern Argentina. Maria Coleta F.A. de Oliveira considers itinerant laborers and resident farmworkers in the coffee and sugar plantations of São Paulo, emphasizing women's livelihood strategies. Magdalena León de Leal and Carmen Diana Deere consider the sexual division of labor in Colombian communities in transition between peasant production and proletarianized labor. Esther Hermitte and Malvina Segre examine women working in textile weaving in northeastern Argentina, their relation to the national market, and the patron-client relations that persist between weavers and capitalist middlemen. Beatriz Elba Schmukler discusses the role of women who work in small groceries and shops selling basic staples. Arakcy Martins Rodrigues writes on women in blue-collar families in greater São Paulo. Zahidé Machado Neto writes on female children and adolescent workers in a proletarian neighborhood of Salvador, Brazil, and their double exploitation as both women and children. The volume concludes with Neuma Aguiar's theoretical framework for understanding the productive activities realized by women within the home.

19. **Aguiar, Neuma, ed. (1990).** *Mujer y crisis: Respuestas ante la recesión.* Rio de Janeiro/Caracas: DAWN/MUDAR/Nueva Sociedad. 131 p.

The essays in this volume address the impact of economic recession and structural adjustment policies on women in Latin America, emphasizing the effect on women's participation in the labor market. Neuma Aguiar provides a general outline of the effect of the crisis on women's participation in the labor force and household composition, and the impact of social policy on women. Orlandina de Oliveira considers women's participation in the labor force in Mexico during the 1970s and 1980s, emphasizing the effects of modernization, inequality, economic restructuring, and recession. Zuleica Lopes Cavalcanti de Oliveira studies the effects of economic and social change on the incorporation of family members into the workforce in Brazil, comparing families of different sizes and types and in different regions of the country. Suzana Prates discusses women's participation in the workforce in Uruguay over the last three decades, arguing that participation has not only grown during phases of both economic expansion, but also during periods of recession. Claudia Serrano M. considers women's subsistence strategies in the context of rising unemployment in Chile, discussing changes in household organization, the formation of women's organizations, and women's relationship with state social programs. Cheywa Spindel discusses the impact of the recession of 1981–1984 on women's wage labor in Brazil, noting that women's relative participation in the labor force increased during that period and continued to increase during the recuperation period following the recession.

20. **Barrig, Maruja, ed. (1985).** *Mujer, trabajo y empleo.* Lima: Asociación de Defensa y Capacitación Legal. 294 p.

This book contains papers presented at the seminar "Mujer, Trabajo y Empleo" sponsored by ADEC in October 1985. Each article is accompanied by detailed critiques and commentaries by three or four other authors. Nora Galer discusses reproductive work, presenting some conceptual tools to help understand the sexual division of labor, the image of the family, and the social conceptualization of work. Comments are provided by Jeanine Anderson, Amelia Fort, and Roberto Miró Quesada. Delma Del Valle writes on the effects of economic crisis on women and employment and the tendency for the female working population to be pushed into the informal sector. Comments are made by Narda Henríquez, Joel Jurado, and Franciso Cerdera.

Three articles on women in manufacturing are included in the collection. Ana María Yáñez discusses the reasons capitalist enterprise favors employing female labor. Virginia Guzmán and Patricia Portocarrero discuss the sexual division of labor within the production organization of the electronics industry. Violeta Sara-Lafosse writes on home workers in the textile industry. Commentaries on these three articles are presented by Marcela Chueca, Oscar Dancourt, and Pedro Galin. Eliana Chávez discusses women in the informal sector and the factors behind women's participation in ambulatory commerce. Romeo Grompone, Violeta Sara-Lafosse, Carlos Wendorff, and Félix Lossro comment on this final article.

21. **Chant, Sylvia** (1991). *Women and Survival in Mexican Cities: Perspectives on Gender, Labour Markets and Low-Income Households*. Manchester: Manchester University Press. 270 p.

This study explores the complex interrelationships between household structure and women's labor force participation in Mexico, based on three case studies of cities with different types of economies: Querétaro, León, and Puerto Vallarta. The author argues that most research on women's labor force participation focuses either on supply or on demand factors: "family-centered" research considers how gender relations in the household affect the supply of women workers while "workplace-centered" studies examine the gender division of labor in formal and informal labor markets.

Chant's contribution is to explore both sides of this equation at the same time. On the one hand, she considers the kinds of jobs women have in each of the three cities and the general market conditions under which women's employment levels rise and fall. On the other hand, she correlates a number of household variables—such as household structure, education, migrant status, and fertility rates—with women family members' participation in the labor force. The author then explores how the two questions are related in a variety of ways, analyzing how women's labor force participation affects household structure and organization, and attempting to understand whether supply or demand factors are more important in determining women's likelihood of being employed outside the home. The study also includes a longitudinal analysis of the Querétaro case—based on earlier research by the author—which examines how women's participation changed during the recession of the 1980s.

22. **Cooper, Jennifer, et al.** (1989). *Fuerza de trabajo femenina urbana en México*. 2 vols. Mexico, D.F.: Coordinación de Humanidades, UNAM; Miguel Angel Porrúa. 805 p.

This work is an outcome of a seminar on the urban female workforce in Mexico held at the UNAM School of Political and Social Sciences in November 1987. It is divided into two volumes: "Características y Tendencias" and "Participación Económica y Política." The first volume contains two sections. The first section, which covers the general characteristics of urban women's work in Mexico, includes six case studies. Orlandina de Oliveira discusses women's employment in Mexico during the recent economic recession. Rodolfo Cruz Piñeiro and René Zenteno Quintero write on the socio-demographic characteristics of women workers in Tijuana. Beatriz Castilla, José Gamboa, Arcadio Sabido, and Beatriz Torres discuss women's work in Yucatán. Edgar López Garza's essay concerns discrimination, segregation, and inequality in the case of women workers in Nuevo León. Irma Martínez Jasso's chapter considers the wage differentials between men and women in Monterrey. Teresa Rendon and Carlos Salas supply the commentaries on the essays in the first section.

The second section of the first volume includes three essays on demographic change and women's participation in the labor force. Carlos Welti discusses women's economic participation and fertility in Mexico City. Alejandro Córdova, Gustavo Leal, and Carolina Martínes consider the effects of demographic change on the health of women workers in urban areas. Rodolfo Corona, Ana María Chávez, and Héctor Hernández Bringas write on female interstate migration between 1950 and 1980. Commentaries are offered by Brígida García and Josefina Aranda Bezaury.

The second volume contains three sections on women in different economic sectors. Five chapters compose the section on women working in industry: María de la Luz Macías writes on the gender division of labor and wage differentials in manufacturing in the Federal District, Guadalajara, and Monterrey. María Patricia Fernández-Kelly considers technology and women's employment on the Mexican-U.S. border. Rubi Jiménez Betancourt's essay concerns recent changes in women's participation in maquiladora industries. José Antonio Alonso considers urban marginality and clandestine female labor. Jussara Teixeira writes on the health of women industrial workers. Commentaries are supplied by Patricia Arias and Enrique de la Garza Toledo.

Five chapters appear in the section on women in the service sector. Following a general overview by Estela Suárez, Pablo Serrano Vallejo presents a case study of women working in telephone services. Guadalupe Cortés discusses Telmex operators. María Eugenia Valdés Vega considers primary school teachers in Mexico City. Mercedes Carreras discusses women in academe. Elia Ramírez comments.

Two essays focus on organizing and resistance among urban women workers. Sara Lovera presents an overview of workers' organizations, and Jennifer Cooper considers the relationship between technological change and resistance among telephone operators. Commentaries are provided by Esperanza Tuñon and Carmen Lugo.

The final section includes four chapters on women's work and social and cultural change. Alejandra Massolo considers women's role in the formation of popular urban social movements. José Manuel Valenzuela Arce writes on the daily life and culture of women working in the maquiladoras of northern Mexico. María Antonieta Torres Arias uses concepts from Freudian psychoanalysis to examine women's sense of identity. Marta Lamas discusses the social basis for the gender division of labor and wage differentials. Eli Bartra and Graciela Hierro provide the commentaries on this section.

23. **Bruschini, Maria Cristina A.** (1985). *Mulher e trabalho: Uma avaliação da década da mulher*. São Paulo: NOBEL/Conselho Estadual da Condição Feminina. 147 p.

This book attempts to assess the improvements made in Brazil during the U.N. Women's Decade (1975–1985). Official statistics are analyzed to identify changes in women's participation in the workforce. Several other factors are also considered (with emphasis on São Paulo state) including family demographics and education, as well as broader issues such as the sexual division of labor, wage inequities, working conditions, unemployment, and social welfare. A special section is devoted to the most disadvantaged groups of women workers, emphasizing the position of domestics, rural workers, women household heads, and black women.

24. **Bruschini, Maria Cristina A., and Fúlvia Rosemberg, eds.** (1982). *Trabalhadoras do Brasil*. Volume 2 of *Vivencia: Historia, sexualidade e imagens femininas organizadoras*. São Paulo: Brasiliense; Fundação Carlos Chagas/Ford Foundation. 203 p.

This collection contains seven essays on Brazilian working women of diverse kinds. In their introductory chapter, Bruschini and Rosemberg discuss women's participation in the labor market, "occupational ghettos," and wage discrimination in particular. Selene Herculano dos Santos writes on university-educated women in government enterprises. Jane Felipe Beltrão analyzes the relationship between work and the body (both its social representation and its physical use) for women working in Brazil nut processing factories in Belém, Pará. Heleieth Iara Saffioti and Vera Botta Ferrante examine the lives and work of women in rural households of São Paulo. Stela Fernandes Eigenheer's considers the transformation of labor relations between peasants and large landholders and its effect on the sexual division of labor of peasant families in the Alto Jequitinhonha region of Minas Gerais. Maria Ignez Silveira Paulilo analyzes rural women workers, both family laborers and itinerant farmworkers, in an agricultural region of the northeastern state of Paraíba. Jany Chiriac and Solange Padilha discuss the characteristics and limitations of urban women's organizations.

25. **Cisneros, Antonio C., Carlos Koch, and Germán La Fuente** (1984). *La mujer trabajadora: Sus necesidades y criterios sobre la vida familiar*. Estudios de Promoción Femenina no. 3. La Paz: Centro de Investigaciones Sociales. 131 p.

This book presents the results of a study of working women's family life, reproduction, family planning, and work, based on interviews with 600 working women. The book considers the general labor profile in Bolivia, women's participation in the workforce, working women's legal rights, women's health service needs, family relations in households where women work, time management, and domestic tasks, the perceptions of women about their health, men's perceptions of women's work, and actions which would improve the health and family life of working women.

26. **Costa, Letícia B.** (1984). *Participação da mulher no mercado de trabalho*. São Paulo: Instituto de Pesquisas Econômicas. 153 p.

The first part of this book is a historical analysis of women's participation in Brazil's labor force between 1940 and 1977. The first section includes a descriptive analysis of aggregated data in terms of female labor supply and demand. The second section aims at a more explanatory analysis, establishing correlations between labor force participation and women's domestic work, socioeconomic position, family structure, education, and salaries. The shorter, second part of the book includes a similar analysis with regard to the evolution of women's participation in the labor force in São Paulo state as reflected in data from the 1970 and 1980 censuses.

27. **Ehlers, Tracy Bachrach** (1990). *Silent Looms: Women and Production in a Guatemalan Town*. Boulder, CO: Westview Press. 177 p.

Based on more than a decade's research, this anthropological study considers how rapid economic expansion and increasing political violence affected women's lives in a Guatemalan town. San Pedro Sacatepéquez is a busy Indian commercial center where women constitute the majority of the traditional labor force, particularly in textile production. The author explores how, as rapid changes occurred there, women lost much of the traditional autonomy they had selling their products on the local market. She also examines how gender relations changed as intermarriage began to replace the more balanced relations of indigenous couples with Ladino *machismo*. Chapters include a general ethnography of the town, a detailed case study of female family labor in a local general store, an examination of the activities of female traders and of women in the small-scale weaving industry, and a lengthy examination of relationships between women and men. This final chapter explores a variety of issues related to male authority, courtship, marriage, parallel marriage, and women's feelings about sex.

Jelin, Elizabeth, and María del Carmen Feijoó (1980). *Trabajo y familia en el ciclo de vida femenino*. See 15.

28. **Souza-Lobo, Elisabeth** (1991). *A classe operária tem dois sexos: Trabalho, dominação e resistência*. São Paulo: Brasiliense.

This volume—produced after the author's tragic death in 1991—compiles the principal theoretical works of Souza-Lobo in three areas. The first area concerns the relationship between the sociology of factory work and gender. Here she analyzes the gender division of labor in factories and in union organizing. She also considers the relationship between factory work and domestic work and studies the social consciousness and self-representations of women workers. One essay compares some of these issues with parallel cases in Japan. The second area encompasses the sociology of knowledge. Here, Souza-Lobo explores how the social sciences have theorized about women workers, the sexual division of labor, the relations between men and women, the category of "gender," and "women's history." The third area concerns women's social movements and questions of equality and difference. She writes on the history of feminism in Brazil; the specificity of the women's movement with respect to other movements; new forms of women's resistance and discourse; the construction of women's citizenship and its expression in the new Brazilian constitution of 1988; and new research goals for the study of women's movements. This last section also provides theoretical material on women's identity and on inequality. A final essay explores the relationship between women's participation in social movements and their political representation.

29. **Zylberstajn, Hélio, Carmen Silvia Pagotto, and José Pastoré (1985).** *A mulher e o menor na força de trabalho.* São Paulo: NOBEL; Ministério do Trabalho. 168 p.

This study concerns women and children workers in families living in extreme poverty, defined as earning less than one-fourth of the official minimum salary per month. The book includes a bibliography of studies about women and children. The main body of the work analyzes official statistics in order to identify where working women and children live, what their principal occupations are, how many hours they work, how much they earn, what their contribution to the family income is, and what other factors characterize families in which women and children work. Several case studies of poor families in which children work are also presented.

Blue-Collar Work

30. **Benería, Lourdes, and Martha Roldan (1987).** *The Crossroads of Class and Gender: Industrial Homework, Subcontracting, and Household Dynamics in Mexico City.* Chicago: University of Chicago Press. 204 p.

The major theme of this work on women informal industrial workers in Mexico is how class and gender are articulated in both household and workplace. The authors examine a series of focal issues including the relationship between female employment and the larger economy; the connection between the domestic market and sexual divisions of labor; the process of female proletarianization; and changes in women's awareness of their subordinate position in society. The authors analyze the macroeconomic structure in which subcontracting and women's work are placed. They also detail the household conditions in which homework takes place and the reasons why women predominate in this sector. A historical analysis of the evolution of family, class, and gender issues further explains women's insertion in industrial homework. Finally, the authors consider in-depth the relationship between women's work and the renegotiation of gender relations in the household and the factors constraining the women's struggle.

31. Conselho Estadual da Condição Feminina, Centro de Memória Sindical (1985). *Mulheres operárias.* São Paulo: Nobel. 128 p.

This book contains the impressions and stories of five women with regard to their experiences in union organizing. In four sections, each woman's testimony about a particular theme is presented: (1) trajectories leading them to work in the factory; (2) the double workday at home and in the factory; (3) concepts of what it means to be a women; (4) specific experiences with the union. In a final section, a conversation among the five women is reproduced.

Moser, Anita (1985). *A nova submissão: Mulheres da zona rural no processo de trabalho industrial.* See 42.

32. Saffioti, Heleieth I. B. (1981). *Do artesanal ao industrial: A exploração da mulher. Um estudo de operárias têxteis e de confecções no Brasil e nos Estados Unidos.* São Paulo: Editora HUCITEC. 184 p.

The main body of this book discusses the changes in Brazil's textile and garment industries over time, and the consequent changes in the role of women working in those sectors. The first chapter discusses the historical trends of women's participation in Brazil's labor force and the effects of mechanization and industrialization on this participation. Wage discrimination is also discussed. The second chapter describes the industrialization of the São Paulo region, considering employment structure, agricultural modernization, and urbanization. The third chapter provides an account of the textile industry in Brazil, particularly São Paulo. The fourth, fifth, and sixth chapters are based on the analysis of fieldwork carried out in two factories. Details on the livelihood conditions of the factory women are discussed, including analysis of family relationships, education, and income. The women's work, lives, and their expectations for the future are also considered. The seventh chapter compares Brazilian conditions with those of North American women textile workers. The author notes that despite the higher living standards and greater legal status of the North American workers, they bear much in common with Brazilian working women, in particular their subordinated position with respect to men and their "double workday." A major theme of the book is that modernization, rather than improving the status of women, reproduces their subordinated condition. The research in the United States was carried out in collaboration with Helen Icken Safa.

Souza-Lobo, Elisabeth (1991). *A classe operária tem dois sexos: Trabalho, dominação e resistência.* See 28.

33. **Wilson, Fiona** (1990). *De la casa al taller: Mujeres, trabajo y clase social en la industria textil y del vestido, Santiago, Tangamandapio*. Zamora: El Colegio de Michoacán. 238 p.

The author discusses the introduction of a new manufacturing industry in a central western Mexican community and its effects on gender relations and family structure. Much of the first part of the book concerns the political-economic context of this process: industrial restructuring and expansion, urbanization and semi-proletarianization, and the production process of workshop industries. The author also considers labor relations and resistance strategies in detail. The second part of the book emphasizes the impact of these changes on family life. One chapter is devoted to class and gender relations outside the workshops, in particular family and community relations. In the final chapter, synthesizing her case study, the author constructs a preliminary model of the expansion of workshop industry and its effects on gender relations.

Informal Work

34. **Berger, Marguerite, and Mayra Buvinić, eds.** (1988). *La mujer en el sector informal: Trabajo femenino y microempresa en América Latina*. Caracas: Editorial Nueva Sociedad. (English edition: *Women's Ventures: Assistance to the Informal Sector in Latin America*. West Hartford, CT: Kumarian Press, 1989).

This collective work on women in microenterprises in Latin America contains essays covering four basic areas: (1) a review of the informal sector; (2) training and technical assistance policies; (3) case studies of microenterprise credit programs; and (4) evaluations of the success of assistance programs in reaching women. As a whole, the essays are practical in character, aimed at formulating and evaluating assistance programs.

The chapter by Margaret Lycette and Karen White reviews the importance of credit for women and the problems women have in gaining access to credit. Jaime Mezzera provides a general theoretical framework for studying the informal sector. Silvia Escobar's case study of La Paz, Bolivia, places this framework into a particular context, describing the informal economy as a whole in that city.

Several articles discuss particular kinds of programs for microenterprises: María Otero reviews the "solidarity group mechanism," Cressida S. McKean discusses technical assistance and training, and María Mercedes Placencia considers the effectiveness of training programs, using for reference two programs in Ecuador. A series of case studies of microenterprise credit programs are included as well: Rebecca Lynn Reichmann compares two integrated private voluntary associations, ADEMI in the Dominican Republic and Progreso in Lima, Peru, evaluating their respective abilities to reach women; Luz María Abreu describes a woman-specific credit program in rural Dominican Republic; Women's World Banking describes its international support program for women entrepreneurs, while Margarita Guzmán and María Clemencia Castro evaluate a particular Women's World Banking project in Cali, Colombia; María Eugenia Arias evaluates the Peruvian Rural Development Fund's effectiveness in including women; essays by Jorge F. Landívar and by Mayra Buvinić, Marguerite Berger, and Cecilia Jaramillo evaluate the Ecuadorian Development Foundation's success in promoting microenterprises, comparing the results for male- and female-owned businesses. The Spanish edition also contains an article by Mayra Buvinić, Marguerite Berger, and Stephen Gross, which presents the results of an ICRW evaluation of the Peruvian Urban Small Enterprise Development Fund's ability to include women.

35. **Bunster, Ximena, and Elsa M. Chaney (1985).** *Sellers and Servants: Working Women Working in Lima, Peru.* New York: Praeger. 258 p.

This work presents and interprets the results of a study of women migrants in Lima, Peru. The book concentrates on street vendors and domestic servants. The study was conducted using an innovative research technique, described in the Epilogue. The authors found that combining the use of photographs with open-ended interviews gave depth to the conversations and helped those interviewed to be more precise in their responses.

The first chapter addresses a series of issues related to domestic workers, including the persistence of domestic service in industrializing society, the history of servant occupations in Peru, the migration experience, and domestic service in the context of the Lima labor market at large. The second chapter explores the experience of women street vendors, discussing their personal characteristics, their own impressions of their experience, and identifying a series of difficulties street vendors face in establishing and maintaining business. The viability of cooperative markets in improving business conditions is also explored. The third chapter locates women workers within the context of motherhood, family, and community, discussing the problems of combining work and family, housing issues, and the links working women maintain with community groups. The fourth chapter addresses the exploitation of working children, considering children's views of why they work, how work contributes to a child's socialization in sexual inequality, solidarity and class consciousness among working children, their perceptions of marriage and fertility, health care, schooling, and the views of working mothers about the work of their children.

Paid Domestic Work

Bunster, Ximena, and Elsa M. Chaney (1985). *Sellers and Servants. See 35.*

36. **Chaney, Elsa M., and Mary García Castro, eds. (1989).** *Muchachas No More: Household Workers in Latin America and the Caribbean.* Philadelphia: Temple University Press. 486 p.

This book is the first major anthology on domestic workers in Latin America. In the introduction, Elsa Chaney and Mary García Castro outline several important issues in the study of women domestic workers. The main body of the volume contains twenty-two contributions divided into five sections. Part I contains three historical pieces. Elizabeth Kuznesof provides a history of domestic service in Latin America between 1492 and 1980. B.W. Higman examines the history of domestic work in Jamaica, and Sandra Lauderdale Graham writes on domestic workers in Rio de Janeiro during the 1870s. Part II contains six case studies of domestic service today. Mónica Gogna writes on domestics in Buenos Aires. Mary García Castro considers the case of Bogotá. Margo L. Smith investigates former domestic workers in Peru. Cornelia Butler Flora examines the representation of domestics in the Latin American *fotonovela*. Patricia Mohammed discusses household servants in the Caribbean and Shellee Colen discusses the experience of West Indian domestic workers in New York City.

Part III consists of three chapters on the relationship between domestics and the feminist movement in general. Isis Durate considers the relationship between middle-class women and domestics in the Dominican Republic. Mary Goldsmith explores domestic workers' organizations in Mexico. Hildete Pereira de Melo discusses the conditions of domestic workers in Rio de Janeiro and the relationship between domestics and middle-class feminists who employ them.

Part IV includes five chapters on domestic workers' organizations and the state. Suzana Prates examines whether such organizations in Montevideo succeed in increasing collective consciousness among domestic workers. Thea Schellekens and Anja van de Schoot consider the process of organizing domestic workers in Peru. Thelma Gálvez and Rosalba Todaro consider the way the organization of paid domestic labor constrains worker mobilization. Magdalena León describes and analyzes the experience of a domestic worker's project in Colombia. Elena Gil Izquierdo writes on the impact of the Federation of Cuban Women in educating domestic workers in Cuba.

Part V contains testimonies and narratives by domestic workers themselves. The chapter by Anazir Maria de Oliveira and Odete Maria de Conceição (with Hildete Pereira de Melo) outlines the history of the domestic workers' movement in Rio de Janeiro. The contribution by SINTRASEDOM (National Union of Household Workers, Colombia) discusses the evolution of this labor union. Adelinda Díaz Uriarte's autobiography tells the life story of a union leader in the Peruvian domestic workers' movement. Aída Moreno Valenzuela reviews the history of the household workers' movement in Chile. Mary García Castro analyzes pamphlets, posters, and other documents by domestic workers' organizations throughout Latin America.

For a more complete discussion of this literature, see Chapter 7 in this volume.

37. Santos, Ely Souto dos (1983). *As domésticas: Um estudo interdisciplinar da realidade social, política, econômica e jurídica.* Porto Alegre: Editora da Universidade; Cáritas Brasileira. 201 p.

The author argues that, following the European experience, Brazilians find domestic work tiresome and undignified and are increasingly unwilling to do it.

The book examines from a variety of disciplinary perspectives the roots of this negative stereotype, exploring how people view domestic workers and how domestics view themselves. The first chapter is a historical analysis of domestic work, beginning with slaves. The second chapter explores the representation of domestic workers in literature. The third chapter, which considers domestics from a sociological standpoint, incorporates primary and secondary statistical data, emphasizes how domestic servants see themselves and how others see them, and examines organizations that assist domestic workers. The fourth chapter surveys laws and legislation relating to domestics.

IV. Rural Women's Work

Aguiar, Neuma, ed. (1984). *Mulheres na força de trabalho na América Latina: Análises qualitativas.* See 18.

38. Benería, Lourdes, ed. (1982). *Women and Development: The Sexual Division of Labor in Rural Societies.* International Labor Office, World Employment Programme. New York: Praeger. 257 p.

Two chapters in this anthology pertain specifically to Latin America. In "Peasant Production, Proletarianization, and the Sexual Division of Labor in the Andes," Carmen Diana Deere and Magdalena León de Leal discuss the sexual division of labor in agricultural production in three Andean regions, emphasizing the importance of economic conditions in explaining the variations among the regions and types of production organization. Kate Young's chapter, "The Creation of a Relative Surplus Population: A Case Study from Mexico," considers the evolution of a rural surplus population in an isolated region of Oaxaca, and the factors driving many young women to migrate from the region.

Bronstein, Audrey (1982). *The Triple Struggle: Latin American Peasant Women.* See 3.

Bruschini, Maria Cristina A. (1985). *Mulher e trabalho: Uma avaliação da década da mulher.* See 23.

Bruschini, Maria Cristina A., and Fúlvia Rosemberg, eds. (1982). *Trabalhadoras do Brasil.* See 24.

Bourque, Susan C., and Kay Barbara Warren (1981). *Women of the Andes: Patriarchy and Social Change in Two Peruvian Towns.* See 14.

Centro de Investigación y Estudios de la Reforma Agraria (1989). *La vida cotidiana de la mujer campesina.* See 5.

39. Deere, Carmen Diana, and Magdalena León, eds., (1987). *Rural Women and State Policy: Feminist Perspectives on Latin American Agricultural Development.* Series in Political Economy and Economic Development in Latin America. Boulder, CO:

Westview Press. 282 p. Spanish edition: *La mujer y la política agraria en América Latina*. Bogotá: Siglo Veintiuno, 1986. 290 p.

This volume assembles papers presented in a seminar titled "Feminist Theory, State Policy and Rural Women in Latin America," convened at the Kellogg Institute of International Studies, University of Notre Dame, in 1985.

In the Introduction, Magdalena León and Carmen Diana Deere review the literature on rural women and state policy and discuss the impact on women of policies ranging from import substitution to debt crisis policy. María Soledad Lago discusses the effect of the neoliberal development model in Chilean agriculture. Belkis Mones and Lydia Grant consider the impact of the agrarian crisis and agricultural development policies on rural women in the Dominican Republic. Cheywa Spindel writes on the social invisibility of women's work in Brazilian agriculture, emphasizing rural women wage workers. (The Spanish version of this study is much more detailed.) Lourdes Arizpe and Carlota Botey discuss the effects of both specific agricultural policies and generalized processes, especially proletarianization, on peasant women in Mexico. Magdalena León outlines agricultural policy in Colombia in relation to rural women, discussing agrarian reform, integrated rural development programs, and new policies aimed directly at peasant women. Lynne Phillips discusses agrarian reform in Ecuador and its effects on gender relations. Luz Padilla, Clara Murguíalday, and Ana Criquillón examine the impact of the Sandinista agrarian reform on the subordination of rural women, analyzing how rural women were incorporated into the reform and the resulting changes in livelihood conditions and work organization. Jean Stubbs and Mavis Alvarez write on women's roles in the cooperativization of agriculture in Cuba. Carmen Diana Deere reviews agrarian reform in Latin America and the Caribbean, discussing gender differentials in the benefits of reform, mechanisms that exclude women, and the need for women's participation in rural development. Elsa Chaney discusses the role of women in integrated rural development projects. Drawing examples from the Dominican Republic and Jamaica, she argues that intensive gardening projects have the greatest potential. Cornelia Butler Flora writes on alternative ways to increase women's income, based on the cooperative, community development, and welfare models. María de los Angeles Crummet investigates rural women and migration in Latin America, considering different policies and analytical frameworks.

Two essays are found only in the Spanish edition: Lidiethe Madden discusses the situation of peasant women in Costa Rica, considering, in particular, factors of self-perception and culture and the limitations that agrarian policy imposes on women; Fiona Wilson assesses the impact of the capitalization of agriculture on women, changing productive and reproductive roles, and the position of women within unequal social relations.

40. **Flórez, Carmen Elisa, et al. (1983).** *El papel de la mujer campesina en el desarrollo rural.* Documento CEDES no. 80. Bogotá: Centro de Estudios sobre Desarrollo Económico, Facultad de Economía, Universidad de los Andes. 216 p.

The research published in this book, financed by the Colombian Ministry of Agriculture, investigates the role of women in agriculture, using both the analysis of national statistics and case studies. The first section examines the impact of three variables—employment, income, and education—on the macro-regional level, using official statistics. The second section, which questions the usefulness of the politically defined, administrative regions described in the first section, identifies three types of sub-regions according to the form of production most characteristic of each area: modern, traditional, and transitional. The third section analyzes case studies in each type of region, using secondary sources. The structures of production, family life, and the sexual division of labor are compared.

41. **León de Leal, Magdalena, et al.** (1980). *Mujer y capitalismo agrario: Estudio de cuatro regiones colombianas*. Bogotá: Asociación Colombiana para el Estudio de la Población. 295 p.

This book contains eight essays on the impact of capitalist agricultural development on women in rural Colombia. There are three studies by Magdalena León de Leal and Carmen Diana Deere. The first is an introductory piece which makes both theoretical and empirical observations about the sexual division of labor, and which presents a historical analysis of capitalist development in Colombian agriculture. Their second essay compares capitalist agricultural development in four regions: Fredonia, Sincelejo, El Espinal, and García Rovira. Their third chapter, which concludes the volume, discusses the process of rural women's proletarianization and changes in the sexual division of labor in different agricultural activities. The book also includes a case study by Diana Medrano S. of women's work in coffee plantations in Antioquia as capitalist production expands into the region. Of the two contributions by Clara González G., the first discusses the expansion of large-scale livestock ranching and the corresponding changes in household organization and the gender division of labor, and the second compares the organization of the peasant household as an economic unit in the regions of Enciso and El Espinal. Lilián Motta de Correa provides a detailed history of the Alto Magdalena region, emphasizing changes in the labor market and in the household division of labor as capitalist agriculture develops. Ingrid Cáceres G. examines changes in the division of labor in minifundio peasant households, with reference to capitalist development in García Rovira.

42. **Moser, Anita** (1985). *A nova submissão: Mulheres da zona rural no processo de trabalho industrial*. Porto Alegre, Brazil: EDIPAZ. 124 p.

This work analyses the changes that took place in a small rural community in the interior of southern Brazil after a large, modern garment factory opened. This plant absorbed the bulk of female labor in the region, which had been employed in subsistence agriculture. The work includes a theoretical discussion of the importance of tapping women's labor for capital accumulation and industrialization as well as a detailed account of the changes in the region. The author also discusses the organization of work within the factory, the controls placed on the workers' capacity to raise consciousness and make demands, and the general impact of the factory on the livelihood of women workers.

43. **Rojas, Raquel** (1986). *Kuña Paraguay: La mujer en la domesticidad rural*. Asunción: Centro Paraguayo de Estudios Sociológicos. 60 p.

This book discusses the role of Paraguayan women in both the rural economy and in the household. The author analyzes the effects of agricultural modernization on these roles, the relationship between family production and entrepreneurial production, and the long-term potential for family agriculture in Paraguay. Rojas also describes relationships between people both within the household and among households and the multiple roles women play as domestic workers, mothers, and farm producers. Special attention is given to young women and their experiences with paid and unpaid work, migration, and motherhood. The book ends with a discussion of the roles of ideology, values, and education among rural women.

44. **Ruchwarger, Gary** (1989). *Struggling for Survival: Workers, Women, and Class on a Nicaraguan State Farm*. Boulder, CO: Westview Press. 128 p.

This case study considers both class and gender relations on the Oscar Turcios state farm in northwestern Nicaragua, where 60 percent of the permanent workers and 75 percent of the temporary workers were women. The sections on class examine the emergence of new class divisions in postrevolutionary Nicaragua, as "managerial," "coordinator," and "working" classes developed. The section on gender explores issues related to the particular concerns of women workers. The author outlines the gender division of labor on the farm; considers the conflict women faced between family life and the ideology of production that prevailed during the period; analyzes how male supervisors and union leaders perceived women workers; and explores how women workers responded differently from men to various aspects of production organization on the farm, such as the incentive system used.

Valdés, Ximena, et al. (1983). *Historias testimoniales de mujeres del campo*. See 13.

45. **Valdés, Ximena** (1988). *La posición de la mujer en la hacienda*. Santiago: Centro de Estudios de la Mujer. 136 p.

The author analyzes the changing roles of women in agriculture between 1930 and the 1960s, when the Chilean agrarian reform took place; the role of women in tenant farming; and wage occupations commonly held by women on the haciendas, especially the work of cooks, dairy workers, and farm laborers.

46. **Valdés, Ximena, and Paulina Matta** (1986). *Oficios y trabajos de las mujeres*

de Pomaire. Santiago: CEM; PEHUÉN. 321 p.

This work is divided into two sections. The first, by Valdés, is a sociohistorical analysis of women and pottery making in Pomaire, Chile. The author notes that as Indian peasants in the region slowly lost access to the land, pottery making was the only way to resist the forces expelling them from the countryside. Because large haciendas principally employed men, pottery making, which was traditionally carried out by both males and females, became increasingly dominated by women. This picture has begun to change, as hand-crafted pottery faces competition from mechanized factory production. The ascendency of these pottery factories, which employ mostly men, is pushing women out of pottery making as well. The second part of the book, compiled by Matta, is a collection of life histories of the women interviewed for the study.

V. Organizations and Social Movements

Alegría, Claribel, and D.J. Flakoll (1983). *No me agarran viva: La mujer salvadoreña en lucha*. See 1.

47. **Alvarez, Sonia E. (1990).** *Engendering Democracy in Brazil: Women's Movements in Transition Politics*. Princeton: Princeton University Press. 304 p.

This volume explores the emergence of the women's movement in Brazil in the 1970s and 1980s. The study begins with a discussion of how that emergence was related to the changes in women's social roles and consciousness that took place during authoritarian rule. Alvarez argues that repressive social policies drew women of all social classes into the political opposition. She then describes the rise of women's organizations in the periphery of Brazil's major cities during the 1970s and 1980s, arguing that organizations that originally addressed women's practical needs gradually radicalized to incorporate a critique of women's status in general.

Later chapters analyze the relationship between the women's movement and the political opposition to the authoritarian regime. Alvarez considers how, in the context of democratization, newly formed political parties incorporated women's issues into their agendas. As those parties have gained power with the fall of the military regime, Alvarez argues that women's issues have been co-opted by parties and the state, leading to the reinforcement of existing gender-power arrangements. The volume ends with a consideration of how women's movements have confronted this new problem.

48. **Andreas, Carol (1985).** *When Women Rebel: The Rise of Popular Feminism in Peru*. Westport, CT: Lawrence Hill and Co. 234 p.

Andreas aims at providing a sociological and historical analysis of the factors underlying the development of women's movements in Peru, emphasizing the deep-seated sources of collective power among Peruvian women. The book presents facts and events which the author believes have been extremely important for women's history in Peru, but which have been commonly hidden from public view. An introductory chapter on the history of Peruvian women is followed by chapters describing women in different regions and varying types of communities and their experience with organizing. The second chapter describes the effects of foreign economic penetration on the experience of women in the coastal fishing town of Chimbote. The third chapter discusses the work and political life of indigenous Andean women, emphasizing women's confrontation with and eventual participation in male-dominated peasant unions. The fourth chapter treats community organizing among popular sectors in cities. The fifth chapter explores women's work in the urban "peripheral sector," emphasizing the contradictions arising from the fact that women both compete with men and ally with them against the state in labor unions. The sixth chapter examines the physical and cultural destruction of indigenous groups in the Amazon and Andean regions, accompanied by the destruction of the nonpatriarchal cultural values of pre-Columbian cultures. The author describes the rise of (eventually armed) resistance, led mostly by women, to combat this destruction.

49. **Blondet, Cecilia** (1986). *Muchas vidas construyendo una identidad: Las mujeres pobladoras de un barrio limeño*. Lima: Instituto de Estudio Peruanos. 66 p.

This book traces the history of a group of women who migrated to Lima from the countryside between 1940 and 1960, and who eventually became community leaders in the poor neighborhood of San Martín de Porres. Blondet locates the origins of community action in the daily life of the city, as isolated female migrants began to develop a network of reciprocal community relations. Eventually, Mother's Organizations (Clubes de Madres) emerge, which, Blondet argues, have the potential to evolve into a larger women's movement. Such an evolution is inhibited, however, by the fact that these organizations have not yet transcended the limits of the family and have not challenged the subordinated condition of women in society.

50. **Blondet, Cecilia** (1991). *Las mujeres y el poder: Una historia de Villa El Salvador*. Lima: Instituto de Estudios Peruanos.

This book recounts the twenty-year history of a social movement in Villa El Salvador, a suburb of Lima, as it evolved from squatter invasion to neighborhood movement, focusing on the role played by women. Blondet describes the squatter invasion and the political and social conditions of the 1970s that were propitious to the emergence of a strong community movement, allowing Villa El Salvador to consolidate into a legitimate neighborhood and eventually a municipality. She outlines the role of women in this movement from its beginning, analyzing the personal evolution of inexperienced women who began to find their own voices, to gain self-esteem, and to learn to organize and lead. Eventually, they formed an autonomous association, the Popular Confederation of Women of Villa El Salvador, which, among other activities, ran a number of "popular kitchens." Blondet tells the story of how vertical, authoritarian, and clientelist forms of organization emerged within this movement and how, eventually, those forms were replaced by more democratic ones.

Bourque, Susan C., and Kay Barbara Warren (1981). *Women of the Andes: Patriarchy and Social Change in Two Peruvian Towns.* See 14.

51. Miller, Francesca (1991). *Latin American Women and the Search for Social Justice.* Hanover, NH: University Press of New England. 324 p.

This historical survey examines the role women have played in Latin American social life over several centuries, focusing in particular on women activists in all kinds of social movements. The first chapter explores methodological issues pertinent to the history of women. The author then outlines generally the role of women during the years of European contact, the colonial period, the independence wars, noting how in each era, important women figures appeared, such as the *heroínas* of the independence period. An entire chapter is dedicated to how women have been educated throughout Latin American history. The remainder of the book focuses on women's activism during the twentieth century, with a particularly long section on the "second wave" of feminism since the mid-1970s. One chapter discusses early feminist activism associated with the international feminist movement, much of which concerned women's rights in the workplace. Another chapter considers the populist era, when women were very active in nationalist movements for social justice. The chapter on women and socialist revolutions tells detailed stories about several important women activists and revolutionaries, and documents the role they played in a movement that largely subordinated feminist concerns. The longest section of the book explores the period since the mid-1970s, during which Latin American women have increasingly participated in the new international feminist movement. This chapter examines the relationships between middle-class and working-class women activists and among national feminist movements in different countries as well as the emergence of a specifically Latin American feminism.

52. Chungara, Domitila de (1982). *La mujer y la organización.* Cuzco: Centro las Casas. 50 p.

This pamphlet, written for Bolivian working women, in particular peasants, is an effort at consciousness raising. Beyond a more general discussion of why women should organize and the presentation of a series of proposals on practical aspects of organizing, the pamphlet describes the emergence and development of Housewives Committees in La Paz. The author details her personal experience in the women's struggle.

53. Escobar, Arturo, and Sonia E. Alvarez, eds. (1992). *The Making of Social*

Movements in Latin America: Identity, Strategy, and Democracy. Boulder, CO: Westview Press. 383 p.

This collection of essays includes three on women's movements and feminism. Norma Stoltz Chinchilla's chapter analyzes the debate over the "second wave" of Latin American feminism that emerged in the mid-1970s and Marxism, focusing on the impact of democratic and pluralist ideas on both schools of thought. Amy Conger Lind writes on popular women's organizations in Ecuador, arguing that through the collectivization of reproductive work, women become politicized about gender relations. The essay by Nancy Saporta Sternbach, Marysa Navarro-Aranguen, Patricia Chuchryk, and Sonia E. Alvarez outlines the recent history of the Latin American feminist movement, challenges the assumption that Latin American women do not define themselves as feminists, and argues instead that a distinctive feminist model has emerged in the region.

54. **Galer, Nora M., and Pilar Núñez C., eds. (1989).** *Mujer y comedores populares.* Lima: Servicios para el Desarrollo (SEPADE). 297 p.

The main contributions to this anthology on Peruvian women's participation in collective kitchens are the following: Pedro Lizarzaburu provides a background essay on food access and assistance in Peru; José Maguiña argues that collective kitchens have been fundamentally responsible for containing malnutrition in Peru despite severe economic crisis; Martha Cuentas outlines the activities of FOVINA, a government support program for the collective kitchens which helps them to organize into consumer co-optives; Josefina Huamán presents a microeconomic analysis of the kitchens, arguing that they operate efficiently in much the same ways as businesses function; Violeta Sara-Lafosse discusses the effects of women's participation in the movements on their family life and self-perception; Ofelia Montes López considers the relation between the collective kitchens and external agencies that provide training and assistance; and Maritza Villavicencio discusses how participating in the kitchens affects women's household relationships and integration into the community. The volume also contains several short program descriptions. In addition, each essay is accompanied by two brief commentaries.

55. **Instituto de Capacitación Política (1984).** *Participación política de la mujer en México: Siglo XX.* Mexico, D.F.: ICAP. 262 p.

The first part of this book provides a detailed history of the women's movement in Mexico, from the emergence of embryonic groups early in the twentieth century to the development of large, political movements. The rest of the book reproduces a series of programs, speeches, statutes, and actions by feminist leaders from the Partido Revolucionario Institucional (PRI). Much attention is given to the evolution of the Agrupación Nacional Femenil Revolucionaria (ANFER).

56. **Jaquette, Jane S., ed. (1989).** *The Women's Movement in Latin America: Feminism and the Transition to Democracy.* Boston, MA: Unwin and Hyman. 215 p.

This book brings together essays on the role of women in the transition from dictatorship to democracy in Latin America during the 1980s. Jane Jaquette's introduction reviews the history of the women's movement in Latin America and outlines the characteristics of "bureaucratic authoritarianism." In her chapter on Brazil, Sonia Alvarez explores how a massive women's movement emerged during the 1970s and 1980s in the context of a repressive, conservative political regime. María del Carmen Feijoó discusses the decline of the women's movement in Argentina after the crisis of transition to democracy passed. Carina Perelli writes on the traditional, conservative, and unorthodox participation of women in Uruguay's transition from military rule. Maruja Barrig examines Peru's feminist movement, emphasizing the contradictions between the aspirations of women's popular organizations and the aims of feminist leaders and discussing the difficulties in bringing about large-scale mobilization and integration of small women's groups. Patricia M. Chuchryk investigates the women's movement in Chile and its relationship with political groups in opposition to the authoritarian regime, considering as well prospects for the evolution of feminism in Chile within the context of democracy. Jaquette's conclusion reviews the origins, goals, and strategies of the various movements presented in the book and speculates on future possibilities for women, feminism, and democracy in Latin America.

57. **Jelin, Elizabeth,** ed. (1990). *Women and Social Change in Latin America.* Geneva: United Nations Research Institute for Social Development; London: Zed Books. 226 p.

This collection contains six case studies and an overview of women's participation in social movements in Latin America. In a short forward to the volume, Lourdes Arizpe places the issues presented in the book within a framework of the changing nature of politics and social relations in contemporary Latin America. Elizabeth Jelin's introduction deals with defining conceptual tools for studying social movements and popular participation and proposes a guide for research. In her case study of a poor neighborhood in Lima, Peru, Cecilia Blondet tells the story of the experience of migrant women with collective action. This study was also published separately. (See reference 49.) Teresa Pires de Rio Caldeira examines the role of women in social movements in São Paulo. María del Carmen Feijoó and Mónica Gogna write on the transformations undergone by the women's movement in Argentina during the transition from dictatorship to democracy. Thelma Gálvez and Rosalba Todaro discuss women's participation in union organizations in light of the free market economic model of post-1973 Chile. Rosario León investigates the participation of Bolivian peasant women in unions and social movements. The essay prepared by the Andean Oral History Workshop (compiled by Silvia Rivera Cusicanqui) discusses the role of Aymara and Quechua women in Indian insurrections in Bolivia. In the concluding chapter, Elizabeth Jelin ties together some of the main points in the case studies, emphasizing the distinctions between public and private, the nature of the struggle for equality in each case, and the historical significance of the women's struggle.

58. **Larguía, Isabel, and John Dumoulin** (1983). *Hacia una concepción científica de la emancipación de la mujer.* Havana: Editorial de Ciencias Sociales. 168 p.

The authors present a Marxist-Leninist theory of women's subordination, discussing, among other issues, women's production for use, visible versus invisible work, production versus reproduction, the sexual division of labor, and the impact of capitalist development on the condition of women. Special emphasis is given to the experience of discrimination against women in prerevolutionary Cuba and the role of women in the Cuban revolution.

59. **Murguíalday, Clara** (1990). *Nicaragua, revolución y feminismo (1977–89).* Madrid: Editorial Revolución. 314 p.

This book traces the history of the women's movement in Nicaragua, focusing on the period since the 1979 revolution. The volume begins with a discussion of the effects of industrialization and urbanization on women in the prerevolutionary period and describes the participation of women in prerevolutionary movements and in guerrilla activities. Murguíalday then addresses the social policies enacted by the Sandinista government in the early revolutionary period (1979–1984), arguing that since women's needs coincided with the government's basic objectives, those policies were fairly effective. The author also outlines the formation of AMNLAE, a broad-based Sandinista women's organization. She argues that although initially successful, the organization failed to press forward with ideological struggles, limiting itself to practical "women's issues." The volume then takes up the later revolutionary period (1985–1989), during which, according to the author, war and economic difficulties were accompanied by an increase in the subordination of women. The author considers how this process affected women's domestic and working lives and describes the emergence of new women's struggles and mobilization, despite a generalized retraction of the feminist movement. The volume ends by discussing the reorganization of AMNLAE in 1987, and the subsequent improvement in its effectiveness as the organization democratized and developed new ties with base women's movements. The volume also includes interviews with eight Sandinista feminists on the success of the Nicaraguan women's movement, on the role of AMNLAE, and on the relationship between feminism and Sandinismo.

60. **Randall, Margaret** (1980). *No se puede hacer la revolución sin nosotras.* Caracas: Editorial Ateneo de Caracas. 179 p.

The body of this book consists of interviews with women revolutionaries in different countries, including Brazil, Nicaragua, Peru, and Cuba. The author also outlines the history of women's participation in the Cuban revolution and recent advances in the Cuban feminist movement.

61. **Sara-Lafosse, Violeta** (1984). *Comedores comunales: La mujer frente a la crisis*. Lima: Servicios Urbanos y Mujeres de Bajos Ingresos. 101 p.

In this short volume, Sara-Lafosse discusses the expansion of communal kitchens in Lima. She explores their organizational patterns and evaluates their ability to realize their objectives. The study also examines the effects of the kitchens on the women who participate in them, with reference to changes in family life, health and nutrition patterns, social and feminist consciousness, and material conditions.

62. **Stone, Elizabeth, ed.** (1981). *Women and the Cuban Revolution: Speeches and Documents*. New York: Pathfinder Press. 156 p.

This book contains excerpts from speeches on women by important figures and groups in Cuba. Vilma Espin discusses the history of women's participation in the Cuban revolution. Two speeches by Fidel Castro, one from 1966 and the other from 1980, discuss women's role in political life at two points in time. The book also includes a speech presented at the first congress of Cuba's Communist Party which outlines the party's principles and goals with respect to women.

63. **Tabak, Fanny** (1983). *Autoritarismo e participação política da mulher*. Rio de Janeiro: Graal. 171 p.

In this collection of essays, Tabak touches on a series of themes related to women's participation in politics and authoritarianism in Brazil. The author describes the progress of women's movements over the last several decades. She also considers how the dictatorship influenced the political socialization of women through controlled information, education, and outright repression, and reflects on the nature of women's resistance (or lack of resistance) in light of this socialization. Other themes are women's roles in policy making in Brazil; the ability of feminist groups to influence Brazil's political arena; the relationship between the feminist movement and political parties; and the capacity for large groups of women to be mobilized for political participation.

64. **Tabak, Fanny, and Moema Toscano** (1982). *Mulher e política*. Rio de Janeiro: Paz e Terra. 133 p.

This book contains three essays. The first, by Tabak and Toscano, presents the results of a study of women voters in Rio de Janeiro during the 1978 election. It addresses the motivations behind female voters' choices, the significance they attribute to their participation in elections, and the specific priorities and preoccupations these women expressed. The second chapter, by Toscano, is a more general discussion of women in politics in Brazil. The author examines the roots of women's negligible participation in politics and reviews the experience of women candidates for elected office. In the third essay, Tabak outlines the history of the women's campaign for the right to vote and discusses the participation of women in the Rio de Janeiro legislature.

65. **Tamez, Elsa, ed.** (1986) *Teólogos de la liberación hablan sobre la mujer*. San José,

Costa Rica: Editorial Departamento Ecuménico de Investigaciones. 183 p. (English edition: *Against Machismo*. Oak Park, IL: Meyer Stone Books, 1987.)

Tamez conducts short interviews with male liberation theologians on their views of women and oppression and the Catholic Church. The individuals interviewed are Juan Luis Segundo, Julio de Santa Ana, Jorge Pixley, Hugo Assmann, Gustavo Gutiérrez, José Míguez Bonino, Enrique Dussel, Rubem Alves, Carlos Mesters, Milton Schwantes, Frei Betto, Leonardo Boff, Pablo Richard, Raúl Vidales, and Mortimer Arias.

VI. General Studies: Anthologies and Regional Studies

66. Blondet, Cecilia, ed. (1987). *Mujer y sociedad: Perspectivas metodológicas*. Enfoques Peruanos; Temas Latinoamericanos. Lima: Fundación Friedrich Naumann; Instituto de Estudios Peruanos. 124 p.

This book was compiled as part of an effort to give greater rigor and clarity to the methodology used in studying women. The introduction defines and discusses some basic analytical concepts. M. Teresita de Barbieri investigates the economic and social importance of unpaid domestic work, initiating a discussion of the relation of such work to Marx's labor theory of value. Her research compares interviews with working women, nonworking housewives, and women of different socioeconomic classes in Peru. María del Carmen Feijoó and Elizabeth Jelin ask whether the poverty that has been increasingly visible in Argentina since democratization began is new, or whether it is merely an expression of what had been repressed in the past. To answer this question, the authors trace the history of women, poverty, and the women's movement in Argentina. Catalina H. Wainerman and Martín Moreno address some of the technical and conceptual problems in detecting women's participation in the labor force and present evidence of the failure of censuses to identify women's participation. The authors make detailed recommendations for alternative research practices, including interviewer training techniques, questionnaire formulation, and identification of periods of reference.

67. Bohman, Kristina (1984). *Women of the Barrio: Class and Gender in a Colombian City*. Stockholm: Department of Social Anthropology, University of Stockholm. 373 p.

This study of La Rosa, a popular neighborhood in Medellín, Colombia, discusses the economic, social, and ideological factors behind women's subordinated position in society, emphasizing the extent to which women have the power to control their own lives and careers. Three major themes are discussed: material conditions, kinship, and ideology. The work includes an analysis of the region's history, with particular reference to women's work both in the countryside and city. The processes of urbanization and rural-urban migration and the development of poor peripheral neighborhoods are detailed and the relationship between kinship structures and migration is discussed. Insight into the specifics of women's "life situations" is provided through the description of numerous women's life stories and experiences. The author also describes family, neighborhood, and friendship networks that are articulated by women. Finally, various aspects of social interaction and ideology are considered, including the formation of social organizations and work groups; religious beliefs; perceptions of sexuality, motherhood, and suffering; the influence of mass media; and female protest movements.

Ehlers, Tracy Bachrach (1990). *Silent Looms: Women and Production in a Guatemalan Town.* See 27.

68. Nash, June, and Helen Icken Safa, eds. (1986). *Women and Change in Latin America: New Directions in Sex and Class.* South Hadley, MA: Bergin & Garvey. 372 p.

This anthology emphasizes women's production for the market and the relationship between productive work and women's reproductive roles. In the introductory section, June Nash surveys the research on women's work in Latin America, and Neuma Aguiar presents a number of research guidelines, especially for analyzing official statistics on women's work.

Four studies consider women's role in production for the market and in social reproduction. Frances Rothstein examines the effects of modernization on children in a Mexican community, arguing that as industrialization takes place, children are less integrated into the adult world and parents devote greater energy to their children than in the past. Florence Babb argues that the work of Andean market women cannot be categorized as merely the extension of their reproductive roles into society at large, but must be seen as an integration of productive and reproductive roles. Lynn Bolles studies how working-class households in Jamaica cope with an insecure and inadequate wage economy, arguing that male partner/spouse households have greater access to resources and less dependence on the informal sector than do female-headed households. Helen Safa shows how rapid export-based industrialization in Puerto Rico has favored female employment and explores why newer industrial employers prefer young, single women from rural areas.

Five essays address women in the context of industrial and agricultural change. Heleieth Saffioti compares case studies of a small garment factory with skilled labor and a large, highly automated textile factory with unskilled labor in Brazil, to identify the effect of technological change on women's participation in Brazil's industrial labor force. Marianne Schmink analyzes the sexual division of labor in an industrial community in Brazil, describing the types of strategies that households of different economic status pursue. Judith-Maria Buechler discusses the organization and development of small-scale enterprises run by women in La Paz, Bolivia, considering the relationship between these firms and both industrialization and political crisis in Bolivia. Carmen Diana Deere compares the participation of rural women in agrarian reform in Peru, Chile, and Cuba, arguing that Cuba was more successful than Peru and Chile in incorporating women into the process. Cornelia Butler Flora and Blas Santos examine semi-proletarian peasant households in the Dominican Republic affected by an agricultural development project which was redesigned to involve women in production.

Three studies deal with women migrants. Mary García Castro analyzes how Colombian migrant women in New York developed consciousness regarding their situation in the labor market and in the family. Margalit Berlin explores the employment strategies of Colombian women migrants working in Venezuelan industries and discusses the relationships among workers and between workers and management. Patricia Pessar uses the case of Dominican migrants in the United States to create a "gender free model of the settlement process," identifying how gender ideologies change within immigrant households.

Finally, three chapters consider women's participation in political life. Ximena Bunster-Burotto analyzes sexual torture of female political prisoners in Argentina, Chile, and Uruguay. Gloria Ardaya Salinas shows how the women's movement in Bolivia has been an important element of Bolivian social movements in general and of national life as a whole. Isabel Larguía and John Dumoulin study the struggle for women's equality in Cuba, arguing that significant advances have been made in the postrevolutionary era.

69. **Weil, Connie, ed. (1988).** *Lucha: The Struggles of Latin American Women.* Minneapolis, MN: Prisma Institute. 201 p.

This volume consists of two essays that place Latin American women's struggles for livelihood in the context of changing global conditions and four case studies reflecting different aspects of the lives of poor women in Latin America. The chapter by Barbara Knudson and Connie Weil analyzes global demographic and socioeconomic statistics, locating Latin America in that context, showing how different regions within Latin America vary and drawing out the implications for women. June Nash focuses more specifically on global economic trends in her discussion of the effects of capital penetration and technological change on poor women's household strategies. Nancy J. Black shows how Quiché Mayan women of the Guatemalan highlands have been described over time by anthropologists. Marilyn Bowman discusses the role Guatemalan migrant women in both the Mexican and the U.S. economies, outlining what she refers to as the formation of a "new proletariat" of "undocumented women." Valerie Estes's contribution concerns women factory workers in Bolivia and how their jobs affect their family lives. The chapter by Benjamin S. Orlove explores the life story of a young woman in a small town in highland Peru, examining the life choices she faced, in an attempt to understand what led her to suicide.

VII. Bibliographies on Women in Latin America

70. **Agramont Virreira, Miriam, et al. (1986).** *Bibliografía de la mujer boliviana, 1920–1985: La Paz, Sucre, Cochabamba y Santa Cruz.* La Paz: Ediciones CIDEM. 158 p.

71. **Alfaro, Teresa** (1982). *Relación bibliográfica: Tesis sobre la mujer peruana*. Lima: Asociación Perú Mulher. 19 p.

72. **Arteaga, Ana María, et al.** (1985). *Mujeres populares: 20 años de investigación en Chile*. Santiago: Centro de Estudios de la Mujer. 226 p.

73. **Arteaga, Ana María** (1986). *La mujer en Chile: Bibliografía comentada*. Santiago: Centro de Estudios de la Mujer. 284 p.

74. **Ashby, Jacqueline Anne, et al.** (1985). *Women, Agriculture, and Rural Development in Latin America*. Muscle Shoals, Alabama: International Fertilizer Development Center; Cali: Centro Internacional de Agricultura Tropical. 171 p.

75. **Bartra, Eli, et al.** (1983). *Mujer: Una bibliografía*. Mexico, D.F.: Universidad Autónoma Metropolitana Xochimilco. 129 p.

76. **Bergmann, Emilie, et al.** (1990). "Bibliographical Update: Women, Politics, and Culture in Latin America." In **Emilie Bergmann et al., eds.**, *Women, Culture, and Politics in Latin America*. Berkeley: University of California Press. Pp. 182–231.

77. **Byrne, Pamela R., and Suzanne R. Ontiveros, eds.** (1986). "Women in Latin America and the West Indies." In *Women in the Third World: A Historical Bibliography*. Chapter 6. Santa Barbara, CA: ABC-Clio Information Services. Pp. 70–121.

78. **Centro Informação Mulher** (1984). *Boletim CIM*, July 1984. São Paulo.

79. **Consejo Nacional de Población** (1986). *Bibliografía sobre la mujer*. Mexico: Consejo Nacional de Población; Comisión Nacional de la Mujer. 248 p.

80. **Corvalán, Graziella, and Mabel Centurión** (1987). *Bibliografía sobre estudios de la mujer en el Paraguay*. Asunción: Centro Paraguayo de Estudios Sociológicos; Grupo de Estudios de la Mujer Paraguaya. 39 p.

81. **Rosero, Rocio, and Jackeline Contreras** (1988). *Bibliografía sobre la mujer en el Ecuador*. Quito: ILDIS. 164 p.

82. **Stoner, Lynn** (1989). *Latinas of the Americas: A Source Book*. New York: Garland. 692 p.

83. **Studer, Hans Martin** (1983). *Trabajo femenino y resistencia en América Latina: Una bibliografía comentada, especialmente referente a México, Venezuela, Colombia, Ecuador, Perú y Bolivia*. Arbeitspapiere 29. Bielefeld: Universität Bielefeld; Universitätsschwerpunkt Lateinamerikaforschung. 125 p.

Country Index

Argentina, 6, 15, 66
Bolivia, 25, 69, 70, 83
Brazil, 8, 9, 10, 18, 23, 24, 26, 28, 29, 31, 32, 37, 47, 60, 63, 64, 78
Chile, 6, 7, 11, 13, 16, 17, 45, 46, 72, 73
Colombia, 40, 41, 67, 83
Cuba, 58, 60, 62
Ecuador, 53, 81, 83
El Salvador, 1
Guatemala, 4, 27, 69
Latin America, general, 3, 12, 18, 19, 34, 36, 38, 39, 51, 53, 56, 57, 65, 68, 69, 74, 76, 77, 82
Mexico, 21, 22, 30, 33, 55, 75, 79, 83
Nicaragua, 44, 59, 60
Paraguay, 6, 43, 80
Peru, 2, 14, 20, 35, 48, 49, 50, 52, 54, 60, 61, 66, 69, 71, 83
Uruguay, 6
Venezuela, 60, 83

Author Index

Agramont Virreira, Miriam, 70
Aguiar, Neuma, 18, 19
Alegría, Claribel, 1
Alfaro, Teresa, 71
Alvarez, Sonia E., 47, 53
Andreas, Carol, 48
Arteaga, Ana María, 72, 73
Ashby, Jacqueline Anne, 74
Barrig, Maruja, 2, 20
Bartra, Eli, 75
Benería, Lourdes, 30, 38
Berger, Marguerite, 34
Bergmann, Emilie, 76
Blondet, Cecilia, 49, 50, 66
Bohman, Kristina, 67
Bourque, Susan C., 14
Bronstein, Audrey, 3
Bruschini, Maria Cristina A., 23, 24
Bunster Burrotto, Ximena, 35
Burgos-Debray, Elisabeth, 4
Buvinić, Mayra, 34
Byrne, Pamela R., 77
Centro de Investigación y Estudios de la Reforma Agraria, 5
Centro Informação Mulher, 78
Centurión, Mabel, 80
Chaney, Elsa M., 35, 36
Chant, Sylvia, 21
Chungara, Domitila de, 52
Cisneros, Antonio C., 25
Consejo Naciónal de Población, 79
Conselho Estadual da Condição Feminina, Centro de Memória Sindica, 31
Contreras, Jackeline, 81
Cooper, Jennifer, 22
Corvalán, Graziella, 80
Costa, Letícia B., 26
Deere, Carmen Diana, 39
Dumoulin, John, 58
Escobar, Arturo, 53
Ehlers, Tracy Bachrach, 27
Feijoó, María del Carmen, 15
Fisher, Jo, 6
Flakoll, D.J., 1
Flórez, Carmen Elisa, 40
Galer M., Nora, 54
García Castro, María (Mary), 36
Instituto de Capacitación Política, 55
Jaquette, Jane S., 56
Jelin, Elizabeth, 15, 57
Koch, Carlos, 25
La Fuente, Germán, 25
Larguía, Isabel, 58
León, Kirai de, 7
León de Lea, Magdalena, 39, 41
Mafei, Maristela, 8
Magenzo, Salomón, 16
Matta, Paulina, 46
Miller, Francesca, 51
Moser, Anita, 42
Murguíalday, Clara, 59
Nash, June, 68

Núñez C., Pilar, 54
O'Gorman, Frances, 9
Ontiveros, Suzanne R., 77
Pagotto, Carmen Silvia, 29
Pastoré, José, 29
Patai, Daphne, 10
Raczynski, Dagmar, 11
Randall, Margaret, 12, 60
Rojas, Raquel, 43
Roldan, Martha, 30
Rosemberg, Fúlvia, 24
Rosero, Rócio, 81
Ruchwarger, Gary, 44
Safa, Helen Icken, 68
Saffioti, Heleieth I. B., 32
Santos, Ely Souto dos, 37

Sara-Lafosse, Violeta, 61
Serrano, Claudia, 11
Souza-Lobo García, Elisabeth de, 28
Stone, Elizabeth, 62
Stoner, Lynn, 82
Studer, Hans Martin, 83
Tabak, Fanny, 63, 64
Tamez, Elsa, 65
Toscano, Moema, 64
Valdés, Ximena, 13, 45, 46
Valdés Enchenique, Teresa, 17
Warren, Kay Barbara, 14
Weil, Connie, 69
Wilson, Fiona, 33
Zylberstajn, Hélio, 29

Index

Abandoned women, in the labor force, 51
Acción Democrática-M-19, 140
ACEP (Asociación Colombiana para el Estudio de la Población). *See* Colombian Association for Population Studies (ACEP)
Africa
 implementation of structural adjustment policies in, 24
 poverty in, 21
Age at first marriage, rise in, 53
Agency for International Development (USAID), 61
Aging, among domestic workers, 116
Agriculture
 commercialization of, 48–49
 Peruvian economic measures and, 64
Alianza Popular Revolucionaria de América (APRA), administration of Peru by, 62
Amasando la Esperanza (Kneading Hope)
 formation of, 37, 38
 goals of, 39
AMNLAE. *See* Luisa Amanda Espinoza Women's Association (AMNLAE)
Amplio, Frente, 140
AMPRONAC. *See* Women's Association to Confront the National Problematic (AMPRONAC)
ANECAP (Asociación Nacional de Empleadas de Casa Particular). *See* National Association of Workers in Private Homes (ANECAP)
Argentina. *See also* Buenos Aires, Argentina; Itatí, Argentina; Lomas de Zamora, Argentina; Moreno, Argentina
 daily life in, 163

domestic worker organizations and unions in, 117, 188
"economy of solidarity" in, 34–35
hyperinflation in, 32–33
increased number of women in the labor market in, 33–34
social change in, 163
women's responses to debt crisis in, 31–44
Arizpe, Lourdes, 113
Asistencialismo, 68
Asociación de Trabajadoras del Hogar, 119
Assassinations, by Sendero Luminoso, 75
Association of Domestic Workers, 119
Association of Household Workers, 126–127
ATC. *See* Women's Secretariat of the Agricultural Workers' Association (ATC)

Baker Plan, 14
Barrantes, Alfonso, 61–62
Barrig, Maruja, 142
 on the changing relationship between women's movements and the state in Peru, 137–138
Belaúnde, Fernando, 60
Benería, Lourdes, 138, 139, 140–141
Bercovich, Clelia, 127
Betrayals, by political parties, 71
Biases, in structural adjustment policies, 22–24
Blue-collar work, 170–172
Bolivia. *See also* La Paz, Bolivia
 advice to working women of, 181
 domestic worker organizations in, 118
 soup kitchens in, 18
Brady Plan, 15

Bravo, Rosa, 123
Brazil. *See also* Rio de Janeiro, Brazil
　child care facilities in, 124–125
　domestic worker organizations in, 118
　domestic work in, 174–175
　drafting of new constitution by, 144
　expanding citizen rights in, 143
　interest payments of, 14–15
　life stories of women from, 161
　productive and reproductive roles of women in, 187–188
　rural workers in, 177–178
　textile and garment industry of, 171
　urban women of, 168, 169
　violence against rural workers of, 160
　women's movements in, 179
　women's participation in politics of, 185
Budget adjustments, of households, 19
Buenos Aires, Argentina
　case studies of women's situations in, 36–41
　community development projects in, 5
　social change in, 163
　women's responses to the debt crisis in, 31–44
Bunster, Ximena, 115–116

Caldeira, Teresa, on expansion of social rights, 142–143
California, migrations from Mexico to, 48–49
Caminando Juntas, 119
Campesinas (*campesinos*), 111, 126
　life among, 107–110
Capital interests
　responsiveness of structural adjustment policies to needs of, 23–24
　as served by the Peruvian state, 68–69
Capitalist economy
　criteria for evaluating, 22–23
　effects on poor classes, 138
　livelihood in, 2–3
CARITAS. *See* Catholic Church
Casas de la Mujer, 98
CASED (Colectivo de Acción Solidaria con Empleadas). *See* Collective for Action in Solidarity with Domestic Workers (CASED)
Catholic Church. *See also* Young Catholic Workers (JOC)
　family assistance activities in Chile, 108–109
　family assistance activities in Peru, 59, 61, 62, 64, 82–83
　family assistance activities in Uruguay, 120
　opposition to family planning by, 53
　oppression of women by, 186
CCTH (Centro de Capacitación para Trabajadoras del Hogar). *See* Training Center for Household Workers (CCTH)
CELADE (Centro Latinoamericano de Demografía). *See* Latin American Center for Demography (CELADE)
CEM (Centro de Estudios de la Mujer). *See* Center of Women's Studies (CEM: Chile); Women's Studies Center (CEM: Argentina)
Center for Household Workers, 108
Center of Women's Studies (CEM: Chile), 109, 114–115, 128
Chamorro, Violeta de, 99
Checras, Peru, social change in, 162–163
Chiapas, Mexico, uprising in, 21, 22
Childbearing, 52–53
Child care facilities, for domestic workers, 124–125
Children
　avoiding malnutrition among, 61–62
　effects of structural adjustment policies on, 19, 43–44
Chile. *See also* Conchalí, Chile; Graneros, Chile; Santiago, Chile
　agrarian reform in, 178–179
　domestic worker organizations and unions in, 117, 118–119
　effects of structural adjustment policies on, 21
　military coup in, 160
　peasant life in, 107–110, 163–164
　social change in, 163–164

structural reforms in, 14
women's life in, 160, 161, 162
Chilean National Statistical Institute, 123
Chiuchin, Peru, social change in, 162–163
"Cities of women," 35
Citizen rights, 1, 3, 4–5
feminist perspectives on, 142–145
in Peru, 67–71, 137–138
Clubes de Madres, 180
Cocinas Familiares. See Family Kitchens
Collective actions
in Peru, 59
struggle for livelihood and, 2–3
Collective for Action in Solidarity with Domestic Workers (CASED), 115
Collective kitchens, 61, 62–65, 185. *See also* Family Kitchens
corporativism of, 71–72
families and, 64
leaders of, 73–74
as political entities, 72–73
Collective of Masaya, 98
Collective of Matagalpa, 98
Collective solutions to debt crisis, 31–44
Colombia, 186–187. *See also* La Rosa, Colombia; Medellín, Colombia
domestic worker organizations in, 119
effects of structural adjustment policies on, 22
rural workers in, 177
studies of domestic workers in, 128
Colombian Association for Population Studies (ACEP), 128
Colombian Ministry of Agriculture, 177
Comedores, social structures including, 65–67
Comedores del pueblo, 62
Comedores populares, 18, 61, 142. *See also* Family Kitchens
Communism, Sendero Luminoso and, 87
Community-based economic organizations, women's emergence in, 5
Community-development projects, in Buenos Aires, 36–38
Community standards, livelihood and, 1–2
Compañeras (compañeros), 88, 108

CONAPRO. *See* Nicaraguan Confederation of Professionals (CONAPRO)
Conchalí, Chile, life stories of women from, 161
Confederation of Domestic Workers, 110
Confederation of Latin American and Caribbean Household Workers (CONLACTRAHO), 109, 110
in Argentina, 118
becoming affiliated with, 130
bulletins published by, 130
child care facilities under, 124–125
in Colombia, 119
creation of, 121–122
goals of, 122
housing cooperatives and, 125
leadership training under, 123
studies of domestic workers by, 123–124
throughout Latin America, 120
"Conference of Nicaraguan Women for Unity in Diversity," 99–192
Conformism, among domestic workers, 111
CONLACTRAHO (Confederación Latinoamericana y del Caribe de Trabajadoras del Hogar). *See* Confederation of Latin American and Caribbean Household Workers (CONLACTRAHO)
Construction Workers Federation, 109
Consumerism, citizenship and, 70
Consumption, 1, 2
effects of debt crisis on, 32
Contraceptive use, 53
Coordinadora de Organizaciones del Area de la Mujer, 126–127, 128
Coordinating Office of Household Worker Unions of Metropolitan Lima (COSINTRAHOL), 110, 127–128
Coordination of Women's Groups, 119
Coordination of Women's Organizations, 126–127
Corporativism, 70
of collective kitchens, 71–72
COSINTRAHOL (Coordinadora Sindical de Trabajadoras del Hogar de Lima Metropolitana). *See* Coordinating Office of Household Worker

Unions of Metropolitan Lima
(COSINTRAHOL)
Costa Rica
  domestic worker organizations in, 119
  effects of structural adjustment policies
    on, 22
Courtship patterns, 52–53
Crime. See also Violence
  resulting from structural adjustment
    policies, 18
"Crisis of development," in Latin America,
  14, 155–156
"Crushing of labor," 12–13
Cuba, women's movements and politics in,
  184, 185
Currency devaluation, Latin American
  foreign debt crisis and, 11

Daily life, 162–164
  restructuring of, 19–21
Debt. See Foreign debt
Debt crisis. See also Foreign debt
  Argentine women's responses to, 31–44
  feminist strategies for dealing with,
    137–145
  political parties and, 71
  responses of Peru to, 59–75
  social impact of, 32–33
"Democratic deficit," 24
Democratic discussions, adoption of structural adjustment policies without,
  23–24
Democratic rule, 3
Democratization of Latin America, 139
Desdibujamiento, 137, 139
Development Alternatives with Women
  for a New Era (DAWN), 140
Díaz, Adelinda, 110, 121
Dictatorships, 159–160
Direct Assistance Program (PAD), 62, 65
Disease, increases in, 21
Disinformation, sown by Sendero Luminoso, 86–88
Domesticity
  effects of structural adjustment policies
    on women's, 18–19, 20
  women's emergence from, 1

Domestic power, within migrant-labor
  families, 53–54
Domestic work, 173–175
  characteristics of, 110–113, 113–116
  disparagement of, 113–116
  lack of legitimacy for, 129
  low status of, 128, 129
  slavery and, 110–111
  working conditions in, 113–116
Domestic workers, 173–175
  efforts to organize, 130
  future plans for, 122–125
  low social status of, 114, 128, 129
  opportunities for, 129–130
  organization of, 117–122
  political activism among, 125–130
  publications concerning, 111–113,
    120–122
  struggles of, 129-130
  studies of, 123–124
Dominican Republic
  documenting domestic work conditions
    in, 115
  domestic worker organizations in, 119
  effects of structural adjustment policies
    on, 22
  feminist organizations in, 126–127
Duarte, Isis, 115

Eastern Europe, implementation of structural adjustment policies in, 24
Economic Commission for Latin America
  (CEPAL), 32
Economic crisis. See Debt crisis; Foreign
  debt
Economic rights
  feminist perspectives on, 142–145
  women's struggle for, 3
Economies, internationalization of
  domestic, 12
Economy Network, 101
"Economy of solidarity," 2, 22–23, 31
  emergence of, 34–35
Editorial Nueva Sociedad, 121
Education
  government cuts in, 17
  government subsidies to, 11–12

of household workers in Lima, Peru, 127–128
Peruvian government spending on, 68
of poor women in Peru, 82–83
Education Network, 101
Education of children, livelihood and, 2
Efficiency, evaluating, 22–23
Elitism, in Peru, 69–70
Elson, Diane, on the social effects of structural adjustment policies, 23
Employment. *See* Unemployment; Wage work; Working classes; Working wives; Working women
Empowerment of women, 40–41, 50–51, 53–54, 141, 156
　in Nicaragua, 91–102
　in Peru, 137–138
Empregada, 126
Environment Network, 101
Epidemics, increases in, 21
Episcopal Church, 38
Equality, ideology of, 69–70
Esfuerzo propio, 68
Estado de compromiso, 69
Ethnicity biases, in structural adjustment policies, 22
"Eugenia," 158
European Economic Community (EEC), 140
Exogamy, 53
Exports, 12

Families. *See also* Households
　circumstances of impoverished, 38–39, 168–169
　collective kitchens and, 64
　formation of, 52–53
　reproductive activities of, 65–67
　women's labor supporting, 20, 49–51, 81
　women's roles in, 41
"Family-centered" studies, 166
Family honor, 49–50
Family Kitchens, 59, 60–63. *See also* Collective kitchens
　conflicts with other collective kitchen programs, 61
　dismantlement of, 62
　organization of, 60–61
Family patrimony, women's share in, 50
Family planning, 53
Family sizes, decline in, 53
Family wage. *See also* Wages
　livelihood and, 2
Fatalism, among domestic workers, 111
Favelas, life stories of women from, 160
Fear, sown by Sendero Luminoso, 86–88
Federation of Bolivian Household Workers (FENATRAHOB), 118
Female unemployment. *See also* Working women
　in Peru, 63–65
Feminism, 137–145, 155. *See also* Women's movements
　Dominican Republic and, 126–127
　María Elena Moyano and, 89–90
　North American, 142
　politics and, 144–145
　poverty and, 138–145
FEM magazine, 115
FENATRAHOB (Federación de Trabajadoras del Hogar de Bolivia). *See* Federation of Bolivian Household Workers (FENATRAHOB)
"Fideo-making," 141
Field labor, women involved in, 51
Figueroa, Blanca, 112, 127–128
Filial duties, of unmarried daughters, 54
Fixed incomes, 11
FLACSO. *See* Latin American Social Science Research Faculty (FLACSO)
Food distribution, in impoverished Peru, 6, 62–67
Food riots, resulting from structural adjustment policies, 18
Foreign debt. *See also* Debt crisis
　interest on, 14–15
　Latin American crisis with, 11–25
　ratio to GNP of, 15–17
　table of changes in, 16
Foreign exchange, Latin American foreign debt crisis and, 11
FOVINA, 182

Freseras, 49–51, 51–52, 55
Friends of Household Workers, 130
FSLN. *See* Sandinista National Liberation Front (FSLN)
Fujimori, Alberto, 83–84
"Fuji-shock," 84

Gálvez, Thelma, 109, 114, 115, 123
García, Alan, 62, 68
García, Rutté, 112
García Castro, Mary, 115, 129
Gender impacts
 among migrant-labor families, 53–54
 of structural adjustment policies, 25, 47–55
Gender-specific citizen rights, 137–138
"Glass of Milk" program, 61–62, 120
Global restructuring processes, effects on rural communities in Michoacán, Mexico, 5–6
Gogna, Mónica, 115
Goldsmith, Mary, 115
"Good Times." *See* The 1980s
Government spending, effects of cuts in, 11–12
Graneros, Chile, peasant life in, 107–110
Gremio, 125
Gross National Product (GNP)
 drop in workers' share of, 32
 ratio of foreign debt to, 15–17
Guatemala
 domestic worker organizations in, 119
 urban women of, 169
 women's struggles in, 188
Guzmán, Abimael, capture of, 80–81

Health
 decline in standards of, 21
 government cuts in support for, 17
Health Network, 101
Historic Program of the FSLN, 92
Hogar de la Empleada, 108
Hogar de paso, 120
Household income, 1, 162–164
Households, 162–164. *See also* Families
 circumstances of impoverished, 38–39
 effects of structural adjustment policies on, 17–22
 neighborhood-based survival activities and, 33
 reproductive activities of, 65–67
 struggles for livelihood in, 1–2, 18, 138–139, 157–158
 women as heads of, 52
Household work. *See* Domestic work
Household workers. *See also* Domestic workers
 organizing, 107–130
 struggles of, 107
Housewives Committees, 181
Housework. *See* Domestic work
"Housework for Pay in Chile: Not Just Another Job" (Gálvez & Todaro), 115
Housing
 in Argentine popular neighborhoods, 36–38
 government cuts in support for, 17
Housing cooperatives, for domestic workers, 125
Hurtado, Yenny del Carmen, 110
Hyperinflation, in 1980s Argentina, 32–33

Illiteracy, among working women, 94
Imports, 12
Impoverishment. *See also* Poor classes; Poverty
 of poor classes in Peru, 82–83
 of working classes, 3
Industrialization, effects of, 47–55
Industrial revolution, effects of, 22
Inefficiency, 13
Inflation, 11, 12–13
 in 1980s Argentina, 32–33
Institute of Promotion and Formation of Household Workers, 120
Institutionality, in social movements, 75
Instituto de Promoción y Formación de Trabajadoras del Hogar, 120
"Intellectual work," Nicaraguan leaders' rejection of, 96
Inter-American Foundation, 119
Interest on foreign debt, 14–15

INDEX 199

International capital institutions, responsiveness of structural adjustment policies to needs of, 23–24
International Domestic Workers' Day, 122
Internationalization of domestic economies, 12
International Monetary Fund (IMF), 11, 59
　criticisms against, 21
　intervention in Peru by, 83–84
　responsiveness of structural adjustment policies to needs of, 23–24
Invisibility of domestic workers, 129
Itatí, Argentina
　effects of non-governmental organizations on, 43
　formation of, 36–37
　goals of non-governmental organizations in, 41
　improving women's performance in, 41–42
　PRODIBA's goals in, 39
　women's wages in, 40

Jelin, Elizabeth, 112–113, 115
JOC (Juventud Obrera Católica). *See* Young Catholic Workers (JOC)
Journeying Together, 119

Kneading Hope
　formation of, 37, 38
　goals of, 39

Labor
　marital status and women's, 47–48
　Peruvian social policies and, 68
　sexual division of, 42
Labor costs, 12–13
Labor laws, regarding domestic work, 114
Labor market
　drop relative to GNP in, 32
　incorporation of women into, 33–35
　increased number of persons in, 18–19
La Paz, Bolivia, working women in, 181, 187–188
La Rosa, Colombia, 186–187

Las Madres de la Plaza de Mayo movement, 4, 160
Latin America
　charitable activities of the JOC in, 117
　democratization of, 139
　deterioration of economies of, 15–17
　domestic workers in, 173–174
　effects of structural adjustment policies in, 11–25
　emerging markets of, 13–14
　experiences of women's organizations in, 137–138
　fate of, 138–139
　feminist scholars of, 142–143
　foreign debt crisis of, 11–25, 155–156
　growth rate of, 17
　increased number of women in the labor market in, 33–34
　interest payments of, 14–15
　non-state solutions to problems of, 139–145
　political ethos of, 3
　productive and reproductive roles of women in, 187–188
　role of women in politics of, 182–183
　rural workers in, 175, 176
　studies of domestic workers in, 123–124
　urban women of, 165–166
　women in microenterprises in, 172–173
　women in social life of, 181
　women's movements in, 182, 184
　women's struggles in, 188
　working classes of, 164–165
Latin American Center for Demography (CELADE), 123
Latin American Social Science Research Faculty (FLACSO), 123
Latin American Studies Association
　XI Congress of, 121
Laws, concerning collective kitchens, 74
Leaders, Sendero Luminoso attacks against political, 84–90
Leadership development, 41, 42
　training workshops for, 123
Legal rights, women's struggle for, 92–93
León, Magdalena, 128
León, Mexico, urban women of, 166

Lima, Peru
  collective kitchens in, 72–73, 185
  domestic workers of, 112
  living in the slums of, 158
  organization of Family Kitchens in, 60–63
  organization of "Glass of Milk" program in, 61–62
  Sendero Luminoso activities in, 6, 79–90
  women migrants in, 173
  women's movements in, 180
Livelihood, 1–3, 4–5
  in Latin America of the 1980s, 2–3, 17–22
  women's struggles and, 1, 138–139, 155, 157–158
Living standards
  effects of inflation on, 12–13
  effects of structural adjustment policies on, 18
  effects of women wage-earners on, 47–55
  erosion of, 32–33, 65–67
  women's striving toward higher, 79–80
Lomas de Zamora, Argentina, food service program in, 127
Looting, 33
  effects on quality of life, 38–39
  in Moreno, Argentina, 37–38
Lost Decade. *See* The 1980s
Luisa Amanda Espinoza Women's Association (AMNLAE), 91
  creation and early goals of, 92–93
  following defeat of the Sandinista regime, 99–102
  formation of, 184
  goals of, 93–97
  loss of legitimacy of, 93
  unresponsiveness of, 95–96
  work methods of, 97–99

Machista culture, 94
Madres educadoras, emergence of, 36
Madre Tierra (Mother Earth), formation of, 38

Male-dominated political systems. *See also* Patriarchy
  strategies for dealing with, 137–145
Male opposition to working women, 48–51
  Nicaraguan politics and, 97–99
"Managed adjustment" policies, 24
Manliness, working women as questioning, 49
Mapuche communities, 162
Marginalization, of domestic workers, 116–117
Marital status, women's jobs appropriate to, 47–48, 54–55
Market, structural adjustment policies and, 12
Market economies, Peru among, 68–69
Market-related efficiency criteria, evaluating structural adjustment policies with, 22–23
Marriage, 52–53
Marriage market, 50
Marshall, T.H., 142–143
Mayobamba, Peru, social change in, 162–163
Medellín, Colombia, 186-187
"Meica," 107
Men, working women without, 51
Menchú, Rigoberta, 159
Mercado Común del Sur (MERCOSUR), 140
Metropolitan Union of Workers in Private Homes (SINCATRAP), 109–110, 118, 124, 125
Mexico. *See also* Chiapas, Mexico; León, Mexico; Michoacán, Mexico; Puerto Vallarta, Mexico; Querétaro, Mexico; Quiringuicharo, Mexico
  alternatives to structural adjustment policies in, 24
  blue-collar workers of, 170–171
  effects of structural adjustment policies on, 21–22
  expanding citizen rights in, 143
  household restructuring in, 20
  Latin American foreign debt crisis and, 11–12

INDEX

migrations to California from, 48–49
productive and reproductive roles of women in, 187–188
solidarity program (PRONASOL) of, 22–23
structural reforms in, 14
urban women of, 166, 167–168
women's movement in, 182
working-class life in, 172
Mexico City
  labor-market studies in, 18–19
  urban women of, 167–168
Michoacán, Mexico
  effects of global restructuring processes on rural communities in, 5–6
  industrialization and changing gender roles in, 47–55
Microenterprises, 35, 172–173
Middle class, effects of structural adjustment policies on, 19–20
Migrant women, 188
Migration. *See* Wage-labor migration
Military state, in Peru, 60–62
"Mini-factories," 38
Mobility, of poor women, 63–64
Modernization, 12
MOMUPO (Movimiento de Mujeres Pobladoras), 160
Money, livelihood and, 2
"Moral economy" of social relations, 1–3
Moreno, Argentina
  effects of non-governmental organizations on, 42–43
  goals of non-governmental organizations in, 39, 41
  impoverished neighborhoods in, 37
  improving women's performance in, 41–42
  women's wages in, 40
Mother Earth, formation of, 38
Mothers
  social roles of, 41
  as teachers' assistants, 36
  as working women, 51–52
Mothers' Organizations, 180
Motivations, of impoverished women, 39–40

Movimiento-al-Socialismo, 140
Moyano, María Elena
  feminist perspective of, 89–90
  as an inspiration to the poor women of Peru, 79–90
  murder of, 79

National Action Party, 60
National Association of Workers in Private Homes (ANECAP), 118, 125
  operations in Chile, 108–110
National Commission of Comedores (CNC), 66
  politics and, 72–73
National Domestic Workers Union, 119
National Farmers' and Ranchers' Union (UNAG), Women's Section within, 97–98
Neighborhood-based survival activities
  Sendero Luminoso and, 88–90
  of women, 33
Neighborhood commissions, formation of, 37
Neighborhood movements, 141
  in Peru, 82
Neighborhoods
  formation of popular, 36–38
  Sandinista consideration for, 94
Neo-locality, among migrant-labor families, 53
Nett, Emily, 112
Networks of activity, 101
Nicaragua
  women in politics of, 184
  women's movements in, 6–7, 91–102
  women workers in, 178
Nicaraguan Confederation of Professionals (CONAPRO)
  National Women's Commission within, 98
Non-governmental organizations (NGOs), 34–35, 141, 179–186
  in Argentina, 127
  in Chile, 108–110
  for domestic workers, by country, 117–122
  goals of, 39

impacts of, 40–41
nature of, 42–43
in Peru, 82–84, 137–138
reorganization of, 137–138
results of, 42–43
UNICEF and, 37, 38
North American Free Trade Agreement (NAFTA), 140
Nutrition, decline in standards of, 21

Olla comun, 18
Opus Dei movement, 117–118
Oscar Turcios state farm, 178

PAD. See Direct Assistance Program (PAD)
PAIT. See Temporary Income Support Program (PAIT)
Paraguay
  child care facilities in, 125
  domestic worker organizations in, 119–120
  women workers in, 178
Paraguayan Peasant Movement, 160
"Pasta factories," wages paid by, 40
Pastoras, 126
Paternalism, toward the poor in Peru, 69–70
Patriarchy. See also Male-dominated political systems; Manliness
  women's struggle against, 1, 4–5, 6–8, 91–102, 138
Patriotic Military Service (SPM), 95
Patronas, 126, 128, 129, 130
Peasant classes. See also *Campesinas* (*campesinos*); Poor classes
  life among, 107–110
Performance, improving women's, 41–42
Peru, 186. See also Checras, Peru; Chiuchin, Peru; Lima, Peru; Mayobamba, Peru; Santa Leonora, Peru; Villa El Salvador, Peru
  domestic work conditions in, 115–116
  domestic worker organizations in, 120
  economic crisis of, 6, 59–75
  erosion of social functions of the state in, 137–138

expansion of the military state in, 60–62
isolation of legitimate leadership of, 75
malnutrition in, 182
popular struggle against the government of, 60–62
social change in, 162–163
social policies of, 67–71
social spending in, 65–67
soup kitchens in, 18
women's movements in, 179–180
Perú-Mujer project, 110, 127–128
Pobladoras, 126
Political parties, in Peru, 71–74
Political repression, in Guatemala, 119
Political rights, women's struggle for, 3, 138–139
Politics. See also Power
  among AMNLAE, women, and the Nicaraguan state, 97–102
  authoritarian, 159–160
  collective kitchens' aversion to, 72
  community, 141
  feminism and, 144–145
  of gender, 95–96, 137–145
  of livelihood, 4–5
  local, 140–141
  National Commission of Comedores and, 72–73
  in Nicaragua, 95–96
Poor classes. See also Impoverishment; Poverty
  domestic workers as members of, 128–129
  employment of, 63–65
  expansion of, 17–22
  impoverishment of, in Peru, 82–84
  mobility of, 63–64
  segregation of, 4
  Sendero Luminoso attacks against, 86–87
  as of strategic importance to Sendero Luminoso, 80
  struggle for social rights of, 74–75, 155
  struggles of, 137–145
  suffering of, 70
  survival strategies of, 33–35
  women as part of, 4, 94

Populism, in Peru, 69–70
Portocarrero, Gonzalo, on suffering by the poor, 70
Poverty. *See also* Impoverishment; Poor classes
    case studies of extreme, 170
    feminist strategies for dealing with, 138–139
    impacts of non-governmental organizations on, 40–41
    skyrocketing, in Peru, 65–67
Power. *See also* Domestic power; Empowerment of women; Politics
    in Nicaraguan state, 96–97
Pragmatism, toward Peruvian poor, 69–70
Privatization, of the struggle for survival, 18
Production, 1
Productive activities, 33, 43–44
Programa de Desarrollo Integral de Buenos Aires (PRODIBA)
    formation of, 37
    goals of, 39, 40, 41
Programa Nacional de Solidaridad (PRONASOL), 22–23
Projects. *See* Community-development projects
Publications, concerning domestic workers, 111–113
Public spending, decreases in, 59
Pueblos. See Neighborhoods
Pueblos jóvenes, in Lima, Peru, 6
Puerto Vallarta, Mexico, urban women of, 166

Quality of life, deterioration of, 21
Querétaro, Mexico, urban women of, 166
Quiringuicharo, Mexico, case study of working women in, 47–55

Racial biases, in structural adjustment policies, 22
Religion. *See also* Catholic Church; Episcopal Church
    as motivating working women, 108–109

Reproductive activities, 33, 43–44
    of families, 65–67
Residential patterns, within migrant-labor families, 53
Rhodes, William, on the Latin American debt crisis, 14
Right to vote, among impoverished Peruvians, 69
Rio de Janeiro, Brazil, women's participation in politics of, 185
Rumors, sown by Sendero Luminoso, 86–88
Rural villages, 175–179
    impact of women wage-earners on economies of, 47–55
Rural workers, 175–179
    violence against, 160

Sacrifice, by the poor classes, 70
Salaries. *See also* Wages
    of impoverished women, 40
Sandinista National Liberation Front (FSLN), 91
    creation of AMNLAE by, 94–97
    historical roots of, 91–92
    women's organizations supported by, 97–99
Sandinista regime
    AMNLAE and, 93–97
    Nicaraguan women's movements following defeat of, 99–102
    women's movements and, 6–7, 91–93
Sandinista Revolution, women's movement in Nicaragua and, 91–93
Santa Leonora, Peru, social change in, 162–163
Santiago, Chile, daily life in, 163–164
Santo Domingo. *See* Dominican Republic
Savings and Loan Cooperative, 118
Seasonal labor, 48
Self-esteem
    among collective kitchen leaders, 73–74
    employment and, 35–36
    improving women's, 35-36, 41–42
Sendero Luminoso, 6
    attacks against women's organizations by, 84–90

communism and, 87
deleterious activities in Peru, 59, 75
goals of, 80–81
importance of women's organizations to, 80, 84–90
political violence engendered by, 79–90
Servicios Quillay, 119
Settlements. *See* Neighborhoods
Sexual division of labor, 42
Sexuality Network, 101
Shining Path, 6. *See also* Sendero Luminoso
deleterious activities in Peru, 59, 75
SINCATRAP (Sindicato de Trabajadoras de Casa Particular). *See* Union of Workers in Private Homes (SINCATRAP)
Sindicato Nacional de Trabajadoras del Servicio Doméstico, 119
Sindicato Nacional de Trabajadores Domésticas, 115
SINTRASEDOM, 123, 128
Slavery
domestic work and, 110–111
domestic working conditions as similar to, 113–114
"Social emergencies," 32–33
impoverished households in, 38–39
in Peru, 64–65
women's responses to, 35–36
Social institutions, in Peru, 71–74
Social life
effects of structural adjustment policies on, 20, 22–23
impact of debt crisis on, 32–33
Social marginalization, of domestic workers, 116–117
Social movements, 179–186
incorporation of the poor into, 4
institutionality in, 75
political parties and, 71
women's struggle against, 1, 138–139
Social policies, of Peru, 67–71
Social relations
impacts of non-governmental organizations on, 40–41
livelihood and, 1–2

Social rights
feminist perspectives on, 142–145
struggle of poor classes for, 74–75
women's struggle for, 3, 92–93
Social Security system, of Peru, 68
Social services. *See also* Agency for International Development (USAID); Catholic Church; Collective kitchens; Community-based economic organizations; Community-development projects; Direct Assistance Program (PAD); Family Kitchens; "Glass of Milk" program; Kneading Hope; National Commission of Comedores (CNC); Non-governmental organizations (NGOs); Programa de Desarrollo Integral de Buenos Aires (PRODIBA); *Pueblos júvenes*; Soup kitchens; Temporary Income Support Program (PAIT); UNICEF; Welfare programs
decline in spending on, 64–65
decline of, in Peru, 81–84
inability of state to perform, 71
Social tensions, resulting from structural adjustment policies, 18
Solidarity. *See* Collective for Action in Solidarity with Domestic Workers (CASED); "Economy of solidarity"
Somoza dictatorship, human rights violations of, 92
Soup kitchens, 18. *See also* Collective kitchens; Family Kitchens
Souza-Lobo, Elisabeth, 141, 145
on women in Latin American society, 169–170
Spinsters, in the labor force, 51
SPM. *See* Patriotic Military Service (SPM)
Standard of living. *See* Living standards
State. *See also* Argentina; Bolivia; Brazil; Chile; Colombia; Costa Rica; Cuba; Dominican Republic; Guatemala; Latin America; Mexico; Nicaragua; Paraguay; Peru; Uruguay; Venezuela
debt crisis and collapse of, 71
effects of non-governmental organizations and, 43

looking beyond, 139–145
"municipalization" and "provincialization" of, 139
renunciation of role as provider of universal services, 65–67
retreat from social obligations by, 3, 59, 74–75
women's struggle against, 1, 7, 138–139
State-civil society relations, 42–43
Strawberry packing plants, women laborers for, 48, 49–51
Structural adjustment policies (SAPs), 5
alternatives to, 24–25
biases of, 22–24
effects on public spending in Peru, 59
evaluating with market-related efficiency criteria, 22–23
future of, 43–44
goals of, 74–75
government spending and, 11–12
harshness of, in Peru, 83–84
in Latin America, 11–25, 59
in Peru, 67–71, 74–75
social costs of, 17–22
unequal application of, 18
Struggles, 155, 157–158
Sub-national organizations, 140–141
Subsistence-related organizations, 74–75
Suffering, of the poor classes, 70
Supra-national organizations, 139–140
Survival strategies, among impoverished households, 33

Teachers' assistants, women as, 36
Teenagers, effects of structural adjustment policies on, 19
Temporary Income Support Program (PAIT)
decline in, 64
effects on Peru of, 62–65
Terrorism. *See* Violence
The 1980s
debt crisis in Peru during, 60–67
emergence of Latin American women's rights during, 3
lack of Latin American growth during, 17–22, 32–33

women's responses to, 33–35
women's social roles during, 35–36
Theologians (male), on Catholic Church's oppression of women, 186
Third World countries, implementation of structural adjustment policies in, 24
Todaro, Rosalba, 109, 114
Top-down political organization, Nicaraguan state as, 96–97, 97–102
Trade liberalization, 12
Training, 41, 42
Training Center for Household Workers (CCTH), 120, 124
"Triple struggle" of Latin American women, 158–159

UNAG. *See* National Farmers' and Ranchers' Union (UNAG)
Unemployment, in Peru, 63–65
UNICEF
economic development evaluations by, 22, 23
non-governmental organizations funded by, 37, 38
Unions, 171. *See also* Non-governmental organizations (NGOs); Women's organizations
United States, financial "rescue" of Mexico by, 11
Universal rights
feminist perspectives on, 142–145
women's struggle for, 3
U.N. Women's Decade, 168
Urban life
incorporation of the population into, 3–4
women in, 3–4, 35
Uruguay, domestic worker organizations in, 120

Vaccination campaigns, 83
Valdez, Theresa, 123
Vaso de Leche program. *See* "Glass of Milk" program
Venezuela
domestic worker organizations in, 120

effects of structural adjustment policies on, 22
Villa El Salvador, Peru, social movement in, 180–181
Villas, formation of, 36–38
Violence
  engendered by Sendero Luminoso, 79–90
  resulting from structural adjustment policies, 18, 21
Violence Network, 101

Wage-labor migration, 48–49
  alterations in family formation patterns resulting from, 52–53
  alterations in residential patterns resulting from, 53
  among domestic workers, 111, 116–117
  women's burdens resulting from, 52
Wages, 6
  declines in, 64–65
  inflation and, 11, 12–13
  paid to impoverished women, 40
Wage work, 157–158
  involving Mexican women, 47, 54–55
Welfare programs
  in Argentina, 35
  collapse of, in Peru, 82–84
Welfare rights struggles, 142
Welfare state, erosion of, 138, 139
Widows
  in the labor force, 51
  women as virtual, 52
Women, 155–158. *See also* Domestic workers; Household workers; Mothers; Working women
  and alternatives to structural adjustment policies, 24–25
  burdens imposed upon, 20–21, 52, 82–84
  case studies of Argentine, 36–41
  education of poor, 82–83
  effects of structural adjustment policies on, 5, 43–44
  emancipation of, 96–97
  empowerment of, 40–41, 50–51, 53–54, 91–102, 137–138, 145, 156

as heads of households, 52
  impoverished, in 1990s Peru, 65–67
  improving performance of, 41–42
  increased numbers in labor market, 18–19
  jobs and marital status of, 47–48
  in the labor market, 33–35
  as leaders of collective kitchens, 73–74
  life stories of, 158–162
  male opposition to labor by, 48–51
  manifesto of poor, in Peru, 69–70
  migrant, 188
  motivations of, 39–40
  as operators of collective kitchens, 61
  peasant, 159
  in Peruvian welfare programs, 62–65
  productive and reproductive activities of, 33, 43–44
  responses to the debt crisis by, 31–44
  roles of, 47
  in rural life, 175–179
  under the Sandinista regime, 94–95
  social roles of, 40–41
  struggles of, 1, 3, 4–5, 6–7, 64, 82–84, 91–102, 137–145, 158–159
  suffering of poor, 70
  in urban life, 3–4, 35, 164–175
  wages earned by, 6
Women's Association to Confront the National Problematic (AMPRONAC)
  creation of, 92
Women's Houses, 98
Women's movements, 144–145. *See also* Feminism
  characteristics of women in, 94
  in Nicaragua, 91–102
  in Peru, 59–75, 72
Women's organizations, 171
  emergence of, 20–21
  resistance to Sendero Luminoso by, 75, 79–90
  Sandinista political support of, 94–95, 97–99
Women's Patriotic Alliance, 91–92
Women's Proclamation, 95, 96
Women's Secretariat of the Agricultural Workers' Association (ATC), 97–98

Women's Studies Center (CEM: Argentina), 127, 128
Workers' Party, in Brazil, 140
Working classes
  impoverishment of, 3
  livelihood strategies among, 164–165
Working conditions, for domestic workers, 113–116
Working wives, 51–52
Working women. *See also* Female unemployment; Women
  of Lima, Peru, 158
  male opposition to, 48–51
  without men, 51
  need for cooperation among, 100–102
  in Nicaragua, 92–93
"Workplace-centered" studies, 166
World Bank, 3
  and alternatives to structural adjustment policies, 25
  criticisms against, 21
  responsiveness of structural adjustment policies to needs of, 23–24
Worthiness, among the poor classes, 70

Young Catholic Workers (JOC), 112. *See also* Catholic Church
  assistance for domestic workers through, 117
  charitable operations in Chile, 108
  charitable operations in Paraguay, 119–120
  charitable operations in Peru, 120

Zurutuza, Cristina, 127